WHAT CHRISTIAN LEADERS ARE SAYING ABOUT *BEYOND BELIEF TO CONVICTIONS*

"Today's teens are quick to say that they believe something to be true. However, these so-called beliefs never translate into action. *Beyond Belief to Convictions* confronts young people with the Person of Truth, Jesus Christ, and challenges them to live out this truth based on a personal, intimate relationship with him. When truth becomes a conviction in one's life, that person will act on those beliefs regardless of the consequences. This is a book that should be read by every Christian—both young and old alike. If its message is not taken to heart, we could lose the next generation to the false philosophies of this world."

> **DR. GLEN L. SCHULTZ,** *director of Christian schools for LifeWay Christian Resources and author of* Kingdom Education: God's Plan for Educating Future Generations

"Josh McDowell's relational apologetic presents Christianity as it really is— an intellectually compelling and emotionally satisfying relationship with God. *Beyond Belief to Convictions* is a critically needed resource for today's family and the church."

> **DR. GARY SMALLEY,** *founder and chairman of the board of the Smalley Relationship Center and author of* Food and Love

"Postmodern thinking is rampant among today's young people, and it isn't going to get better unless parents and Christian leaders take a stand. In an easy-to-read style, Josh McDowell and his coauthors offer constructive ways to counter postmodernism's deadly influence. Their emphasis on the historical witness of the Christian faith reminds us of the great importance of a well-formed Christian worldview."

> **CHARLES W. COLSON,** *founder of Prison Fellowship Ministries and author of* How Now Shall We Live?

"In a day when so many young people are wrestling with the idea of absolute truth and floundering in a sea of moral relativity, *Beyond Belief to Con-*

victions shines like a beacon. This book sheds the clear light of understanding on the internal struggles teens and young adults face today—and shows how to respond with convincing proof for the reliability of Scripture and the truth and love of Christ. It's a 'must read' for any Christian who cares about youth!"

BILL McCARTNEY, *founder and president of Promise Keepers*

"Josh's powerful relational apologetics presents truth that is to be objectively known and relationally experienced."

DR. DAVID FERGUSON, *director of Intimate Life Ministries*

"Addressing parents and all who reach out to young people, this volume is fresh-bread-and-butter McDowell, a masterful resource for ministry to postmodernism's junior victims. The fresh bread is simple, solid, rational, relational, Bible-based argument, while the butter is autobiography and parabolic fiction, showing how knowing Christ and the Bible changes people for the better. The bread is good, and the butter upgrades its taste. Here is a basic tool for truth and life—one I am glad to recommend."

DR. JAMES I. PACKER, *professor of theology at Regent College and author of* Knowing God *and* Concise Theology

"Historically, *ethics* has been the outflow of *beliefs*. Today's morass of moral and intellectual relativism and the confusion it creates, however, separates ethics and beliefs. Facing this, Josh McDowell and his coauthors have put a powerful tool in the hand of today's Christian leadership. I strongly recommend this dynamic resource to foster and fuel a clear-headed and penetrating mind-set—the kind that can help you and me speak to our generation more effectively and with greater impact."

DR. JACK W. HAYFORD, *founding pastor of The Church on the Way and chancellor of The King's College and Seminary*

"Josh has helped all of us—not just our kids—to move out of our heads into our hearts by putting our beliefs to work. If you want to start living your faith rather than just believing, this book is for you."

DR. STEPHEN ARTERBURN, *founder of Women of Faith and author of* Flashpoints

"Through the years our passion has been to see God raise up that 'next generation' of younger leaders who have a Great Commission passion fueled by a Great Commandment lifestyle. Josh's new book clearly addresses the relational apologetics that is needed for this next generation. I highly commend it to you, knowing the impact it will have not only on your own life but also on the lives of those you lead. Every person, young and old, can greatly benefit from the wisdom and insight contained in this work."

DR. DANN SPADER, *executive director of Sonlife Ministries*

"Who is more qualified than Josh McDowell to come up with the completely new paradigm of 'relational apologetics'? Together with his coauthors, Josh urges us to move beyond belief to convictions. Throughout his ministry McDowell has provided the incontrovertible evidence that believers need (faith is the evidence of things not seen). Now, in this book, comes the clear presentation of the relational meaning of that evidence in terms of an undying personal trust in Jesus Christ. This is solid apologetical reading and a timely promise of genuine help to a generation growing up with the threat of postmodernism."

DR. D. JAMES KENNEDY, *senior minister of Coral Ridge Presbyterian Church and chancellor of Knox Theological Seminary*

"Josh McDowell has sounded an alarm. If we don't act soon, we may lose a whole generation of young people to postmodernism. But Josh also points us to an effective path to reach and rescue that generation—through what he calls relational apologetics. Here is a profoundly practical way to pass on a real and relevant faith in God."

DR. HOWARD G. HENDRICKS, *chairman of the Center for Christian Leadership and author of* Living by the Book

"Josh McDowell is certainly right in his concern that, in too many cases, beliefs are not being translated into convictions. This book will undoubtedly be an important factor in changing that situation. Using refreshing narratives, the book clearly addresses the fundamental beliefs of Christianity and shows how those beliefs can be translated into life-transforming convictions. I applaud the authors, both for their concern and for this proactive way of addressing it."

DR. JOHN N. OSWALT, *research professor of Old Testament at Wesley Biblical Seminary and author of* Called to Be Holy: A Christian Perspective on Biblical Holiness

"Josh McDowell, a leading authority on the mind of contemporary youth, addresses arguably the most dangerous threat not only to young people but to everyone—postmodernism's relativizing of truth. Building on his earlier demands for objective truth set forth in works like *The New Evidence That Demands a Verdict*, McDowell presses on to the biblical demand that truth believed must be experiential: a conviction of life. In an engaging, practical, and powerful way he shows that such Christian belief means living in a relationship with the person of Christ, who is the Truth. Anyone interested in understanding something of today's culture—and more important in influencing young (and old) to a solid biblical faith in the midst of that murky culture—will find this book of great value."

>**DR. ROBERT L. SAUCY,** *distinguished professor of systematic theology at Talbot School of Theology and author of* Scripture: Its Authority, Power, and Relevance

"The church was long overdue for someone to articulate the uniqueness of Christ in a way that communicates to the worldview of postmodernism. In sharp contrast to their predecessors, postmoderns no longer ask, 'Is Christianity true?' They believe all religions are equally true. What they are asking is, 'Does Christianity work?' Josh and Bob do an outstanding job at showing that Christianity indeed 'works' because it is 'true.'"

>**DR. BILL JONES,** *professor of evangelism and missions at Columbia International University and president of Crossover Communications International*

BEYOND BELIEF
TO CONVICTIONS

• • •

JOSH D. McDOWELL
BOB HOSTETLER

• • •

TYNDALE HOUSE PUBLISHERS
WHEATON, ILLINOIS

Visit Tyndale's exciting Web site at www.tyndale.com

Beyond Belief to Convictions

"The Making of an Individual" diagram in chapter 1 is taken from Glen Schultz, *Kingdom Education* (Nashville: LifeWay Press, 1998), 40. Used with permission.

Some material in chapter 6 is adapted from Josh McDowell, *The Disconnected Generation: Saving Our Youth from Self-Destruction* (Nashville: Word, 2000). Used with permission.

The charts that appear in chapter 8 are adapted from a chart used in Josh McDowell, *The New Evidence That Demands a Verdict* (Nashville: Nelson, 1999), 38. Used with permission.

Interior designed by Dean H. Renninger

Edited by Lynn Vanderzalm

Library of Congress Cataloging-in-Publication Data

McDowell, Josh.
  Beyond belief to convictions / Josh D. McDowell, Bob Hostetler.
    p. cm.
Includes bibliographical references.
ISBN 0-8423-8009-4 (hc)—ISBN 0-8423-7409-4 (sc)
1. Apologetics.   2. Postmodernism—Religious aspects—Christianity.
I. Hostetler, Bob, date   II. Title.
BT1103 .M33 2002
239—dc21   2002006066

Printed in the United States of America

07   06   05   04   03   02
8   7   6   5   4   3   2   1

CONTENTS

Part Three
THE BIBLE: GOD WANTS US TO KNOW HIM
AND BE LIKE HIM

Part Four
THE RESURRECTION: GOD WANTS US TO TRUST HIM, NO MATTER WHAT

Part Five
TAKING THE NEXT STEP

ACKNOWLEDGMENTS

A work of this magnitude could not have been developed and written without the extraordinary contribution of many people. I wish to thank the following people for their collaborative involvement in this project:

Dave Bellis, my friend and colleague for twenty-five years, for being one of my coauthors. Dave hammered out the theme and focus of the book and kept me "on message" throughout. While he collaborated with me and Bob Hostetler to write the many drafts for this book, he requested that his name not appear on the front cover. He says he doesn't need the recognition since he doesn't aspire to author any books of his own, but I certainly recognize both his ownership of this message and his writing skills to help deliver this work to you.

Bob Hostetler for being my other coauthor. Bob labored through the collaborative process to generate draft after draft with Dave. I cannot say enough about Bob's talents and abilities to take written concepts and make them come alive on a printed page. And while I have been in awe of his writing skills for many years, it is his heart to serve and make Christ known that I admire most.

Meg Flammang and the Barna Research Group, Ltd., for conducting research specifically for this book and for the "Third Millennium Teens" research, which added so significantly to this work.

Dr. Robert Saucy, Dr. Walter Russell, Dr. John Oswalt, Tom Madden, and Jane Vogel for their insightful analysis regarding the theological perspective presented in this book.

Dr. David Ferguson for what his life and the biblical message he proclaims has meant to the authors' lives and to this book. David and his wife, Teresa, spent the larger part of two years ministering to me about the passionate heart of God and his purpose for each of us to love him and one another. I can't say enough about David and Intimate Life Ministries and how his living example of godliness has affected my life. His influence is felt throughout the pages of this book. (For more information about Intimate Life Ministries, see appendix C.)

Sean McDowell, Jonalyn Grace Taylor, Kyle Strobel, Gary Hartke, Dann Spader, and Bill Jones for their perceptive input on the cultural and youth relevance of the book.

Win Clark, Bob George, Kay and John Johnson, Bill Riley, Stan Brown, Bill Furman, Cherie Hawk, Darryl Gray, Hoyte Brown, Gary and Kay Manka, Deb Saas, Annie Hellwig, Charles and Elizabeth Foley, Chris and Christina Owens, Kathy Pechan, Ryan and Jill Hartsock, Deb and Jock Pitts, Robin Hostetler, Doug Shope, Glen Johnson, Brian Martin, Tom Troke, Heather and Christopher Adkins-Lamb, Bob and Karen Evans, and Mark Killian for participating in the focus group and providing insights that made the message of the book easier to understand and more practical to apply.

Dr. Glen Schultz, Sherry Tiede, Ed Stewart, David Hone, Tammy and Dave Bellis II, Jann Saulsberry, Bart Larson, Fred Lynch, Joey Paul, Deborah Jackson, Dottie McDowell, Terri Ferguson Snead, Heather Pott, Tally Whitehead, and Peter Meadows for their careful review of the manuscript and practical guidance in helping Dave, Bob, and me clarify the meaning and practical application of each chapter.

Kevin Johnson and Jamie Puckett for assisting in the writing process to mold and shape the book into its final form.

Ron Beers and Ken Petersen of Tyndale House Publishers for their patience, encouragement, and vision for this book.

Lynn Vanderzalm of Tyndale House Publishers for her analytical skills, structural understanding of a good book, perception of what makes written content compelling, and her overall partnership in molding and shaping every aspect of this work. Lynn is more than an editor, and I deeply respect her devotion to this project and her commitment to excellence.

And, finally, to the many Tyndale House people who have engaged in copyediting, internal design and layout, cover design, and the myriad of details that are required to bring a book to press, I thank you.

Josh McDowell

PART ONE

THE LOSS OF CONVICTIONS: A CONDITION IN OUR CULTURE

CHAPTER 1

A Crisis of Beliefs

As the three Christian leaders gathered before dawn in a place they thought to be secret, their prayer time together was interrupted by the sounds of crashing and shouting. The authorities had made repeated efforts to persuade the believers to recant their loyalty to Jesus Christ . . . and had failed. But this time there were no discussions. In seconds, the Christians were surrounded by a cadre of Roman soldiers, lifted to their feet, shackled, and led away to an unknown destination.

After several anxious hours of imprisonment, the Christians were brought out before a raucous crowd in the arena of the Colosseum. Their eyes scanned the stadium, blinking away disbelief at the thousands of eager thrill seekers awaiting the spectacle of a grisly execution.

Still in chains, the group stood before the proconsul, who ordered them to renounce their faith in Jesus, God's Son.

"Swear that Caesar is Lord," the proconsul demanded. "Renounce your false beliefs, and I will release you." He added a warning. "Fail to swear the oath, and you will face the lions."

One among the followers of Christ stepped forward. "I have committed my life to Jesus Christ, the Son of the living God," he said. "If he wills that I die today, so be it. But I cannot renounce him."

"Nor can I," spoke the second man in a loud voice.

"I will serve only Christ," said the last.

The proconsul hesitated only a moment before lifting his hand with a flourish. "Then you have made your choice," he said. He nodded his head, and the soldiers opened the gates. The crowd erupted in a bloodthirsty frenzy as the lions appeared in the arena and focused their hungry gazes on their prey.

DANGERS IN A TWENTY-FIRST-CENTURY COLOSSEUM

The rolls of history are filled with the names and accounts of Christians who, like the men described above, stood strong for their beliefs in Jesus Christ—even in the face of torture and execution. They chose death for what they believed rather than renounce their firm faith in the one true God.

In many ways, our young people today must endure a twenty-first-century Colosseum. They may not face literal lions, but they quite possibly encounter more ethical and moral temptations, greater spiritual battles and more intense emotional and relational struggles than any other generation in history. I know that your prayer—like mine—is that our kids will be strong in spirit and character, able to resist the pressures of a godless culture so that no matter what happens, they can live lives we can be proud of—lives that are pleasing to God and others. We want them to become "mature and full grown in the Lord," as the apostle Paul said, so that they "will no longer be like children, forever changing [their] minds about what [they] believe because someone has told [them] something different or because someone has cleverly lied to [them] and made the lie sound like the truth" (Ephesians 4:13-14).

But we worry that the values we are trying to instill within our children will be countered somehow. What strikes fear in our hearts is the possibility that our young people will fall prey to the wrong crowd, succumb to the cultural pressures, and make wrong choices that will bring pain and suffering to their lives. We're concerned that all the warnings, cautions, and biblical teachings we offer our children won't be enough to ground them and keep them standing strong. And we have ample reason for alarm.

WHY BELIEFS MATTER

I don't need to alarm you by quoting statistics that indicate what our kids are doing. If you're a parent, pastor, youth worker, educator, or anyone interested in today's young people, you see what's happening; you sense the danger. Our children today face unprecedented pressure. They are exposed to sexual temptation, school violence, alcohol, illegal drugs, and a variety of influences that threaten to undo all that we teach them. And while we need to fear what our kids could be tempted to do, we need to be more concerned with what our kids are led to believe.

And while we need to fear what our kids could be tempted to do, we need to be more concerned with what our kids are led to believe.

You see, the way our kids behave comes *from* something. Their attitudes and actions spring from their value system, and their value system is based on what they believe. In his book *Kingdom Education,* my friend Dr. Glen Schultz, a Christian educator, says, "At the foundation of a person's life, we find his beliefs. These beliefs shape his values, and his values drive his actions."[1] Glen illustrates this through a pyramid that graphically makes the point that our visible actions are a direct result of our beliefs and values (see diagram).[2]

THE MAKING OF AN INDIVIDUAL

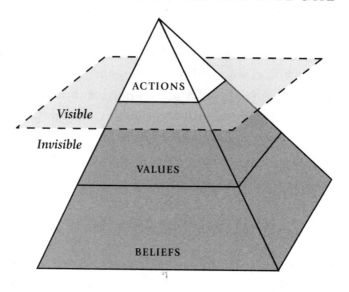

Research shows, for example, that kids who *believe* that premarital sex is morally right are far more likely to be sexually active. Their beliefs shape their values, and their values lead them to exhibit specific attitudes and actions.

This is precisely why, for example, many studies (among them our own study of more than 3,700 kids who regularly attend church) reveal that young people who lack a basic biblical belief system are

- 225 percent more likely to be angry with life
- 216 percent more likely to be resentful
- 210 percent more likely to lack purpose in life
- 200 percent more likely to be disappointed in life[3]

Their beliefs create values that result not only in certain attitudes but also in specific behaviors. That's why research has shown that kids—otherwise good kids from good families—who don't possess a biblical belief system are

- 36 percent more likely to lie to a friend
- 48 percent more likely to cheat on an exam
- 200 percent more likely to steal
- 200 percent more likely to physically hurt someone
- 300 percent more likely to use illegal drugs
- 600 percent more likely to attempt suicide[4]

While this may be disturbing it should not surprise us, because our actions flow out of our values, which arise from our beliefs. But what may surprise you is that the majority of our young people don't even hold to a biblical belief system. Our kids, even those from solid Christian homes and churches, have distorted beliefs about God and the Bible, beliefs that are having a devastating rippling effect into every aspect of their lives.

OUR KIDS' DISTORTED BELIEFS

Now I realize that many parents and gatekeepers will tell me that they have good kids and they're so impressed with the attitudes of their young people. And, in part, research bears this out. Even after the terrorist attacks of September 11, 2001, the studies show our kids have maintained an impressive set of personal priorities. Research we commissioned from the Barna Research Group after the 2001 terrorist attacks reveals the following:

- 65 percent of today's young people want a close relationship with God.[5]
- 49 percent want to make a difference in the world.[6]
- 79 percent consider having close personal friends as a high-priority goal for their future.[7]

Based on the research, if I had to summarize in one sentence what I believe kids want, I would say *they want a healthy, relationally significant life on earth and a home in heaven.* Today's young people appear to be the most occupationally and educationally ambitious generation ever, and they possess a high degree of spiritual interest. The "Third Millennium Teens" study (also performed by the Barna Research Group) reports that "4 out of 5 teens (80 percent) say that their religious beliefs are very important in their life."[8]

But because you and I care about the future of our young people, we must look at what our kids are really believing in three areas—their beliefs about God, truth, and reality. For it is what our kids believe that will eventually define everything they come to be, as well as determine the most important choices they make in life. And what our kids currently believe is alarming.

1. Our Kids Are Adopting Distorted Beliefs about God

Gather a group of teenagers together—good Christian kids—and ask them, "Who do you think God is?" "What do you think God is like?"

What kinds of answers do you suppose you'll get? They probably won't differ much from those reported by Rob Rienow, a youth minister at Wheaton Bible Church, Wheaton, Illinois, in a *Newsweek* cover story titled "What Teens Believe":

> Their answers were as individual as the kids themselves. One thought God was like his grandfather: "He's there, but I never see him." Another took a harder view, describing "an evil being who wants to punish me all the time." Two more opinions followed. Finally, the last teen weighed in: "I think you're *all* right, because that's what you really believe." In other words, as Rienow relates it, God is whatever works for you. On this, all of the youth agreed.[9]

This generation may be open and vocal about their faith—even to the point of wearing their Christian witness on T-shirts and WWJD bracelets—but many of them are defining God in their own ways. In the Barna "Third Millennium Teens" research we've already quoted, 70 percent of the teenagers surveyed were active in some church youth group, and 82 percent identified themselves as Christians. We are talking about your youth and mine—good Christian kids from good Christian homes and churches. The study revealed these conclusions:

- The vast majority of our teens (80 percent) believe that God created the universe.
- 84 percent believe that God is personally involved in people's lives.

Yet, in spite of these orthodox views,

- 63 percent also believe that Muslims, Buddhists, Christians, Jews, and all other people pray to the same god, even though they use different names for their god.[10]

And what did these teens say they believe about Jesus?

- 87 percent of our kids believe Jesus was a real person who came to earth, and 78 percent believe he was born to a virgin.
- Yet nearly half (46 percent) believe he committed sins, and over half (51 percent) say he died but *did not* rise from the dead![11]

And in their minds is Christianity the only way to salvation?

- 48 percent of teenagers today believe that it doesn't matter what religious faith you associate with because they all believe the same principles and truth.
- 58 percent believe that all religious faiths teach equally valid truth.[12]

Your child or youth group may believe that Jesus really lived and that he was actually born of a virgin. Your son or daughter may even be among the minority who believe that Christ rose from the dead. But the vast majority of our own kids (65 percent) either believes or suspects that there is "no way to tell which religion is true"![13] Their view of God is so distorted that they're not convinced that the Jesus of the Bible is the way, the truth, and the life for "all the children of the world."

It is not that our kids are rejecting Christianity as they know it—they have simply been influenced to redefine it according to their cultural setting. They are putting together their own religious canon in a smorgasbord style. They are led to believe it is better to pick and choose from various ideas, concepts of God, and religion around them until they construct a tailor-made "faith," one that's just right for them. They are being encouraged to piece their faith together themselves; that way it will be theirs personally, and it will offend no one.

They are putting together their own religious canon in a smorgasbord style.

As *Newsweek* reporter John Leland discovered, "Even more than their baby-boomer parents, teenagers often pick and choose what works for them. . . . As they sample from various faiths, students have become more accepting of each other's beliefs, even when those beliefs are stringent. Clayton, a high-school junior, says he is known among his classmates as 'the religious guy,' but this does not make him the odd man out. Clayton, 17, an evangelical Christian, is one of a growing minority of teenagers who are vowing to defer sex until marriage. 'There really is an atmosphere of whatever you think is OK,' he says. 'Just don't tell me what to think. I'll figure it out myself.'"[14]

Clayton, like many of our Christian kids, may be taking a temporary stand for some good things. But how they determine what is true (and what is good) is alarming. Today's culture encourages our young people to "figure it out" themselves, and what most are "figuring out" is a little truth here and a little error there until they end up with erroneous beliefs.

2. Our Kids Are Embracing Distorted Beliefs about Truth

Picture a youth-group Bible study. The adult group leader, who has just finished reading a Scripture passage, turns to a student and asks, "Alicia, what does this verse mean?"

Alicia, a professed Christian from a good Christian home, pauses to reflect on the passage. "Well," she begins, after a few moments of careful consideration, "what this verse means to me is . . ."

Chances are, most of us wouldn't even detect the subtle shift in meaning reflected in Alicia's use of the words *to me*. But the importance of those two tiny words must not be underestimated. They are indicative of another dangerous condition that exists among today's Christian young people: Most of them are not looking to the biblical text for truth; they are actually looking within themselves. The majority of today's youth (70 percent) say there is no absolute moral truth.[15]

For the most part, many church and parachurch youth workers have become group facilitators rather than teachers of scriptural truth. And it's not so much because group leaders are not intending to share the meaning of scriptural truth—many are. The problem is that young people simply hear truth through their own "filter," which tells them that all truth is subjectively and personally determined.

For example, listen to Amber, a typical sixteen-year-old Christian from a solid youth group, respond to my questions.

"Is it wrong to engage in premarital sex?" I ask.

"Well, I believe it's wrong for me," she responds.

I probe further. "But do you believe the Bible teaches that premarital sex is wrong for everyone?"

Amber's eyes shift back and forth as she weighs her answer. "Well," she begins slowly, "I know it's wrong for me, and I have chosen not to have sex until I'm married. But I don't think I can judge other people on what they do."

You see, it's not that Amber doesn't believe the Bible provides "a clear and totally accurate description of moral truth." She, like 61 percent of our kids, would say that's exactly what she believes.[16] But she's like the majority of our young people, who have been conditioned to believe that truth is not true for them *until they choose to believe it.* That's why 81 percent of our kids claim that "all truth is relative to the individual and his/her circumstances."[17]

> *Our kids have been conditioned to believe that truth is not true for them until they choose to believe it.*

Now, you might be wondering, "Who's teaching kids these things? And how are they doing it without my knowledge?" The culprit in this case is not a person. It is a philosophy that permeates much of our culture—government, schools, movies, television, and music. It is a widespread cultural mind-set and influence known as postmodernism.

Trying to define and truly understand postmodernism can be a lot like standing in an appliance store trying to watch three or four television shows at once. It defies definition because it is extremely complex, often contradictory, and constantly changing.

In fact, it's fitting that the very term *postmodernism* describes this school of thought by *what it's not.* In other words, postmodernism is the philosophy that succeeded and, to some degree, supplanted modernism, a way of thinking that has itself challenged the Christian worldview for centuries. Whereas modernism rejected religion and superstition in favor of science and reason, postmodernism repudiates any appeal to reality or truth.

So, while postmodernism is tough to pin down, it is possible to summarize its most common beliefs:

- Truth does not exist in any objective sense.
- Instead of "discovering" truth in a "metanarrative"—which is

a story (such as the Bible) or ideology (such as Marxism) that presents a unified way of looking at philosophy, religion, art, and science—postmodernism rejects any overarching explanation of what constitutes truth and reality.

- Truth—whether in science, education, or religion—is created by a specific culture or community and is "true" only in and for that culture.
- Individual persons are the product of their cultures. That is, we are not essentially unique individuals created in the image of God; our identities are defined by our culture (African-American, European, Eastern, Western, urban, rural, etc.).
- All thinking is a "social construct." In other words, what you and I regard as "truths" are simply arbitrary "beliefs we have been conditioned to accept by our society, just as others have been conditioned to accept a completely different set of beliefs."[18]
- Any system or statement that claims to be objectively true or unfavorably judges the values, beliefs, lifestyle, and truth claims of another culture is a power play, an effort by one culture to dominate other cultures.

Our young people, along with the culture at large, have embraced these concepts of truth, and they've done it, more or less, while we were napping. Even the tragic events of September 2001 have not brought a nation back to a recognition of God as the absolute arbiter of truth. In fact, our culture is less inclined to believe in the existence of absolute moral truth than ever before. Before September 2001, Barna's research revealed that only four out of ten adults (38 percent) believed there is absolute moral truth that does not change according to the circumstances. When the same question was asked after the September terrorist attacks, the result was that just two out of ten adults (22 percent) claimed to believe in the existence of absolute moral truth.[19]

While the somewhat sudden dawn of postmodernism has been shaping an entire generation, it has caught many of us—parents, pastors, educators, and youth workers—by surprise. As a result, we have been slow to understand its impact and counter its influence. And because most of our kids seem to have a keen interest in spiritual things, most adults are not alarmed. But as I said before, we have reason for alarm. As the studies show, the postmodern influence has had a profound effect on what our kids believe about God, truth, and reality.

Postmodern influence has had a profound effect on what our kids believe about God, truth, and reality.

Thus, while young people may be willing to believe that Christianity offers *a* "truth," they're not convinced it is *the* truth, the only hope for salvation and relationship with the God of the universe. Also, they are not trying to understand the objective truth of God's Word and live out that truth in their lives. As Andy Crouch, editor-in-chief of *re:generation quarterly*, points out, "The . . . historical truth of a biblical book is not the burning issue [to today's youth], but rather how the Scripture speaks to their situation."[20] Therefore, instead of applying scriptural truth to their lives, our kids are using Scripture merely as a springboard for thought as they attempt to create their own personal "meaning," one that may have little or nothing to do with the objective meaning of the biblical text.

3. Our Kids Are Accepting Distorted Beliefs about Reality

Not only are today's young people adopting a distorted belief about God and embracing a distorted view of truth, they have also become very pragmatic; they want what is real, relevant . . . and "right now." As we've said earlier, kids today place a premium on spiritual things and meaningful relationships.

The problem, however, is that the majority of our young people have become convinced that what is true and relevant is whatever works right now. If Hugh Hefner's motto that "if it feels good, do it" characterized the sixties, today's culture propagates the view that "if it works, it's right for you." According to the Barna studies, 72 percent of our teens believe that "you can tell if something is morally/ethically right for you by whether or not it works in your life."[21]

Today's culture propagates the view that "if it works, it's right for you."

Consequently, our kids feel no need to discuss such abstract ideas as the absolute truth of God's Word; they see little reason to grapple with what they believe about Christ and why. "What's the point?" they would most likely say. "As long as it works for me, that's all I care about." They have bought into a line of reasoning that says, "Don't bore me with your rules, your values, or your belief systems. And don't tell me what to think. I'm supposed to figure out what works myself, in the real world."

Our kids need to see our lives as living examples of the wisdom and practicality of a life that is built on biblical principles of right and wrong. After all, there is a big difference between what seems to work for the moment and what is right. For example: What if cheating on an exam meant the difference between our kids' passing or failing; would it be okay to cheat because it works at the moment? What if stealing could make life easier or better; would they say it is all right to steal? What if lying to friends might avert a big argument; would they think it is better to lie? For many of our kids, the answer is, "Well, if it would work for me right now, it would be 'right.'" That is because most of our kids and many adults as well have bought into a cultural mind-set that says we work out our lives independently of God's absolute standards of right and wrong.

But does that approach actually work in the real world? Not for long, it doesn't. Because in this cause-and-effect world that God created, his absolute ways are what "works." His ways protect us from harm. His ways provide safety and blessing for us. If you possess a biblical worldview (and sadly many adult Christians do not), you would tend to say, "If it's right, it will work," for God is "the fountain of life, the light by which we see" (Psalm 36:9).

Adults who have a biblical perspective know that in this orderly world God created, his ways "work" better than seat-of-the-pants pragmatism; when we try to fashion our own version of reality—and live outside of God's design for us—we will suffer negative consequences.

But the vast majority of our kids don't have that maturity, experience, and biblical worldview. And the adult models that many of our young people have seen have led them to hold distorted beliefs about reality. And their pragmatic "what works right now is right for now" will eventually lead them down a path of self-destruction.

TIME IS RUNNING OUT, BUT THERE IS STILL HOPE

It *does matter* what our kids believe about God and his Word. Their ability to stand strong morally, spiritually, emotionally, and relationally is at stake. The time is now for every denomination, parachurch ministry, local church, and family to ground their children and young people in what we believe as Christians and why we believe it. This is important not just because our kids need to adopt our values but also because their very understanding of the meaning of life depends on it. And that is what this book is all about.

In the pages that follow we will explain how deepened beliefs in God and his Word can so ground a person in his or her relationship with God that they will answer the fundamental questions of life itself: "Who am I?" "Why am I here?" "Where am I going?" It is by leading our young people to truly know the one true God that we will help our kids find their true sense of identity, purpose, and destiny in life. Then they will be fortified spiritually, morally, and emotionally to stand strong in the face of today's culture.

But we must not delay. Time is running out.

Let me put it this way. I have often said, "The youth of today will be the church of tomorrow." But I'm afraid I can't say that anymore because if we don't do something *now* to reeducate our kids in the foundations of the Christian faith, the young people we're counting on to lead the church into the next generation won't even *be in* the church of the next generation!

Our kids' ability to stand strong morally, spiritually, emotionally, and relationally is at stake.

I realize I haven't painted a very pretty picture here. Yet I believe there is still hope. I am hopeful, first, because although our kids do have distorted beliefs about God, truth, and reality, few of them have solidified their positions. The studies reveal that 74 percent of our kids are still trying to figure out the purpose and meaning of their lives, and 63 percent admit that they don't have any set "philosophy about life that consistently influences their lifestyle and decisions."[22] That gives us a wide-open window of opportunity to counter their distorted views and clarify with them what they should believe—and why.

Second, I'm hopeful because there *is* an effective way to counter the cultural conditioning that has distorted our kids' belief systems. I know of no better way to reverse the effect of a postmodern worldview than to bring our kids face-to-face with true biblical Christianity. True Christianity not only effectively counters subjective believing, the loss of moral absolutes, and distorted perceptions of reality; it can also transform a person's behavior so that he or she will no longer be "tossed here and there by waves, and carried about by every wind of doctrine" (Ephesians 4:14, NASB).

That is what you and I want for our young people. We want them to stand strong. We want them to be twenty-first-century expressions of Christ's body, living as "children of God without fault in a crooked and depraved generation, in which [they] shine like stars in the universe" (Philippians 2:15, NIV). But in order for that to happen, we must first help them identify their distorted beliefs and move them beyond their subjective belief system to a set of solid convictions in the one true God. Then we can help them develop an objective faith in God that is real, relevant, and right now.

CHAPTER 2

Beliefs to Convictions

In centuries past, young men and women found the strength to stand up for what they believed, even in the face of pressure and persecution.

Joseph stood strong against an Egyptian temptress, because giving in "would be a great sin against God" (Genesis 39:9).

Daniel refused to compromise his convictions in the face of an antagonistic Babylonian culture.

Peter and John chose to obey God rather than men, though doing so invited persecution.

Others throughout history have done the same, becoming modern-day parallels of those who "shut the mouths of lions, quenched the flames of fire, . . . became strong in battle . . . were mocked, . . . chained . . . killed" (Hebrews 11:33-37).

"So what do we have to do," you might ask, "to equip our children and young people to resist the pressures of a godless culture and stand up for what they believe? Do we simply teach them to believe the right things? Is that the answer?"

That may seem logical, but it's not that simple. Because in today's cultural setting, mere believing isn't enough. In fact, I would go so far as to say even getting our kids to believe in the right things won't be enough.

WHY "BELIEVING" IS NOT ENOUGH

Now, I suspect many people will question my assertion that believing is not enough. I've had parents and other adults react strongly when I've made that statement in the past.

"Josh," they say, "how can you say believing is not enough? I was taught to just believe the right things about God and the Bible, and I turned out okay. Why would it be any different for my kids?"

Allow me to explain. You see, when earlier generations were growing up, most were taught that right was right and wrong was wrong. They were told that certain things were inherently and objectively right and true for all people, for all times, for all places. They were instructed that those things were true, whether or not they chose to live according to them. And they learned that solid beliefs were important and meaningful to their individual lives. And while the popular culture did not always reinforce such messages, it seldom opposed them. It may not have always been easy, but many people resisted the temptations and stood strong for the things they believed. But that is not the case in your child's world.

In fact, I am convinced that the majority of our young people have accepted or adopted Christianity not because they have judged it to be true and thus worthy of acceptance but because Christianity—or at least their own "smorgasbord" version of it— seems to be the best option they've encountered to date. They may have been initially attracted to Christianity for any number of reasons: an exciting youth group, an emotional church camp experience, the influence of a Christian friend, or any number of other factors. Yet it's unimportant to them whether what they believe is true in an objective and absolute sense because they regard truth as something that is subjectively determined, something they are to discover and define on their own.

But what happens when something more exciting or emotionally stimulating comes along? What will keep our kids from changing their beliefs? Or what will happen when they face the great challenges of life and they're morally or ethically at the end of their rope? Will their subjectively determined beliefs hold them steady? Will they make the right choices? The studies (some of which we cited in the last chapter)—as well as our past experience with young people—lead us to conclude that they will not.

Today merely "believing" isn't enough. Not because believing isn't important; it is. But as we stated earlier, in today's culture believing is made out to be more of a preference based on one's subjective feelings at the moment. And that kind of believing isn't enough. Our kids need a deeply held belief in God and his Word, a belief that will root and ground them in the faith so that no matter what tests or trials or storms of life come their way, they will stand strong. We are talking about a belief that goes so deep that it unlocks the secrets to one's very own identity, purpose, and destiny in life. It is a belief that can equip our children to become "twenty-first-century gladiators" who can enter the arena of an antagonistic culture and not crumble under its pressure.

I truly believe that your children and mine live in a culture that is radically different from the one you and I experienced in our formative years. Theirs is more like the culture the early Christians faced two thousand years ago. Today's culture is completely intolerant of anyone who believes in absolute truth—that is, a truth that exists outside ourselves, one that is true for all people, for all times, for all places. Consequently, if our young people assert—or even suggest—that what they believe is absolutely and equally true for everyone, they will face widespread scorn and quite possibly persecution.

Thus, if our kids are going to hold firmly to their faith in such circumstances, it is not enough for them to "just believe" or give mere intellectual assent to certain things about God and the Bible, *even* if those beliefs are correct doctrine. Because of the pressures they face and the influences they reflect, our kids will require something *beyond belief*. In short, we must help them move beyond belief to *convictions*.

DEVELOPING CONVICTIONS ABOUT WHAT WE BELIEVE

To *believe* in something is to "accept it as true, genuine or real."[1] But as we've pointed out, our kids are conditioned by today's culture to think that what is true, genuine, or real is that only when *they accept* it for themselves, subjectively. To the majority of this generation, including our own kids, nothing is objectively true, universally genuine, or actually real in an absolute sense. That is why we must help move our kids beyond a personal, subjective belief to belief with convictions.

To have *convictions* is to be thoroughly convinced that something is true—"the state of being convinced of error or compelled to admit the truth."[2] A conviction goes beyond having a personal preference about something. It goes deeper than a subjective opinion. Having convictions is being so thoroughly convinced that something is absolutely true that you take a stand for it regardless of the consequences. That's the kind of belief in God and his Word our kids need.

That's the kind of belief Daniel had. He stood strong in a Babylonian culture that was antagonistic toward his belief that the God of Israel was the one true God. He was unwilling to compromise his beliefs and practices even though it meant facing a den of ravenous lions. That same kind of committed belief was displayed by his three Hebrew friends (Shadrach, Meshach, and Abednego), who entered a fiery furnace for what they believed and were found still standing.

The apostle Paul had that kind of belief. He was beaten for his faith in Christ; he was stoned and left for dead; he was imprisoned and eventually beheaded. But what did he say? "I am not ashamed; for I know whom I have believed and I am convinced that He is able to guard what I have entrusted to Him until that day" (2 Timothy 1:12, NASB). Paul had convictions. He knew the person he believed in and was so convinced in his mind and persuaded in his heart that he remained faithful to his belief, even to the point of death.

That's the kind of belief several students at Columbine High School had when guns were pointed at their heads and they were asked, "Do you believe in God?"[3] And it cost them their lives.

Having convictions is being so thoroughly convinced that something is absolutely true that you take a stand for it regardless of the consequences.

The morning of April 20, 1999, sixteen-year-old Cassie Bernall handed her friend Amanda Meyer a note that said: "Honestly, I totally want to live my life completely for God. It's hard and scary, but totally worth it!"[4] Later that day she was shot to death.

Rachel Scott was also among those killed. One year earlier she had written in her diary: "I'm not going to apologize for speaking the name of Jesus. . . . I'm not going to hide the light God has put in me. If I have to sacrifice everything, I will."[5] And she did.

It's that convinced, committed kind of belief in God and his Word that each of us is challenged to pursue. We need more than personal opinions or lightly held suspicions about God, truth, and reality; we need convictions. If each of us and our young people are going to risk rejection, persecution, or even worse, we need to be sure that we are committing our lives to something genuine, something true, something real.

It was in that context that Peter wrote,

Don't retaliate when people say unkind things about you. Instead, pay them back with a blessing. That is what God wants you to do, and he will bless you for it. . . . Now, who will want to harm you if you are eager to do good? But even if you suffer for doing what is right, God will reward you for it. So don't be afraid and don't worry. Instead, you must worship Christ as Lord of your life. And if you are asked about your Christian hope, always be ready to explain it. (1 Peter 3:9, 13-15)

Even in the face of persecution, the apostle Peter urged us to be prepared to explain the reason for our hope in Christ, and if each of us is going to develop the kind of convictions that enabled past and present generations to stand strong, our faith must be grounded in the objective truth and relational meaning of the things we believe. Only then will we—and our young people—move beyond mere belief to a set of convictions that will hold us steady in the battles of life.

Our faith must be grounded in the objective truth and relational meaning of the things we believe.

CONVICTIONS: BELIEVING IN WHAT IS OBJECTIVELY TRUE

On the evening of September 10, 2001, nineteen young men read a prayer-laden letter regarding their last night on earth. "Be obedient on this night," the instructions written in Arabic said, "because you will be facing situations that are the ultimate and that would not be done except with full obedience.

"When you engage in the battle," the letter went on to say, "strike as the heroes would strike. As God says, strike above the necks and strike from everywhere . . . and then you will know all the heavens are decorated in the best way to meet you."[6]

The next morning, on September 11, 2001, those nineteen young men gave their lives for what they believed. They hijacked four airliners, used them as flying bombs, and killed more than three thousand innocent people in the worst terrorist attack in the history of the United States. They had a religious conviction that what they were doing was honoring to their god.

Two weeks later, Osama bin Laden, the suspected mastermind behind the attacks, issued this statement: "I bear witness that there is no God but Allah and that Muhammad is his messenger. There is America, hit by God in one of its softest spots. Its greatest buildings were destroyed, thank God for that. There is America, full of fear from its north to its south, from its west to its east. Thank God for that. . . . May God show them his wrath and give them what they deserve."[7]

Those terrorists had deep convictions. From their point of view, they were advancing a just and holy war against evil in the world. They were convinced of "their" truth and were willing to die for it, though, understandably, most Americans were convinced that the terrorists were evil.

Osama bin Laden asserted one truth claim: God was on his side, and the terrorist acts were just. Most Americans, including the president of the United States, asserted another truth claim: God was on America's side, and the terrorists were "evildoers." Bin Laden thanked God for the terror, death, and destruction brought on America. Yet America condemned the terrorists as evil, and "God Bless America" was practically proclaimed the new national anthem.

We know who was right, of course. We're convinced that what nineteen men did in killing more than three thousand people was evil. We're confident that Osama bin Laden wasn't acting righteously when he presumably ordered the deaths of innocent Americans.

But how do we know that? How can we be sure whose view

of God and whose claims about truth are right? It is far more than a philosophical question—and the answer is far more than academic. Those terrorists are a vivid reminder that people can have deepened convictions and still be tragically wrong if the things they believe with conviction are *wrong beliefs*.

People can have deepened convictions and still be tragically wrong if the things they believe with conviction are wrong beliefs.

When faced with competing truth claims, the only way to arrive at a meaningful conclusion is by investigation. Webster's dictionary defines something to be true if it is "in accordance with fact or reality."[8] The careful observer must weigh the claims according to the evidence. If someone makes a claim that something is true, we ought to be able to "test" that claim to see if it is factually true and in accordance with the real world.

The Facts of the Matter

By examining the evidence about God and his Word, you and I and our youth can determine beyond a reasonable doubt that his claims are objectively true. Christianity is a uniquely *factual* truth based on indisputable facts. It is a uniquely verifiable belief because it is based on historical facts that are clearly recognizable by and accessible to everyone. The central question, then, is this: Has the one true God, who is the source of the universe and all that is right and good, revealed himself? And if so, can we know him— and how can we do that?

A certain person in history revealed himself to us and made an extraordinary truth claim. His name was Jesus; he said, "I am the way, the truth, and the life. No one can come to the Father except through me" (John 14:6). Jesus claimed to be God in the flesh. And theologian Clark Pinnock asserted that this claim can be tested by examining the evidences and checking the facts because the facts backing the claims of Christ "are the cognitive, informa-

tional facts upon which all historical, legal, and ordinary decisions are based."[9]

These are the same facts to which Jesus appealed when he
said, "Don't you believe that I am in the Father and the Father is in
me? . . . Or at least *believe because of what you have seen me do*" (John
14:10-11, emphasis mine). Christ wanted his followers to believe
in him for who he claimed to be, and so he appealed to the evidence that established that he was, in fact, the Son of the one true
God. The evidence was and is there to convince our minds that
the claims of Christ are objectively true. To move our kids beyond
belief to conviction, therefore, we must guide them through an
examination of the evidences for what they
believe. Otherwise, neither they nor we will
have a convinced belief that what we believe
is objectively true. In that respect, it is healthy
to require evidence of Christ's claims.

*To move our kids
beyond belief to
conviction, therefore,
we must guide
them through an
examination of the
evidences for what
they believe.*

That is why I don't agree with those who
suggest that the disciple Thomas did something terribly wrong when he insisted on seeing the evidence of Jesus' resurrection. When
he first heard reports that Jesus was alive,
Thomas responded, "I won't believe it unless I see the nail wounds
in his hands, put my fingers into them, and place my hand into the
wound in his side" (John 20:25).

Thomas wanted verification. He wanted to see the evidence
before he committed to that belief. Eight days later, Jesus honored Thomas's request, appearing to him and the other disciples
in the midst of a locked room. Jesus showed himself, saying, "Put
your finger here and see my hands. Put your hand into the wound
in my side. Don't be faithless any longer. Believe!" (John 20:27).

I'm convinced we need more young Thomases—young people
who know why they believe what they believe. Such understanding
is a vital key in developing the right convictions.

The Bible itself repeatedly invites examination. The apostle John, who was there when Thomas saw the risen Christ, recorded that event and added: "Jesus' disciples saw him do many other miraculous signs besides the ones recorded in this book. But these are written so that you may believe that Jesus is the Messiah, the Son of God, and that by believing in him you will have life" (John 20:30-31).

In other words, John recorded some of the evidences that showed Jesus Christ to be the Son of the one true God so that we, like Thomas, could put faithlessness behind us and believe the objective truth with conviction.

The Necessity of Faith

Of course, no matter how thoroughly convincing the evidences are, we still must exercise faith. After all, Jesus invited Thomas to exercise faith; however, the faith Jesus called for was not a blind faith but an informed, intelligent faith, one that was supported by evidence.

We will seldom, if ever, have exhaustive evidence, but we can find sufficient evidence to establish that what we believe is credible and objectively true. We also will seldom find that the evidence will remove all possibility of doubt. Life is filled with questions and circumstances that can test our faith and create momentary doubt.

A man who wanted Jesus to heal his son said to Christ, "'Have mercy on us and help us. Do something if you can.'

"'What do you mean, "If I can"?' Jesus asked. 'Anything is possible if a person believes.'

"The father instantly replied, 'I do believe, but help me not to doubt!'" (Mark 9:22-24).

Though this father believed in Jesus, he confessed that he needed help not to doubt. Even John the Baptist's faith seemed to waver when he was imprisoned and things looked grim. He sent some of his followers to ask Jesus, "Are you really the Messiah we've been waiting for, or should we keep looking for someone else?" (Matthew 11:3).

Remember, this was the same man who, when he first saw Jesus, said, "Look! There is the Lamb of God who takes away the sin of the world! . . . He is the one you are looking for" (John 1:29-33). John had already confessed his faith in Jesus as the Son of God and long-awaited Messiah. Yet, when John was arrested and thrown into prison, he must have wondered why this Jesus wasn't coming to his rescue. Like many of us in difficult times, John the Baptist experienced doubts.

How did Jesus respond to John's questions? He pointed to indisputable facts and events. He told John's disciples, "Go back to John and tell him about what you have heard and seen—the blind see, the lame walk, the lepers are cured, the deaf hear, the dead are raised to life, and the Good News is being preached to the poor" (Matthew 11:4-5).

Jesus reminded John of the *evidence*, the clear indications that Jesus was the Messiah. It was John's objective belief rooted in the reality of Christ as the Messiah that enabled him to stand strong even in the face of death. The trials of life often introduce temptation and doubt into our minds and hearts, but at such times the evidence can anchor us to the objective truth and confirm to us that what we believe is, in fact, true.

Examining the evidence doesn't eliminate the need for faith. No amount of evidence can create a 100 percent certainty. Believing something without evidence is like taking a leap into the dark; faith that is rooted in the truth is like stepping into the light. Noted author and apologist J. P. Moreland aptly defines faith as "a trust in what we have reason to believe is true."[10] A faith that is rooted in the truth that we have reason to believe is objectively true will move us—and our kids—beyond belief to convictions in the one true God.

CONVICTIONS: BELIEVING IN WHAT IS RELATIONALLY MEANINGFUL

Leading our kids to a biblical Christianity that is shown to be objectively true is critical to a faith that will hold them firm and steady in the midst of a godless culture. Yet that is only one side of believing with convictions. The flip side is guiding them to understand the relational meaning of the things they believe.

When Jesus invited his disciples to "believe because of what you have seen me do" (John 14:11), he referred not only to the evidences that make believing a rational, reasonable exercise but also to the context of the invitation. He invites us to believe in a *person.* Believing in Christ and his Word will have a profound and *relational* meaning in each of our lives.

Believing in Christ and his Word will have a profound and relational meaning in each of our lives.

Most of our young people, however, don't understand what their belief in Jesus Christ and the Word of God actually means to their everyday lives. Yes, they may have been told that faith in Christ results in eternal life and involves a call to right living. But the vast majority of our kids see little correlation between the things they believe about God, truth, and reality and their relationships with friends and family, or their future in life. Remember, 74 percent of our kids are still trying to figure out the purpose and meaning of their lives, and 63 percent don't have a clear "philosophy about life that consistently influences their lifestyle and decisions."[11]

Because of the cultural mind-set that prompts today's youth to crave, even demand, what is "real, relevant, and right now," we have a golden opportunity. We can demonstrate not only what is *objectively true* about Christ and his Word but also the *relational meaning* of who Christ is and what he says to us through his Word, a meaning that—as we will show—meets their deepest relational needs and answers the most fundamental questions of life.

DEFINING CONVICTIONS

As we've indicated, people can have convictions in misguided and wrong beliefs—as the terrorist attacks of September 11, 2001, prove. We must help our young people move beyond subjective believing to a conviction in what is objectively true. And those beliefs must be shown to be not only true but also relevant—that is, relationally meaningful to life.

Therefore, our task is to present the Christian faith to our young people in ways that demonstrate that believing is an intelligent exercise of knowing what is both objectively true and relationally meaningful. Having *convictions*, then, can be defined as *being so thoroughly convinced that Christ and his Word are both objectively true and relationally meaningful that you act on your beliefs regardless of the consequences.*

Having convictions is being so thoroughly convinced that Christ and his Word are both objectively true and relationally meaningful that you act on your beliefs regardless of the consequences.

In the pages that follow, we will offer what is needed to overcome our young people's distorted beliefs and lead them to those kinds of convictions. We are not suggesting a complicated formula or regimented catechism for our kids to memorize. Rather, we will provide a clear presentation of the most basic and foundational pillars of the Christian faith—why they are true and how they are meaningful to our lives.

AFTER SEPTEMBER 11, 2001: REASSESSING WHAT'S IMPORTANT IN LIFE

The terrorist attacks of September 11, 2001, have had a profound effect on America—and an entire generation. In the hours and days following that tragedy, people came together to grieve and to give of themselves in ways we had not seen since World War II. Stories of heroism, compassion, and patriotism filled the airwaves and the printed page.

Yet the terrorist attacks of Black Tuesday and the others that followed have done more than stir a collective resolve not to be defeated by fear; they have caused an entire nation to reassess what is really important in life.

In the immediate aftermath of the first terrorist attack, millions of people began reexamining who they are, what they are doing with their lives, and what is truly important to them. One newspaper reported, "Singles without a soul mate are seeking them. Parents without wills are writing them. Couples with conflicts are resolving them. Interviews with matchmaking consultants, marriage counselors, divorce lawyers and other experts make clear that the September 11th attacks—and the fear of more trouble—have instilled a deeper appreciation for the importance of family and intimate bonds."[12]

The national sense of vulnerability and exposure to danger has revitalized our collective need for relationships. Our greater sense of uncertainty in life has heightened our need to know who we are, why we're here, and where we're going. Perhaps never before—and certainly not in our lifetime—has there been a period when more people are focused on what is truly important and meaningful in life. I hope that we as a nation remain focused on that priority.

In today's postmodern culture, many people are no longer asking—or debating—the "big questions" of previous generations. More than anything, they are simply wanting a fulfilled and meaningful life. And that's exactly what Jesus has to offer. "My purpose," Jesus said, "is to give life in all its fullness" (John 10:10).

At its core, the Christian faith is about a relationship with God. That is what provides true meaning to all of our lives. And that is what this book is all about. Everything that Scripture teaches us to believe and to be and to do contains one common thread: an intimate, real relationship with the one true God of the universe. What we will present in the pages to follow is how our understanding of and beliefs about God and his Word establish that relationship. And as we have said, we will discover how that relationship actually answers the fundamental questions to life's meaning: Who am I? Why am I here? Where am I going?

It's not complicated at all. A child can grasp Christ's relational purpose and find it plausible to believe in him. As our young people come to know who Jesus really is, they can more clearly see him as the true Savior of the world, desiring a relationship with them. When you and I and our children understand why the Bible is true, it won't be difficult for us to embrace it as the only true living Word God gave to lead us into a meaningful relationship with him. And when we realize why Christ actually rose from the dead for us, it will become clear that an eternal relationship with God is what Christianity is all about.

So what we will provide here is a fresh framework in which you can present the Christian faith to your kids and to the world around you. It is a way to convey how Christ, the Son of the one true God, and his Word are both true and meaningful to our lives. This will be more than the typical apologetic or defense for Christianity. It will be a *relational apologetic*—rock-solid reasons to believe and a biblical blueprint for living out those beliefs in relationship with others. And it will assist you in moving the young people in your life beyond subjective beliefs to convictions about the one true God and to a meaningful relationship with him. That kind of belief with convictions will open the way for anyone to live life, as Jesus said, "in all its fullness."

> *This book is a* **relational apologetic** *—rock-solid reasons to believe and a biblical blueprint for living out those beliefs in relationship with others.*

As an adult Christian reading this book, you also may find you haven't fully come to understand why you believe what you believe. I find that many Christian adults haven't carefully examined how Christ and his Word are objectively true and relationally meaningful to the point of being able to explain it to others. But if we adults are going to guide our kids into deepened Christian convictions, we must have deepened Christian convictions, too. In fact, you may even find you have unwittingly adopted some of the postmodern mind-set that the younger generation has adopted. In many respects, this book will first equip you—the Christian adult reader—with renewed convictions in Christ and his Word so that you can pass on your faith effectively to the next generation.

Throughout this book we will explore what I call the three fundamental pillars of Christianity:

- Christ's deity and incarnation
- The reliability of Scripture
- The resurrection of Christ

I trust that as we look at these pillars together, you will capture a renewed vision of who Christ is and why he came to earth (Christ's deity and incarnation); I believe you will catch a fresh understanding of how reliable God's Word is and why he so carefully preserved it for you (reliability of Scripture); and, I hope you will be challenged with an optimistic perspective on life and your future as we explore the reality of Christ's death and resurrection (the resurrection of Christ). As we examine each of these together, we will encounter not only the objective truth of these things but also how they are relationally meaningful to our lives—a meaning that, I believe, answers the very fundamental questions of our lives.

"Who Am I?" and the Person of Jesus

In varying degrees, all of us sometimes feel adrift, alone, and alienated from others. Many experts believe such feelings are epidemic—and severe—among today's youth. Most of our kids are not sure who they are, who they belong to, or where they fit in.

Even kids who have the benefit of a relatively functional family still at times wonder, Who am I?

That question slumbers in the heart of every young person and perhaps even in yours. We may not be asking it in those three small words, but our hearts are seeking a vital relational connection. We want to know somehow that we are of value. We want to know we are loved and accepted. Each of us is silently asking, *Who am I?* But few are finding a satisfying answer.

The truth about Jesus *Christ—that he is God who became flesh and lived among us—can unlock the secret to our identity.*

Astonishingly, the answer to that question is also the key that will correct our kids' distorted beliefs about God. The truth about Jesus Christ—that he is God who became flesh and lived among us—can unlock the secret to our identity. The overwhelming evidence of Christ's deity is not only sufficient to convince our minds that it is objectively true but also amazingly meaningful to each of us individually because it enables us to discover our true identity. Encountering that truth and its meaning, as we will in part 2 of this book, will change the way we view God—and ourselves.

"Why Am I Here?" and the Word of God

Every loving Christian parent fears at times that the culture will somehow capture his or her children. Youth workers, Christian educators, and others ministering to young people fear for the youth under their care. As we've said, our kids are fighting against a force that is working to lure them into illicit sex, illegal drug abuse, alcohol use, dishonesty, violence, and a host of other things that will bring heartache and ruin into their lives. We want to protect them from such things and see them living happy, productive, and godly lives.

But our children and young people are too often ill-equipped to resist that force. Their very youthfulness leaves them open to attack because they're still searching for the answer to the question, Why am I here? Their peer group—and much of the culture that surrounds them—proposes various answers, of course, but most of the answers spring from distorted beliefs about truth. But there is another answer to that question, one that not only addresses our kids' distorted view of truth but also leads them beyond belief to conviction about the reliability of God's Word, the Bible.

When we and our kids examine the abundance of evidence for the Bible's reliability and the extraordinary means by which the Bible has been preserved, our minds and hearts will be convinced that the biblical record is an accurate and true reflection of the God who desires a relationship with us. And when we understand what that reliable Word means to our lives, we will discover our God-given purpose in life. Exploring that truth and its meaning, as we will in part 3, will convince us and enable us to urge our kids beyond belief to conviction.

And when we understand what that reliable Word means to our lives, we will discover our God-given purpose in life.

"Where Am I Going?" and the Resurrection of Christ

It doesn't take long for any of us, including our young people, to realize that life is full of disappointments. That's an unavoidable conclusion. And tragedies like the Oklahoma City bombing, the Columbine shootings, and the terrorist attacks in America emotionally reinforce that we live in an uncertain world. But how we and our kids handle the disappointments and heartaches in life is critical. Far too often our tragedies and disappointments in life turn to despondency and despair. We may even become resentful and angry about what has happened. It is far too easy—especially in the highly competitive and cruel world of today's youth culture—for the optimism of a preteen to turn to pessimism in the teen years.

At such times, one fundamental question becomes even more pressing: Where am I going? And neither our kids' distorted beliefs about reality nor the mind-set that dominates today's culture can satisfactorily answer that question for our kids. But there is an answer, and it, too, is tied into one of the three pillars of Christianity.

When we and our kids are led to examine the evidences for the resurrection of Christ, we discover the objective truth of that historical event. But more than that, we discover that the Resurrection is not only objectively true but also profoundly meaningful, particularly in times of disappointment and disaster. In fact, convictions about the truth and meaning of the Resurrection can actually change our entire outlook on life and provide us with such a

The Resurrection can provide us with such a sense of destiny that we and our kids can face life or death, good or evil, triumph or tragedy with a spirit of gratitude, optimism, and courage.

sense of destiny that we and our kids can face life or death, good or evil, triumph or tragedy with a spirit of gratitude, optimism, and courage. That will be the task of part 4 of this book.

MY QUEST FOR LIFE'S MEANING

Believe me, I know firsthand the impact these objective, meaningful truths can have on a life. As a teenager, I was hungry for answers to those three basic life questions: Who am I? Why am I here? Where am I going? I was thirsty to know what life was about. So, as a young student, I started looking for answers.

Where I was brought up, everyone seemed to be into religion. I thought maybe I would find my answers in being religious, so I started attending church. I got into it 150 percent. I went to church morning, afternoon, and evening. But I guess I went to the wrong one because I felt worse inside church than I did outside. I was brought up on a farm in Michigan, and most farmers are very practical. My dad, who was a farmer, taught me that "if something doesn't work, chuck it." So I chucked religion.

Then I thought that education might have the answers to my quest for meaning, so I looked for answers at the university. What a disappointment! You can find a lot of things in the university, but enrolling there to find your identity, purpose, and destiny in life is virtually a lost cause.

I was by far the most unpopular student among the faculty of the first university I attended. I used to buttonhole professors in their offices, seeking the answers to my questions. When they saw me coming, they would turn out the lights, pull down the shades, and lock the door so they wouldn't have to talk to me. I soon realized that the university didn't have the answers I was seeking. Faculty members and my fellow students had just as many problems, frustrations, and unanswered questions as I did. A few years ago I saw a student walking around a campus with a T-shirt that said: "Don't follow me, I'm lost." That's how everyone in the university seemed to me. Education, I thought, was not the answer either.

Prestige must be the way to go, I decided. It just seemed right to find a noble cause, give yourself to it, and become well known. The people with the most prestige in the university were the student leaders, who also controlled the purse strings. So I ran for various student offices and got elected. It was great to know everyone on campus, make important decisions, and spend the university's money doing what I wanted to do. But, like everything else I had tried, the thrill soon wore off.

About that time I noticed a small group of people—eight students and two faculty members—who seemed to be different from the others. They seemed to know who they were and where they were going in life. And they had convictions, which I admired.

Something else about this group caught my attention. It was their attitudes and actions toward each other. They seemed to love each other. But these students and professors not only loved each other, they loved and cared for people outside their group, too. They didn't just talk about love; they got involved in people's lives. It was something totally foreign to me, and I was attracted to it. So I decided to make friends with them.

About two weeks later while I sat talking with some members of this group, the conversation turned to the topic of God. I was pretty insecure about this subject, so I put on a big front to cover it up. I leaned back in my chair, acting as if I couldn't care less. "Christianity, ha!" I blustered. "That's for weaklings, not intellectuals." Down deep, I really wanted what the people in this group had, but my pride didn't want *them* to know that I was so needy. Then I turned to one of the young women in the group and said, "Tell me, what changed your lives? Why are you so different from the other students and faculty?"

She looked me straight in the eye and said two words I never expected to hear in an intelligent discussion on a university campus: "Jesus Christ."

"Jesus Christ?" I snapped. "Don't give me that kind of garbage. I'm fed up with religion, the Bible, and the church."

She quickly shot back, "Mister, I didn't say 'religion,' I said 'Jesus Christ.'"

Taken aback by the girl's courage and conviction, I apologized for my attitude. "But I'm sick and tired of religion and religious people," I added. "I don't want anything to do with it."

Then my new friends issued a challenge I couldn't believe. They challenged me, a pre-law student, to objectively examine the claim that Jesus Christ is God's Son. I thought it was a joke. I thought, *How could something as flimsy as Christianity stand up to an intellectual examination?*

But I took them up on their challenge, mostly out of spite, because I wanted to prove something to them. I spent months in research in an attempt to show that Christ was nothing but a hoax. I started with Scripture. I knew that if I could uncover indisputable evidence that the Bible was an unreliable record, the whole of Christianity would crumble. Sure, Christians could show me that Scripture said Christ was born of a virgin, that he performed miracles, and that he rose from the dead. But if I could find a way to show that Scripture could not be trusted historically, then I could prove Christianity was nothing more than a fantasy made up by wishful religious dreamers.

My research became more and more intense. For a while I dropped out of school to spend time in the historically rich libraries of Europe. And after months of examining historical evidences, I came to one conclusion: If I were to remain intellectually honest, I had to admit that the Old and New Testament documents were the most reliable writings of all antiquity! And that brought me face-to-face with the claims of Christ.

But it wasn't the historical evidence of Christ and his Word that drew me to Christ; it was his love, which had been evidenced in the lives of a handful of Christians. It wasn't logical facts about Christ that caused me to commit my life to him; it was Christ's loving heart, which reached out in mercy to form a relationship with me.

You see, the historical evidence convinced my mind that the Jesus who lived two thousand years ago had to be the one true God. But it was his love that gripped my heart and compelled me to commit my life to Christ. It was God's love that drew me to him. God said, "I have loved you, my people, with an everlasting love. With unfailing love I have drawn you to myself" (Jeremiah 31:3).

So as a young skeptic, that meant that I had to consider the real possibility that this loving Christ actually was who he claimed to be—and that left me with one question: How was I going to respond to Jesus? It was as if Christ was at the door of my life, saying, "Examine the truth about me and become convinced that I am the one true God who loves you and wants a relationship with you.

Know me through my reliable Word, and you will discover the very meaning to life itself."

OUR JOURNEY BEGINS

I believe Jesus Christ is saying the same things to you and me—and our kids—today. We may have acknowledged him as our Savior, but have we examined the evidences for our faith? We may have made a decision to trust Christ, but have we grasped the objective truth and relational meaning of our Christian faith? We may possess many advantages in life, but have we adequately answered those three basic life questions: Who am I? Why am I here? Where am I going?

Christ has those answers, and you and the young people in your life can discover them by moving beyond mere belief to convictions about the person of Jesus, the Word of God, and the resurrection of Christ. Exploring the truth and meaning of these three pillars of the Christian faith will correct our distorted views of God, truth, and reality. Addressing our kids' core beliefs will do more than apply Band-Aid solutions to dangerous and destructive behaviors. It will strike at the root cause of those things and foster the beliefs that will form our children's values, which will in turn shape their attitudes and actions, helping them to avoid the "destruction and misery" that stalk them (Romans 3:16).

As we have indicated earlier, the process of leading our young people beyond belief to convictions is built on a very simple process of understanding why certain things are objectively true and relationally meaningful. And while there is nothing complicated about that, untangling our kids from the complex maze of postmodern thinking will be a challenge. As we proceed through these pages, we will confront those challenges head-on.

However, one book cannot provide all the possible ways to meet those challenges with you, your younger children, preteen, or teenage youth group. That's why we have created a Beyond Belief family of products to help parents, pastors, youth workers, and Christian educators apply the message of this book in specific situations (see appendix A). When appropriate throughout this book, we will refer you to the appendixes, where we will list particular resources that will meet a specific need to better equip you or your young people not only to believe but also to live out biblical Christianity.

We have also chosen three methods of communicating this Beyond Belief message to you. The first is *narrative explanation*. Much of the book is straightforward text in which we identify the issues at stake and offer answers to address the issues. It is through this means that we provide the core message of the book.

Second, we provide *fictional illustration*. At intervals throughout the book we follow three young people, their parents, and their youth leaders as they grapple with distorted beliefs about God, truth, and reality. The fictional elements will help you see how our young people are affected by a postmodern mind-set and how it can be countered with an effective presentation of biblical Christianity. Don't think of these fictional elements as a novel or screenplay but as a means of illustrating how our kids actually think, and how you and I can counter such thinking.

Third, is *my story and personal application*. Throughout these pages, I (Josh) will share how the truth of Christ, his Word, and the Resurrection affected my own life as a way of showing how believing with convictions can affect anyone's life. We also will share how you can apply this message in your own life, family, and ministry, in *"Teachable Moment"* sections. While these application and teachable moment elements are far from exhaustive, we hope they will enable you to catch a vision of how passing on the true faith can be part of your everyday living.

Effectively challenging your child or youth group to live out an authentic Christian faith is perhaps the most exciting journey you can ever take. In doing so, not only will you share in the reward of seeing your young people avoid destruction and misery while answering the most pressing questions in life, but you yourself will no doubt be enriched in the process. I believe that part of the thrill of raising children is the incredible reeducation we parents get, and part of the thrill of passing on your faith to the next generation is the new vitality it can inject into your own faith.

I pray that by the time you finish reading this book, you will not only understand what content and approach is needed to instill convictions in your young people but also will come to know God better, love him more deeply, and trust him more fully. And you, too, may find a deeper, more significant meaning to your own life that will empower you to stand strong in the face of today's culture. Let the journey begin!

PART TWO

THE DEITY AND INCARNATION: GOD WANTS A RELATIONSHIP WITH US

CHAPTER 3

The Truth about Truth

"Part of your freshman orientation," Professor Marks began, "is an explanation of our university's multicultural education policy."

Lauren Johnson leaned forward in her chair, not wanting to miss a thing on her first day of college.

"Multicultural education is inclusive," the professor continued. "A lot of people are on the margins of society because of their race, class, gender, or sexual orientation. Multicultural education is about bringing them to the center, making one nation of many people. And to do that, we must validate each person's experience."

Lauren paused in taking her notes. If she were at Eisenhower High School back home in Westcastle, she would have asked what validating a person's experience really meant, but she decided not to ask—not now, not on her first day.

"We at this university," Professor Marks continued, "legitimize each individual's experience and will not tolerate anything else. We are a community here, and everyone is treated equally. All persons' beliefs, truth claims, and lifestyles are of their own choosing, and they are all equal to each other. Your religious beliefs, for example, are not better or more right than someone else's—they're just different. You must celebrate that difference and respect the other person for having his or her beliefs. Your particular sexual orientation is no better than that of someone else who may have a different orientation. They are both equally right. Your responsibility, as a citizen of this university community, is to celebrate such diversity."

Lauren scribbled furiously as the professor continued speaking in favor of equality, diversity, and tolerance. She thought that some of what she was hearing wasn't what her parents necessarily believed, but it sounded right to her—fair-minded, not judgmental, fully accepting of others' beliefs and views. Those things all made sense to her.

When the orientation session concluded, she linked up with her roommate, Tiffany, and they walked to lunch in the student commons, where they were joined by a second-year student named JD and Nick, a teaching assistant who was a grad student.

"How's the first day going?" Nick asked the two girls as he set his tray of food down on the table.

"Really good," Lauren answered.

"Yeah," Tiffany echoed. "Same here."

"They've just been read the riot act in orientation," JD told Nick, a note of sarcasm in his voice.

"Professor Marks, right?" Nick asked. When the girls nodded, he continued. "Yeah, he can be a bit much sometimes, but it's good to let all the incoming students know that they're expected to respect and validate all viewpoints."

"He sure got his point across," Tiffany said.

"Yeah," Lauren began. She addressed herself primarily to Nick. "I'm just wondering what he really means when he says we should 'validate a person's experience' and celebrate diversity."

Nick nodded as he finished chewing the bite of food he had just taken. "Let me explain," he said, leaning toward the girls. "You girls are of what faith?"

"We're Christians," Tiffany said. Lauren nodded in approval.

Nick turned to JD. "And you're . . . ?"

"Give me a break," JD said. "I'm not into the religious thing at all."

"Okay," Nick said. "That's perfect. You see, we're actually one family of human beings, and if we're going to live in harmony with one another, we've got to validate each other's individual experience. So, if you two girls are going to validate JD's perspective, you have to respect his choice and speak or act in a way that says his point of view is just as valid as yours. He has his view, you have yours, and neither one is right or wrong. That sets you free to celebrate your diversity, and that encourages harmony."

The girls nodded slowly.

"And JD can celebrate those differences by respecting your religious experience, even though he doesn't believe the same thing you do."

"I think I see," Tiffany said. She paused, then looked at the two guys. "What would you two say about celebrating diversity by attending our church youth group meeting next Tuesday over in Westcastle?"

Nick shrugged helplessly. "I teach a class Tuesday nights."

"How about you, JD?" Tiffany pressed.

"I don't think so," JD said with a smile.

"Two words," Lauren said, leaning forward as if she were about to say something important. "Free pizza."

"Not just free," Tiffany said, "but the best pizza you've ever tasted, not like the stuff they serve here!"

JD shrugged. "Now that's tempting," he said. "Pizza is something I can celebrate."

● ● ● ● ●

What Lauren is being subjected to at the university is the cultural mind-set Spanish philosopher Fernando Savater refers to in his book *El Mito Nacionalista*. It is the view that "all opinions are equal.

49

Each one has its point, and all should be respected or praised. That is to say, there is no rational way to discern between them."[1] Thomas A. Helmbock, executive vice president of the national Lambda Chi Alpha fraternity, understands the dangers of this view and offers a cogent analysis of it, calling it *new tolerance*: "The definition of new . . . tolerance is that every individual's beliefs, values, lifestyle, and perception of truth claims are equal. . . . There is no hierarchy of truth. Your beliefs and my beliefs are equal."[2]

If all truth is subjectively created and equal to all other views, then people need to respect the different opinions and beliefs of others. Everyone needs to accept others and not judge them for who they are or for what they believe. So, when we celebrate our individual diversity, we show respect for others, and this produces harmony within the human family. Sounds appealing, doesn't it? Our young people think so, and many of them are adopting this postmodern doctrine.

We have stated that the solution to reversing this mind-set within our children is to lead them beyond belief to conviction. By showing them the evidence for why Christ and his Word are objectively true and meaningful, they will see the error of this cultural doctrine and embrace the truth of Jesus Christ with conviction. But there's a problem.

If our young people have accepted the view that truth is whatever you personally and subjectively believe it to be, why do they need to determine whether any truth is objectively true? If there is no truth that is "more true" than any other "truth," why bother? Why would you want to become absolutely convinced that something is objectively true when you not only don't believe an absolute truth exists but also think that such a viewpoint makes you intolerant of the beliefs of others? When truth is considered to be subjectively created within a person and equal to all others, examining evidence for why something is objectively true is irrelevant, and convictions become unnecessary!

A LIGHT IN THE MIDST OF DARKNESS

I realize we've not presented a bright outlook on the task of moving our kids from belief to convictions. But while postmodernism may have created a cultural atmosphere in which convictions are taboo and evidences seem irrelevant, postmodernism also presents us with a unique opportunity.

One of the primary characteristics of postmodern thought is an emphasis on community and harmony within the human family. This only makes sense, of course. Since—in the postmodern way of thinking—all truth originates in the community in which a person participates, it is natural for a sense of community to be preeminent in the minds of this generation.

In fact, the influence of postmodernism has made today's teenagers the most relational and community-oriented generation in history. The Barna studies on today's youth reveal that relationships score extremely high in the hearts and minds of our young people.[3] My own studies and observations confirm that conclusion. Young people rank "close, personal friendships," "one marriage partner for life," "a close relationship with God," and "influencing other people's lives" so highly that Barna says "one of the distinguishing marks of [today's kids] has been their insistence upon the importance of personal relationships. . . . [They] appear to esteem relationships more highly than has been the norm for more than a quarter century."[4]

The premium our kids place on community and relationships shines a bright light of hope on an otherwise dark set of circumstances. In a world in which convictions are not fashionable and evidences for truth irrelevant, we can capitalize on the culture's desire for relationships and focus on community. Because, as it so happens, the very nature of absolute truth is relational. It addresses our kids' hunger for relationships that really do work. It can answer their heartfelt cry for

> *Truth—absolute truth—is intensely and unavoidably relational.*

community, connectedness, and a sense of belonging. Because truth—absolute truth—is intensely and unavoidably relational.

WHAT IS TRUTH?

Nearly twenty centuries ago, a high government official, trained in politics and the law, asked a question that has echoed all the way into the twenty-first century.

I can see Pontius Pilate, then the Roman governor of Judea, standing in his elaborate palace, bedecked in regal clothes. He posed a set of serious questions to the man who stood shackled between two soldiers.

"Are you the King of the Jews?" Pilate asks. The prisoner was accused of sedition.

This prisoner, unlike most, stands straight in the presence of the governor and looks him in the eyes when he speaks. "I am not an earthly king. . . . My kingdom is not of this world."

"You *are* a king then?" the governor says.

"*You* say that I am a king," the prisoner answers, aware that his interrogator is in a prickly political position, "and you are right." The prisoner looks at the politician with eyes that seem to read the expression not only on his face but of his soul as well. "I was born for that purpose," he goes on, "and I came to bring truth to the world. All who love the truth recognize that what I say is true."

And Pilate responds, "What *is* truth?"[5]

I want you to imagine for a moment that you are in that hall with Pilate and his prisoner. Imagine the words of the governor's question echoing off the marbled walls of that great hall. Imagine the expression on Pilate's face as he poses the question, scornful at first, then turning serious when the answer does not quickly come.

Seconds tick by. Still the prisoner and the governor study each other.

Imagine the governor's thoughts: *Who is this man? Why does he gaze at me so?*

And the prisoner's thoughts: *Have I not just told you? I came to bring truth to the world. Pilate, you are looking at the answer to your own question:* I *am the truth.*

THE PERSON OF TRUTH

Pilate was not just discussing the truth in his Jerusalem palace the day he met Jesus; he was literally looking at it. Truth was standing before him, clothed in human flesh! Jesus Christ, "who came from the Father, full of grace and truth," is the very embodiment and essence of absolute moral and spiritual truth itself (John 1:14, NIV).

You see, moral and spiritual truth isn't so much a concept as it is a person. It isn't so much something we believe as it is someone we relate to. Moral and spiritual truth has flesh. Truth is a person. And, thus, truth is not just conceptual; it is intrinsically relational.

One of *Webster's* definitions of *truth* is "fidelity to an original or standard."[6] For example, when a carpenter says that a floor or a wall **Truth is a person.** is "true," he or she means that it's faithful to the original measurements. But what is the "original" or "standard" for transcendent truth, for the kind of truth Jesus talked about when he said, "I came to bring truth to the world" (John 18:37)?

That standard is Jesus himself. "For by [Jesus Christ] all things were created that are in heaven and that are on earth, visible and invisible, whether thrones or dominions or principalities or powers. All things were created through Him and for Him. And He is before all things, and in Him all things consist" (Colossians 1:16-17, NKJV).

God is the original. He is the origin of all things that are in existence. And if we wish to know if anything is right or wrong, good or evil, we must measure it against the person who is true. "He is the

Rock," Moses said. "His work is perfect: . . . a God of truth and without iniquity, just and right is he" (Deuteronomy 32:4, KJV). You see, it is the very person and nature of God that defines truth. It is not something he measures up to. It is not something he announces. It is not even something he decides. It is something he *is*.

This means that moral and spiritual truth isn't simply abstract or philosophical; it is innately concrete, because truth is a person. It is best understood as a "who," not as a "what." And when we are careful to keep truth within that personal, relational context, it can change everything in the minds and hearts of our young people and the whole postmodern generation!

The apostle James was not talking in abstractions when he wrote: "Whatever is good and perfect comes to us from God above, who created all heaven's lights. Unlike them, he never changes or casts shifting shadows. In his goodness he chose to make us his own children by giving us his true word" (James 1:17-18).

God gave us the true Word—the one who said, "I came to bring truth to the world" (John 18:37)—for one purpose: to make us his own children. The Incarnate Truth came to this earth so that we as the human race could be restored to full fellowship with our Father God. As the apostle John said, "The Word became flesh and made his dwelling among us. We have seen his glory, the glory of the One and Only, who came from the Father, full of grace *and truth*" (John 1:14, NIV, emphasis mine). Thus it was that Jesus told his disciples: "You will know the truth, and the truth will set you free" (John 8:32).

And just a few moments later, Jesus made clear that the truth he had in mind was not only a concept but also a person, when he said: "So if the Son sets you free, you will indeed be free" (John 8:36).

You see, Jesus was not contradicting himself; he was not confused when he said (in verse 32) that "the truth" sets us free and just four verses later (in verse 36) said that it is "the Son" who sets us free. He was not speaking in riddles. He is the one who said, "I am the way, *the truth,* and the life" (John 14:6, emphasis mine). Jesus is the very embodiment of truth.

This is an important realization in our postmodern age—and particularly among our young people, who place such emphasis on relationships and community. They need to understand that truth is not simply an abstract concept; it is not something we create within ourselves. They need to see that truth is intrinsically, inescapably relational because it resides in and springs from a person who loves them and desires a relationship with them, person to person, friend to friend.

Truth is intrinsically, inescapably relational because it resides in and springs from a person who loves them and desires a relationship with them.

A SHIFT FROM "WHAT" TO "WHO"

To counter our young people's faulty thinking about truth—that all moral and spiritual truth is subjective and equal—we must shift the emphasis. What we believe about God or the Bible, or about what's right or wrong, is important. But "what we believe" must be seen in the context of "who we believe." Believing in Christ is about forming a relationship with a real person. Therefore, how we relate to the Person of Truth must become the central issue.

This shift from "what" to "who" will mean a major shift in how we think of Christianity and how we teach our kids the Christian faith. How we relate to moral and spiritual truth should no longer be thought of merely as a philosophical concept or abstract idea but rather how we relate to a person. Scriptural commands and rules should no longer be seen as merely instructions to obey but rather as ways to relate to a person. Evidences for the truth of Christ's deity, his resurrection, and the reliability of Scripture should not be offered as simply an apologetic—giving a defense of what we hold to be true—but they should also underscore the relational meaning of those truths. That is why I prefer to call this a relational apologetic. As we embrace the realization that Jesus is the embodiment of truth and explain the Christian faith as a life lived in relationship with God through Christ, we can counter our young people's faulty perceptions of God, truth, and reality.

Understanding Jesus Christ as the absolute embodiment of truth means that

- Truth could not be subjectively created; truth is and comes from the objective, absolute person of Christ himself. As John wrote:

  "For the law was given through Moses; grace and truth came through Jesus Christ." (John 1:17, NIV)

- Truth could not be relative and change from person to person, from community to community, because Jesus is the incarnation of the God who "never changes or casts shifting shadows" (James 1:17). As the Scripture says:

  "Jesus Christ is the same yesterday, today, and forever." (Hebrews 13:8)

- All truth could not be equal because Jesus didn't claim to be "a" truth, one that is equal to all others. His claim was exclusive; he claimed to be the one and only truth, the only way to God. "I am *the* way, *the* truth, and *the* life," he said. "No one can come to the Father except through me" (John 14:6, emphasis mine). Those are not the words of someone who is "one among many," someone who is "equal" to all others; those are the words of one who has no equal. He is the incarnation of him who said:

  "I am the Lord; there is no other God. I have prepared you, even though you do not know me, so all the world from east to west will know there is no other God. I am the Lord, and there is no other." (Isaiah 45:5-6)

A RELATIONSHIP WITH CHRIST
DEFINES COMMUNITY

This, then, is what we must do to lead our young people beyond belief to conviction: We must transform their mistaken, misguided perceptions of truth by leading them to encounter the one and only true Person of Truth—Jesus Christ.

As we introduce them to the Person of Truth, who wants them to experience his love personally, they will begin to understand how this relationship draws them into an all-inclusive community—the body of Christ (see 1 Corinthians 12:12-27). But while Christ's offer of a relationship with God might be compelling, it wouldn't be real and lasting if he weren't true.

When that realization ripens, we then point our young people to the historical evidence that establishes Jesus Christ as the one and only true and perfect God of the universe. They will be motivated to investigate these evidences because if Christ isn't who he said he was—and if he didn't rise from the dead and if the Bible can't be trusted—none of what they experience is a reality. It would be only a figment of their meaningless faith. For "if we have hope in Christ only for this life, we are the most miserable people in the world" (1 Corinthians 15:19).

Leading your young people beyond belief to convictions is an exciting and rewarding process. By God's grace and our help, our kids can become so thoroughly convinced in their minds and hearts about what they believe about Christ that they will commit to him regardless of the consequences. And the next step in this process is to look at what will convince our young people that Christ is the Son of the one true God.

CHAPTER 4

How True Are Christ's Claims?

"Hey, I've got to run," JD said as he stood. "It was good to meet you, Lauren. And good to see you again, Tiff."

"Yeah, good to meet you, too," Lauren responded. "And the invitation still stands to share a pizza with us," she said smiling.

"I just might take you up on it," JD replied as he headed for the door. Nick watched JD leave, then turned back to the girls. "Before you guys go, I just wanted to say that I'm a Christian, too, and so I think I know where you're coming from."

Lauren and Tiffany nodded appreciatively.

"But," Nick continued, "I think too many people make a mistake when they say that Jesus is the only way and things like that. I think the important thing is what Jesus taught about being a person who cares about others, you know?

"I mean, when people make such a big deal about Jesus' being the Son of God, they miss the real point, which is what he taught us. In fact, Jesus never even claimed to be the Son of God; it was his followers who made that claim after he died."

"I never knew that," Lauren said.

"I didn't either," Tiffany said.

"Well, you're at the university now," Nick said. "You're not in Sunday school anymore, Dorothy, if you know what I mean."

• • • • •

Many of our kids are encountering scenes much like the one being played out between Lauren, Tiffany, and Nick. Too often, Sunday school, church classes, and youth groups don't deal with the issues Nick is bringing up, and our young people are unprepared for what they are being told at most universities and colleges. So many of our kids would consider Nick's reasoning pretty sound. After all, the things Jesus taught *are* important . . . and powerful. And he did command all those who follow him to "love each other" (John 15:17).

But Lauren and Tiffany are being misled. University educators commonly tell their students that Jesus made his *teachings* the central issue and never made a claim to deity. It's fairly common to hear people say such things in university environments. The problem is, they're not true.

Jesus *did* claim to be the Son of God, and that claim was central to everything else he said and did.

On one occasion Jesus asked his disciples, "Who do you say I am?"

"Simon Peter answered, 'You are the Messiah, the Son of the living God.'

"Jesus replied, 'You are blessed, Simon son of John, because my Father in heaven has revealed this to you'" (Matthew 16:15-17).

According to the New Testament record, Jesus repeatedly made it clear that he was the unique Son of God, an assertion that did not go unnoticed by the religious leaders of his day. In fact, that was the very reason they tried to discredit and, eventually, put him to death: "So the Jewish leaders tried all the more to kill him. In addition to disobeying the Sabbath rules, he had spoken of God as his Father, thereby making himself equal with God" (John 5:18).

On more than one occasion, Jesus' clear assertion of his own deity caused his fellow Jews to want to stone him. Once, when he told the Jewish leaders, "Your father Abraham rejoiced at the thought of seeing my day; he saw it and was glad," his listeners became indignant: "'You are not yet fifty years old,' the Jews said to him, 'and you have seen Abraham!'

Jesus did claim to be the Son of God, and that claim was central to everything else he said and did.

"'I tell you the truth,' Jesus answered, 'before Abraham was born, I am!' At this, they picked up stones to stone him, but Jesus hid himself, slipping away from the temple grounds" (John 8:56-59, NIV). On another occasion, when Jesus said that he was one with the Father, the Jewish leaders again picked up stones to kill him (see John 10:30-31).

When Jesus asked why they wanted to kill him, they retorted, "for blasphemy, because you, a mere man, *have made yourself God*" (John 10:33, emphasis mine).

Yet another time, Jesus told a paralyzed man, "My son, your sins are forgiven" and again the religious leaders reacted with outrage. "What?" they said. "This is blasphemy! *Who but God* can forgive sins!" (Mark 2:5-7, emphasis mine).

In the final days prior to Jesus' death, he made it clear—even to the Sanhedrin (the Jewish high council)—just who he was: "Then the high priest asked him, 'Are you the Messiah, the Son of the blessed God?' Jesus said, 'I am. . . .'" In response to the proclamation, they "condemned him to death" (Mark 14:61-64).

HOW CAN WE KNOW JESUS WAS AND IS THE SON OF GOD?

The central issue of Christianity is not the teachings of a man called Jesus but the person of Jesus Christ himself. And throughout the Gospel record, Jesus urged his listeners and followers to believe *in him*, not just in his teachings (see John 3:15-16; 8:24; 11:25; 12:46; 20:29).

In fact, the identity of Jesus is utterly crucial to understanding everything he had to say. All that Jesus said and did pointed to his identity as the Messiah, the Son of God, and to the purpose for which he came to earth. If he is not who he claimed to be, then his teachings are either the ramblings of a lunatic who sincerely *thought* he was God (but wasn't) or the words of a liar who *knew* he wasn't God (but said he was).

If his claims are true, however, then he is not a liar or a lunatic—he is Lord! He is the incarnate Son of the one and only creator of the universe, the one who said: "I am the Lord, and there is no other" and "Do not worship any other gods besides me" (Isaiah 45:6; Exodus 20:3).

If his claims are true, however, then he is not a liar or a lunatic—he is Lord!

But can we know whether or not Jesus' claim to be God is true? How can Lauren—or our kids, or any of us—be sure that Jesus Christ is the Son of the one true God?

There is a way. Jesus did not make his claims to deity without also providing sufficient evidence to support his claims. And, more than that, the evidence Jesus provided—in the fulfillment of messianic prophecies, the Virgin Birth, and the miracles—is so overwhelming and compelling that it ought to fill our hearts and souls with awe and wonder at the God-man, Jesus Christ.

One clarification will be helpful before we examine the evidences of Christ's deity. Evidences that point to the truth of the Incarnation are also evidences for the deity of Jesus Christ. The words *deity* and *incarnation*, however, are not synonymous. The Incarnation refers to the miracle of God the Son's becoming human. The word *deity* refers to the identity of the person who is, in fact, God the Son in the flesh. To know that the Incarnation took place, that God revealed himself on earth in a human form, we must identify that person of history—and that person of history is the Deity, the God-man, Jesus Christ.

MESSIANIC PROPHECIES FULFILLED IN ONE PERSON

Imagine agreeing over the phone to meet a distant business acquaintance—someone you've never met in person—at a large business convention.

"How will I know you?" you might ask.

"Well," your associate might suggest, "I'll be carrying a briefcase."

"All right," you reply, then think better of it. "A lot of people will probably be carrying briefcases. Not everyone, but a lot. What color is it?"

"Black."

"That might narrow it down some," you say, "but not enough."

"I'm a redhead," your associate offers.

"That helps," you answer. *Redhead carrying a black briefcase. Still might not be specific enough.* "What will you be wearing?"

A slight hesitation. "A blue blazer. How's that?"

You nod, though you know your colleague can't see you. "That's better. But just to be sure, can you wear red tennis shoes?"

"Very funny. I'll just make sure I'm wearing a name tag with my name in big bold letters."

"That should do it," you answer. *I'll just look for a redhead carrying a black briefcase and wearing a blue blazer with a name tag.* "I should be able to recognize you from a distance, and your name on the tag will seal it."

Identifying the Deity

Now imagine God, several millennia ago, devising the plan to send his only Son to earth to be born as a human infant.

If we could have spoken down the corridors of time, we might have asked, "How will we know him? How will we recognize him as the Messiah, the eternal, incarnate Son of God?"

God might have responded, "I will cause him to be born as an Israelite, a descendant of Abraham (Genesis 22:18; Galatians 3:16)."

"But," we might have protested, "Abraham's descendants will be as numerous as the stars!"

"Then I will narrow it down to only half of Abraham's lineage, and make him a descendant of Isaac, not Ishmael (Genesis 21:12; Luke 3:23-34)."

"That will help, but isn't that still an awful lot of people?"

"Let him be born from Jacob's line, then, eliminating half of Isaac's lineage (Numbers 24:17; Luke 3:23-34)."

"But—"

"I will be more specific. Jacob will have twelve sons; I will bring forth the Messiah from the tribe of Judah (Genesis 49:10; Luke 3:23-33)."

"Won't that still be a lot of people? We still may not recognize him when he comes."

"Don't worry! Look for him in the family line of Jesse (Isaiah 11:1; Luke 3:23-32). *And* from the house and lineage of Jesse's youngest son, David (Jeremiah 23:5; Luke 3:23-31). And then I will tell you *where* he will be born: Bethlehem, a tiny town in the area called Judah (Micah 5:2; Matthew 2:1)."

"But how will we know which person born there is your Son?"

"He will be preceded by a messenger who will prepare the way and announce his advent (Isaiah 40:3; Matthew 3:1-2). He will begin his ministry in Galilee (Isaiah 9:1; Matthew 4:12-17) and will teach in parables (Psalm 78:2; Matthew 13:34-35), performing many miracles (Isaiah 35:5-6; Matthew 9:35)."

"Okay, that should help a lot."

"Oh," God might have responded, "I'm just getting warmed up. He will ride into the city of Jerusalem on a donkey (Zechariah

9:9; Matthew 21:2; Luke 19:35-37) and will appear suddenly and forcefully at the temple courts and zealously 'clean house' (Psalm 69:9; Malachi 3:1; John 2:15-16). Why, in *one day* I will fulfill no fewer than *twenty-nine* specific prophecies spoken at least five hundred years earlier about him! Listen to this:

1. He will be betrayed by a friend (Psalm 41:9; Matthew 26:49).
2. The price of his betrayal will be thirty pieces of silver (Zechariah 11:12; Matthew 26:15).
3. His betrayal money will be cast to the floor of my temple (Zechariah 11:13; Matthew 27:5).
4. His betrayal money will be used to buy the potter's field (Zechariah 11:13; Matthew 27:7).
5. He will be forsaken and deserted by his disciples (Zechariah 13:7; Mark 14:50).
6. He will be accused by false witnesses (Psalm 35:11; Matthew 26:59-60).
7. He will be silent before his accusers (Isaiah 53:7; Matthew 27:12).
8. He will be wounded and bruised (Isaiah 53:5; Matthew 27:26).
9. He will be hated without a cause (Psalm 69:4; John 15:25).
10. He will be struck and spit on (Isaiah 50:6; Matthew 26:67).
11. He will be mocked, ridiculed, and rejected (Isaiah 53:3; Matthew 27:27-31; and John 7:5, 48).
12. He will collapse from weakness (Psalm 109:24-25; Luke 23:26).
13. He will be taunted with specific words (Psalm 22:6-8; Matthew 27:39-43).
14. People will shake their heads at him (Psalm 109:25; Matthew 27:39).

15. People will stare at him (Psalm 22:17; Luke 23:35).
16. He will be executed among 'sinners' (Isaiah 53:12; Matthew 27:38).
17. His hands and feet will be pierced (Psalm 22:16; Luke 23:33).
18. He will pray for his persecutors (Isaiah 53:12; Luke 23:34).
19. His friends and family will stand afar off and watch (Psalm 38:11; Luke 23:49).
20. His garments will be divided and won by the casting of lots (Psalm 22:18; John 19:23-24).
21. He will thirst (Psalm 69:21; John 19:28).
22. He will be given gall and vinegar (Psalm 69:21; Matthew 27:34).
23. He will commit himself to God (Psalm 31:5; Luke 23:46).
24. His bones will be left unbroken (Psalm 34:20; John 19:33).
25. His heart will rupture (Psalm 22:14; John 19:34).
26. His side will be pierced (Zechariah 12:10; John 19:34).
27. Darkness will come over the land at midday (Amos 8:9; Matthew 27:45).
28. He will be buried in a rich man's tomb (Isaiah 53:9; Matthew 27:57-60).
29. He will die 483 years after the declaration of Artaxerxes to rebuild the temple in 444 B.C. (Daniel 9:24).[1]

"As a final testimony, on the third day after his death, he will be raised from the dead (Psalm 16:10; Acts 2:31), ascend to heaven (Psalm 68:18; Acts 1:9), and be seated at the right hand of God in full majesty and authority (Psalm 110:1; Hebrews 1:3)."

What extraordinary lengths God went to in order to help people identify and recognize his only begotten Son!

What extraordinary lengths God went to in order to help people identify and recognize his only begotten Son! Jesus fulfilled sixty major Old Testament prophecies (with about

270 additional ramifications)—all of which were made more than 400 years before his birth. This makes a compelling case for the deity of Christ.

The Probability Factor

Yet we must admit that Jesus was not the only Jew to be born into the tribe of Judah, in the city of Bethlehem, and buried in a rich man's tomb. Is it possible to believe that some of the details of Jesus' life just happened to coincide with all those Old Testament prophecies?

For the answer to that question, we need only turn to the science of statistics and probabilities. Professor Peter W. Stoner, in an analysis that was carefully reviewed and pronounced to be sound by the American Scientific Affiliation, states that the probability of just *eight* prophecies being fulfilled in one person is 1 in 10^{17} (that's 1 in 100,000,000,000,000,000).[2]

Look at it this way: If you were to take 100,000,000,000,000,000 silver dollars and spread them across the state of Texas, they would not only cover the entire state but also form a pile of coins two feet deep! Now, take one more silver dollar, mark it with a big red X, toss it into that pile, and stir the whole pile thoroughly.

Then, blindfold yourself, and starting at El Paso on the western border of the state, walk the length and breadth of that enormous state, from Amarillo in the panhandle to Laredo on the Rio Grande all the way to Galveston on the Gulf of Mexico, stooping just once along the way to pick up a single silver dollar out of that two-foot-deep pile. Then take off your blindfold, and look at the silver dollar in your hand. What are the chances that you would pick the marked coin out of a pile of silver dollars the size of the Lone Star State? *The same chance that one person could have fulfilled just eight messianic prophecies in one lifetime.*[3]

In other words, it is nearly unthinkable to imagine that eight Old Testament prophecies about the Messiah could have come true in one man—let alone the *sixty* major prophecies that were ful-filled in Jesus of Nazareth—unless, of course, he *is* (as he himself claimed) "the Messiah, the Son of the blessed God," the one who was and is and is to come (Mark 14:61; Revelation 4:8).

THE VIRGIN BIRTH

The fulfillment of all those messianic prophecies in one person, Jesus Christ, ought to fill us—and our children—with awe and wonder, and convince even the most skeptical among us of the truth that Jesus is indeed the Son of God, the Incarnate Word. But there is more, much more.

Long before the prophets spoke, before anyone had heard of the Messiah, God erected in the Garden of Eden a signpost that pointed directly to the means by which his Son would be born. God's merciful and masterful plan to restore his relationship with the human family that had turned from him was to enter the hu-man family himself and take the form of a man. God's declaration was made in the wake of Adam and Eve's original sin, in the very first words of judgment God spoke into earth's atmosphere. When God cursed the serpent who tempted Eve, he said: "From now on, you and the woman will be enemies, and your offspring and her offspring will be enemies. He [Christ] will crush your head, and you will strike his heel" (Genesis 3:15).

The natural process of conceiving and giving birth involves the egg of a woman and the sperm, the "seed" of a man. But God, as re-corded in Genesis 3, referred to a *supernatural* process when he promised that the serpent, Satan, would be defeated by the seed of a woman—not the seed of any man.

Scripture foretold that same supernatural process again, seven hundred years before God was born as a child, when the prophet Isaiah said, "The Lord himself will choose the sign. Look! The virgin will conceive a child! She will give birth to a son and will call him Immanuel—'God is with us'" (Isaiah 7:14).

What striking words: "the *virgin* will *conceive*." In the course of nature, virgins don't conceive. Conception requires fertilization of the female's ovum (egg) by the male's gamete (sperm) to form a new cell, called a zygote. The zygote must then implant itself in the lining of the uterus. That single cell then possesses a complete set of chromosomes, having received half its genetic information from each parent—all the information that will guide its development as a new, distinct, individual is being formed.

But God, speaking to the serpent, and again through the prophet Isaiah, promised something that human history had never seen before (or since): A child would be born outside the natural process of conception. Instead, the Holy Spirit of God himself would form, in the dark ocean of a virgin's womb, a child of divine origin! This person would bear the identity of God's Son because God himself would father the child. From that miraculous moment of conception, that child's human form would develop from a single cell to sixty trillion cells and would be brought into the world as Immanuel, "God is with us"! (see Isaiah 7:14; Matthew 1:23).

If that really happened—if the historical Jesus truly was born to a virgin—it would make a compelling case for his deity, wouldn't it? If Jesus was conceived apart from the natural process of conception, we should be satisfied that he pretty much *had* to be God, right? We can see that the Genesis record and Isaiah's prophecy point to a virgin birth for the Messiah, but is there evidence that what had been promised actually came to pass? Is there any reliable way to investigate the circumstances of Jesus' birth?

Let's begin with the historical record. Seven centuries after Isaiah's prophecy, Matthew reported the extraordinary circumstances of the birth of a child called Jesus of Nazareth. He wrote: "Now this is how Jesus the Messiah was born. His mother, Mary, was engaged to be married to Joseph. But while she was still a virgin, she became pregnant by the Holy Spirit. . . . All of this happened to fulfill the Lord's message through his prophet: 'Look! The virgin will conceive a child! She will give birth to a son, and he will be called Immanuel (meaning, God is with us)'" (Matthew 1:18, 22-23).

The Gospel of Luke, the careful historian whose writings have been repeatedly supported by archaeology, records the appearance of the angel Gabriel to Mary and his announcement that she would give birth to the Messiah. Mary answered with a question: "But how can I have a baby? I am a virgin." Gabriel replied, "The Holy Spirit will come upon you, and the power of the Most High will overshadow you. So the baby born to you will be holy, and he will be called the Son of God" (Luke 1:34-35).

A Glorious Irony

But among the most significant evidences of Jesus' virgin birth are those contained in the accounts of how the people of Jesus' hometown, Nazareth, reacted to him after he began his public ministry.

On one occasion, after he had taught in the synagogue, the people he had grown up with said, "'He's just the carpenter, the son of Mary. . . .' They were deeply offended and refused to believe in him" (Mark 6:3). The label "son of Mary" was an unambiguous insult in a society that called children by the name of their fathers—except, of course, in the case of children whose paternity was doubted.

At another time, Jesus' opponents threw a sharply pointed barb at him when they said, "*We* were not born out of wedlock!" (John 8:41, emphasis mine).

That insult and the reference to Jesus as the "son of Mary" imply that it was common knowledge in Jesus' hometown that Jesus had been conceived before Mary's wedding to—and without the help of—Joseph.

In other words, it seems very likely that the circumstances of Jesus' miraculous birth—to a virgin—caused him to be labeled as an illegitimate child in the society of his day. Thus, as a direct result of the unusual circumstances of his birth, he not only accepted the robe of humanity but undoubtedly endured cruel taunts on the playground of his childhood and coarse ridicule from critics as an adult.

In an irony of unbelief, the evidence of his divine *glory* became a smear on his human reputation! This irony persisted in some of the vehemently anti-Christian writings of Jewish rabbis in the years following his death. The rabbis invented a story that cast Jesus as the illegitimate son of a Roman soldier named Panthera, "unintentionally admitting that Jesus was not born of an ordinary marriage," as the third-century theologian and biblical scholar Origen put it.[4]

The evidence for the Virgin Birth not only points to the conclusion that Jesus of Nazareth is who he claimed to be but also shows how thorough was his identification with us.

The evidence for the Virgin Birth not only points to the conclusion that Jesus of Nazareth is who he claimed to be but also shows how thorough was his identification with us. Though he was God, he humbled himself and willingly endured the sneers and scorn of his contemporaries in order to be born of a virgin and fulfill his mission as the Messiah, the Son of God, "the visible image of the invisible God" (Colossians 1:15).

THE MIRACLES OF CHRIST

The fulfillment of messianic prophecies and the miracle of the Virgin Birth are not the only evidences that convince us that the man called Jesus is also the incarnate Son of God.

Jesus himself pointed out that his actions—his miracles—were evidences that he is God's Son.

> "I have testimony weightier than that of John [the Baptist]. For the very work that the Father has given me to finish, and which I am doing, testifies that the Father has sent me." (John 5:36, NIV)

"The miracles I do in my Father's name speak for me." (John 10:25, NIV)

"Even though you do not believe me, believe the miracles, that you may know and understand that the Father is in me, and I in the Father." (John 10:38, NIV)

Jesus clearly intended his miracles to be understood as a validation of his deity. As the apostle Peter said on the Day of Pentecost, "Jesus of Nazareth was a man accredited by God to you by miracles, wonders and signs, which God did among you through him" (Acts 2:22, NIV). And the apostle John, pointing to Christ's deity, reports that Jesus did many other "miraculous signs" that weren't even recorded for us (John 20:30).

Jesus clearly intended his miracles to be understood as a validation of his deity.

But those recorded miracles are not only sufficient to convince us that Jesus was truly who he claimed to be; they ought to impress us with the awesome power and compassion of the Incarnate One, and cause us to exclaim, "A man who could do that is no ordinary man; he had to be God himself!"

The Light of the World

The Gospel of John, the beloved disciple, records an amazing event that was typical in the life of the God-man, Jesus.

I invite you to take a journey with me and imagine being one of Jesus' disciples as we walk along beside him on a sunny Sabbath afternoon. We have just exited the temple, where Jesus had been accused by the religious leaders of being possessed by a demon. They had been so angry that they had come close to stoning him before we made our escape from the temple area.

Walking briskly, we pass a blind beggar sitting cross-legged on the street and proceed some distance before we realize that Jesus has not kept pace with us. We look back and see the Master gazing at the man, who is somewhat of a fixture in the area because he frequently begs at this or other spots in the city. Though few know the beggar's name, most know his circumstance; he has been blind since birth.

Tentatively, we approach the pair—the beggar and the teacher—and wonder why Jesus has stopped here. One of our companions, always impetuous and eager to please, blurts out a question. "Teacher, why was this man born blind?" he asks. "Was it a result of his own sins or those of his parents?"

But Jesus, with characteristic kindness, plants his knees in the dirt beside the man and answers, more to him than to us it seems, "It was not because of his sins or his parents' sins. . . . He was born blind so the power of God could be seen in him."[5]

The irony of Jesus' words echoes off the stone walls of the buildings that surround us. He explains that this man's eyes—which have never seen his mother's smile, never beheld the dazzling white marble of Herod's Temple reflecting the rays of the sun, never watched waves of wind wafting through the golden grain of a wheat field, never gazed on the face of a blushing young girl in love—have been dark all these years so that the power of God can be seen in them today!

We watch, our attention riveted to the man who has lived in darkness and the man who has called himself the light of the world, as Jesus spits in the dust, not once but several times. No one speaks as he forms a mud pack in his carpenter's hands, and patiently, tenderly spreads the mud over the blind man's eyes.

"Go," he tells the man, "and wash in the pool of Siloam."[6] What transpires next defies natural explanation; it even exceeds the comprehension of twenty-first-century medical science. Because when the man obeys Jesus and washs the mud from his eyes in the pool, he can see!

In an instant of time, the most complex organ in the human body was mended. Without a scalpel to gingerly remove the probable cause—a congenital cataract that had clouded the man's lenses—without a tiny suction tube to clear the clouded, jellylike ocean of the vitreous humor, the man's eyes were healed. There was no digital-age technology to reattach the retinas. There was no highly developed serum applied to the complex layer of light-sensing cells at the back of the eyes that allowed 7 million "cones" and 150 million "rods" to once more send their coded messages of light to the brain via the millions of fibers that comprise the optic nerve. And there was no prescribed therapy for permanent amblyopia inside the man's eyes—the underdevelopment of the visual system resulting from decades of disuse.

Twenty-one centuries later, such congenital blindness is often irreparable, even if the surgery were to be performed by the most skilled surgeons in the most advanced operating room of the best hospital in the world. But Jesus, the Galilean carpenter, performed it in an instant, using mud and his own saliva as his only tools.

As fascinating as this healing is—just one among the many miracles Jesus performed—it should not be surprising. Though the task of removing cataracts, reattaching retinas, and reconstructing the ultrasensitive machinery of the human eye is a highly specialized and evolving field of modern medicine, it was no great feat for Jesus of Nazareth—because he is God Incarnate, the architect of the human eye.

WHO BUT GOD?

The healing of the man who had been born blind was more than miraculous to those who first heard about it; to some, it was disturbing. When the news got to the Pharisees, it caused a stir: "Some of the Pharisees said, 'This man Jesus is not from God, for he is working on the Sabbath.' Others said, 'But how could an ordinary sinner do such miraculous signs?' So there was a deep division of opinion among them" (John 9:16).

The healing of the man born blind was mind-boggling to Jesus' critics. Many of the Pharisees had already rejected Jesus as the Messiah. He had not measured up to their political and religious expectations for the Messiah. The kingdom he was proclaiming called for humility, repentance, servanthood, and devotion to the person of God, not devotion to a set of pharisaical rules and regulations. So they wanted nothing to do with Jesus' relational brand of religion. Yet, his miracles presented them with a major problem.

First, the Pharisees called for the healed man to come before them to explain what had happened. Then they called for his parents to confirm that he in fact had been born blind. Finally, they brought the man back again, hoping to resolve the dilemma, because they could not bring themselves to believe what the miracle indicated: that Jesus was more than a man. And yet, they could not explain how a mere man—a sinner like them—could perform such a miracle (see John 9:17-22). To their questions, the man replied: "I don't know whether he is a sinner. . . . But I know this: I was blind, and now I can see! . . . Never since the world began has anyone been able to open the eyes of someone born blind. If this man were not from God, he couldn't do it" (John 9:25, 32-33).

John's account concludes the story:

> When Jesus heard what had happened, he found the man and said, "Do you believe in the Son of Man?"
>
> The man answered, "Who is he, sir, because I would like to."
> [Remember, this man had no idea what Jesus looked like; he had never seen him before!]
>
> "You have seen him," Jesus said, "and he is speaking to you!"
>
> "Yes, Lord," the man said, "I believe!" And he worshiped Jesus. (John 9:35-38)

The evidence of Jesus' deity was conclusive for the man who had been born blind. "I was blind, and now I can see!" he said, citing the evidence that eventually convinced him. "If this man were not from God, he couldn't do it." But Jesus *did* do it; he had the power to perform this and other miraculous works because he was the Incarnate One (see John 1:1). His power simply reflected his identity.

Who else but God has the mastery Jesus demonstrated over the human body, weather, gravity, and even death itself? Who else but the Incarnate One could do the following things:

- Calm a storm (see Matthew 8)
- Make a mute person speak (see Matthew 9)
- Feed five thousand people with five loaves and two fish (see Matthew 14)
- Cast out demons (see Mark 5)
- Walk on water (see Mark 6)
- Bring sight to the blind (see Mark 10)
- Curse a fig tree (see Mark 11)
- Foretell the future (see Mark 14)
- Heal a paralyzed man (see Luke 5)
- Raise a boy from the dead (see Luke 7)
- Heal incurable hemorrhaging (see Luke 8)
- Cleanse lepers (see Luke 17)
- Turn water into wine (see John 2)
- Make the lame walk (see John 5)
- Forgive sin (see John 8)
- Raise a man from the dead (see John 11)

The miracles of Jesus—if we but consider them openly and confront them fairly—ought to do more than convince us that Jesus is who he said he is. His miracles ought to prompt us to wonder, *Who but God can do such things?* They should move us to cry out, like Thomas, "My Lord and my God!" (John 20:28). As Jesus urged his disciples, "Believe that I am in the Father and the Father is in me. Or at least believe because of what you have seen me do" (John 14:11).

The evidences of Christ's deity—the messianic prophecies, his virgin birth, and his many miracles—are recorded for us in precise and powerful detail so that we can believe in him with deepened conviction, being convinced that Jesus Christ is who he said he is.

The evidences of Christ's deity are recorded for us in precise and powerful detail so that we can believe in him with deepened conviction.

But as we've repeatedly stated, evidences that support Christ's deity have limitations for this generation. In the hands of some, who may be convinced that Jesus is the incarnate God yet don't grasp the relational meaning of that truth, truth not only can be misunderstood but also can be misapplied.

• • • • •

"It's great to have you join us, JD," said Duane Cunningham, the youth leader for Westcastle Community Church, as he shook the hand of Lauren's friend.

JD shrugged. "I thought I'd stop in before leaving for Christmas break. I hear you serve some pretty good pizza."

"We think so," said Liz, Duane's wife. "Come on in, and take a seat. The pizza will be coming out shortly."

Duane and Liz Cunningham, volunteer youth workers with the Westcastle Community Church, took their growing ministry to youth very seriously. Duane studied hard to provide solid biblical lessons for group meetings, and Liz's warmth and loving care for each member of the group kept the kids coming back week after week. Their pizza recipe helped as well.

As usual, Duane led the youth group meeting and even succeeded in involving JD in the interaction following his presentation. When the meeting was over, the group members dove into the pizza and soda as they talked and joked with each other. JD stuck fairly close to Lauren, who soon introduced him to her friends Megan and Brent.

"When do you go home for Christmas, JD?" Lauren asked.

"I'm not," JD replied.

"Why not?" Brent asked. "There's no place like home, you know."

"Well, not for me. My mother passed away, and I don't get along with my dad." His tone was leaden. "I'll be visiting a friend."

"So, was your mother a Christian?" Brent asked, taking a bite of pizza.

"Was she what?" JD asked.

Brent quickly chewed and swallowed. "Was your mother a Christian—you know a believer?"

"Brent," Megan groaned in disapproval.

JD flashed a cold expression at Brent. "What's that got to do with anything?"

"Oh, well . . . ," Brent answered, aware now of his insensitivity. "I just wondered if she, well, you know was, uh, before she died did she . . ." Megan's elbow caused Brent to pause. "I guess it doesn't matter. Sorry I asked."

JD stared in apparent disbelief for a moment. He thought he had found a group of people who really cared for him, people he'd like to be around. But Brent had clearly offended him. JD spun quickly and headed out, slamming the door behind him.

CHAPTER 5

The Relational Meaning of the Incarnation

As the door slammed behind JD, his memory raced back to a day eight years earlier, when another door had slammed behind him.

It was a Saturday morning, and an eleven-year-old JD rose before the crack of dawn. He dressed hurriedly and dashed outside to get his morning chores done before the workmen arrived.

A team of men had been working for days to jack up a small house on his parents' farm and prepare it to be moved to a new location. JD's grown brother, Will, was having it moved over the objections of their father. Will had been engaged in a bitter ongoing feud with his father, which had escalated into an all-out war for half of the family farm. Having successfully sued his father, Will had arrived that morning with a sheriff, a deputy, and a court order authorizing Will to move the house.

JD, however, was trying hard to stay out of the family conflict. He hated to see his father and brother fight, but that was between them. Today JD just wanted to savor the excitement of watching an entire house being towed down the road, a spectacle more entertaining to his eleven-year-old mind than a traveling circus.

Then, just as the tractors were being attached to the house, JD's father, drunk as usual, began yelling at Will. The sheriff moved quickly toward the staggering man to prevent an ugly scene.

But it was too late for that. Will, expecting something like this, had arranged for numerous families from that small farming community to be on hand to provide moral support for him. Many of them began chanting obscenities at JD's father as the sheriff restrained the old man.

JD watched in horror, his excitement turning to embarrassment. Frightened by the escalating conflict and humiliated to see his family's feud played out in full view of his friends and neighbors, little JD ran from the shameful scene and into the family's nearby barn. Slamming the barn door behind him, he scrambled into the corn bin and cowered behind an old barrel, wondering if his father or big brother were going to hurt each other—or worse.

As he crouched in the corn, his shame slowly turned to anger. He was angry that his father's drinking brought so much division to the home. He was angry that he so rarely saw his father sober. But more than anything, he was angry that his drunken father brought such pain to his mother's life.

JD spent hours in the barn that day. No one came looking for him. No one seemed even to notice that he was gone.

JD never really asked for much out of life. But he did long for a loving family and a father who cared enough to show an interest in who he was and what went on in his life. But that day in the barn seemed to seal it in his mind: He'd never have a loving family or a caring father. In fact, from that day forward, something began to grip his heart, something that eventually would hold him captive: a consuming hatred for his father.

LONGING FOR A CONNECTION

That house-moving incident really happened. In fact, the JD character in the story has actually been drawn from my own life. That incident happened exactly as it is recorded here; it was over fifty years ago, yet I can clearly remember the day young Joslin David (JD) McDowell sat for hours alone in that barn. The feud between my father and my oldest brother, Wilmot, is just one painful incident among many from my troubled childhood.

I never had any kind of real relationship with my father. I can't recall him ever hugging me during my childhood. I can't remember a single time when he took me somewhere alone just to spend time with me. I don't think he ever told me he loved me as I was growing up. As a result, I felt thoroughly disconnected from him.

And while I always believed my mother loved me, and I know she always tried to be there for me, she had more than she could handle just trying to survive a violent, dysfunctional marriage. I felt compelled to protect her, but because of my father's alcoholism and abusive behavior, I never experienced anything approaching a normal, healthy relationship with her either.

Now, your children, students, or youth group members may not be suffering from the severe loneliness and relational disconnect that characterized my youth. In fact, I pray heartily that their experience is nothing like mine. But too many of our kids today can identify with at least some of my experiences, and many more—even those from Christian homes—are struggling with the same kinds of emotions that characterized my childhood.

Twenty-first-century teenagers experience an alarmingly high degree of loneliness and alienation. Many of them lead lives of quiet desperation and isolation. They may not even know what they're feeling, but they lack a sense of connectedness. Almost half have lived through their parents' divorce. More than that—63 percent—live in households in which both parents work outside the home.[1] On average, they spend 20 percent of their waking hours alone, and they "are isolated to an extent that has never been possible before."[2]

In my travels and speaking, I interact with many young people. I confirm the studies that proclaim teenagers as the loneliest segment of our society. Many tell me things that echo my own childhood experience, like never hearing a father say, "I love you." The question I get most frequently from today's kids is, "Josh, what am I going to do about my dad?" When I ask what they mean, they invariably say, "He won't spend any time with me" or "He doesn't talk to me." Our kids want our involvement in their lives; they want us to be available to them. But sadly, far too many kids are being raised by inattentive parents, and they feel adrift and disconnected.

Our kids also live in a complex and sometimes confusing world. They often live under extreme pressure and demanding expectations, many times self-imposed. And amid the confusion and pressure, they want to know that someone loves them and understands what they're going through. They desperately want adults and their peers to accept them for who they are, yet most haven't figured out who they really are themselves.

It's not just our kids, of course. We *all* long to feel connected with other people. We all know what it's like to feel unaccepted, unloved, misunderstood, and unimportant. We long to hear someone say, "I love and accept you for who you are, I understand what you're going through, and I'll always be there for you, no matter what." All of us—regardless of our age or stage in life—crave that sense of connectedness to someone who truly cares.

Yet most of our young people don't understand that the incarnation of Jesus Christ directly addresses their feeling of disconnectedness. They don't realize how God wants to connect and root them in the security of his love.

Many of our kids (64 percent) believe the gospel is about God's sending his Son to earth to teach them how to be good enough to earn their way to heaven![3] They have a distorted belief about God, and they, like many adults, do not understand the real meaning of God's taking on the robe of flesh and becoming a human being.

THE INCARNATION SAYS "I WANT TO HAVE A RELATIONSHIP WITH YOU!"

Whether we know it or not, the barn door has slammed shut behind all of us. The apostle Paul, writing in Romans, explained the condition of humanity: We all sit alone in a corner without God. We have all sinned and, as a result of our sin, are separated from God and doomed forever (see Romans 3:23; 6:23; Ephesians 2:1). We *all* enter the world relationally disconnected from the Creator, our Father God, and are adrift in life without a sense of meaning.

But God never wanted us to be disconnected from him or from others. His design for us is a life like the one enjoyed by the first man and woman. In the beginning moments of their existence, Adam and Eve lived in a pristine, flowering garden, a world that was theirs to keep and tend. It was a paradise where they could thrive and raise a human family of their own. It was a heaven on earth, where God had provided everything they could possibly need.

But it was more than a physical utopia. It was a land where they lived in perfect harmony with each other and with their Creator—the Trinity of God the Father, God the Son, and God the Holy Spirit. They communed with him there, as a father and as a friend. And that relationship—more than all the fruit-bearing trees, more than all the crystal waters, more than the perfect beauty and comfort of their surroundings—provided everything their human hearts desired. They had love because their love came from God. They had joy because their joy came from God. They had peace because their peace came from God. There was no hunger, greed, fear, or pain because God's holy presence surrounded and filled that perfect place.

Then tragedy struck. A rebellious angel invaded the Garden in the form of a serpent. He introduced confusion, doubt, and suspicion into Eve's mind. He deceived her into believing his words instead of God's words. He convinced her to choose her own way rather than trusting God's way. He persuaded her to eat the only fruit that God had forbidden to her and her husband. And she, having sinned against God, imitated the serpent and became a tempter to her husband. And he followed her into sin.

That act—their willful sin against God, in spite of all the generosity and goodness, love and friendship he had shared with them—resulted in more than Adam and Eve's expulsion from the Garden. The consequences were dreadful and devastating, affecting the planet itself—every plant and animal, extending to every human being who has been born since that day—bringing death to all.

The entrance of sin drove life from the world. Their sin severed their connection to the holy presence of God—who is life itself and from whom all life comes (see John 1:4; 5:26). Gone were Adam and Eve's shared moments of intimacy and happiness with their Father God. Gone were the thrills of laughter they enjoyed together. Gone was their close relationship.

Their sin brought into the world not only the living death of separation from God but also all the symptoms of death—hunger, disease, hatred, and heartache—symptoms that would only end in their physical death and eternal separation from God. Sin and death reigned over the whole human race from that moment forward.

As God watched the children he loved, living this way for generation after generation, "it broke his heart" (Genesis 6:6). But his broken heart was far from helpless, of course. Even in the Garden, he knew how he would respond. Even before the world was created, God devised a masterful and merciful plan (see Revelation 13:8). It was a plan by which he would enter your world, run to your hiding place, throw open the barn door, and shout to you in your aloneness and confusion, "I want you to have a relationship with me!"

God Makes His Move

Imagine God as he watches in grief and sadness while you are born into the very world where he and Adam once walked in perfect relationship. He longs to relate to you as intimately as he once did to Adam and Eve. He wants to take pleasure in you. He wants to see in your eyes the delight that only his life and love can bring you. But that's not possible because you have been dead to him, separated from the life that is found in him, from the moment you were born. Not only that, but God has been watching from the very first moments of your life as you follow in Adam and Eve's footsteps, becoming his *enemy* by repeatedly and selfishly choosing your own sinful ways instead of God's holy ways.

So God makes his move. *He* takes the initiative. You are the one who desperately needs him, but *you* didn't seek *him* out. *You* are the one who should have been crying out for help, saying, "Please, God, do something; I can't live without you, please help." Yet the all-sufficient Lord, who "has no needs . . . [but] gives life and breath to everything, and . . . satisfies every need there is" *wants you* (Acts 17:25). He wants to relate to you—to enjoy and delight and take pleasure in a personal relationship with you.

So he enters your world to cancel the curse of death that has power over you. He "became human and lived here on earth among us" (John 1:14). "Because God's children are human beings—made of flesh and blood—Jesus also became flesh and blood by being born in human form. For only as a human being could he die, and only by dying could he break the power of the Devil, who had the power of death" (Hebrews 2:14). "God's secret plan has now been revealed to us; it is a plan centered on Christ" (Ephesians 1:9). Only the Son of the living God could wrench the power of death out of the hand of his archenemy, Satan, so that God could be reconnected to all creation in a personal, one-on-one relationship.

The Incarnation says: "You may have turned away from me, but I'm not turning away from you. You are so important to me that I will go to extraordinary lengths to have a personal relationship with you. I'll enter your world and become human like you to save you from death and eternal aloneness without me."

That is so important for us—and our kids—to realize. The core of Christianity is far, far more than a set of true propositions; it is the news of "a God *who is passionate about his relationship with you*" (Exodus 34:14, emphasis mine), offering us eternal life and relationship with him through the Incarnate One—Jesus Christ.

Every word God has spoken, every command he has given, every action he has taken has been a means to an end. Because behind God's plan to conquer death is his desire to enjoy an everlasting and personal relationship with you, your children, friends, and loved ones. And the Incarnation shows God's love in action, providing a way to achieve that personal relationship, a relationship that gives you life and restores your true identity as a priceless human being created in God's image. The Incarnation demonstrates God's desire to have a relationship with you. But the relationship God has in mind is not simply some casual acquaintance but one that relates to you on a deep and intimate level. And there are at least four expressions that characterize God's relationship to you—a relationship in which he accepts you unconditionally, loves you sacrificially, understands you intimately, and relates to you continuously.

The core of Christianity is far, far more than a set of true propositions; it is the news of "a God who is passionate about his relationship with you."

1. God Accepts You Unconditionally

This divine passion to relate to you and enter your world isn't based on anything you have done or could do in the future. It is purely the result of God's grace (see Ephesians 2:8). It was extended to you while you were gripped by death, a sinner by birth and an enemy of God (see Romans 5:8-12). Regardless of all you've done—or haven't done—he offers grace. *God accepts you* completely, and in spite of your sin he provides a way back to him.

The revelation of Christ—the gospel story—is about turning

the paradise lost of Genesis into the paradise regained of Revelation, even though none of us deserves it. It is about abolishing your death sentence even though you have done nothing to warrant eternal life in relationship with God. "Life itself was in him," John said, "and this life gives light to everyone" (John 1:4). Yet the basis of receiving such life is nothing we can do; it is strictly a gift from God. The gospel story is about Christ, who *God accepts you completely, and in spite of your sin he provides a way back to him.* took the initiative and entered our world when we were helpless, unable to even ask for help, and showed us grace—favor that was not merited at all.

2. God Loves You Sacrificially

God has demonstrated that he is willing to go to extraordinary lengths to connect with you. He passionately desires a relationship with you, your children, students, youth group members, and other church members. But the significance of the Incarnation goes even further and deeper than that.

Yes, God accepts us without condition. That unconditional acceptance is demonstrated in his willingness to take the initiative and enter our world in order to reclaim and restore our relationship with him, even when "we were dead because of our sins" (Ephesians 2:5).

But God is not only a God who is "rich in mercy" (Ephesians 2:4). He is also holy. The Bible says of God, "Your eyes are too pure to look on evil; you cannot tolerate wrong" (Habakkuk 1:13, NIV). God is so holy that he "cannot allow sin in any form" (Habakkuk 1:13).

Since each of us was born with a sinful human nature, tainted by sin, we are totally unsuitable for a relationship with a holy God. "When Adam sinned," the Bible says, "sin entered the entire human race" (Romans 5:12). "We were born with an evil nature, and we were under God's anger just like everyone else" (Ephesians 2:3).

And, if that were not enough, we even further ruined our chances to relate to God by adding our own sins to original sin. "Adam's sin brought death, so death spread to everyone, for everyone sinned" (Romans 5:12). Each one of us has spent our lives committing "many sins, . . . obeying Satan, . . . following the passions and desires of our evil nature" (Ephesians 2:1-3).

Therefore, even though God's mercy prompts him to accept us even when "we were dead because of our sins" (Ephesians 2:5), his holiness requires that our sinfulness be dealt with. If your death sentence (and mine) is going to be abolished, the issue of our sins must be addressed.

But how? We cannot save ourselves; we are "utterly helpless" (Romans 5:6). "The law of Moses could not save us," Paul said, "because of our sinful nature" (Romans 8:3). But because God is not only holy but also just, he solved the problem in a way that satisfied both his holiness and his justice. The penalty of sin had to be paid: "The wages of sin is death" (Romans 6:23). A sacrifice was needed, but not just any sacrifice would do. In his holiness God would accept only a pure, spotless, sinless sacrifice. And no one on earth—no one in the history of humanity—could fill that bill. So, what could be done?

A Roman playwright named Horace, who lived and wrote in the days of Julius Caesar, criticized the other poets and playwrights of his day. He hated their irritating tendency, every time a problem occurred in the plot of a play, to simply introduce one of the many Roman gods to solve the problem and save the day. So Horace wrote, "Do not bring a god onto the stage unless the problem is one that deserves a god to solve it."[4]

Well, our problem—the horrible, tragic, crippling problem of sin, which separates us from God and the life that is in him—is a problem of that magnitude. It is a problem too big for any human ingenuity or effort. It deserves—in fact, demands—a God to solve it. So "God put into effect a different plan to save us. He sent his own Son in a human body like ours, except that ours are sinful. God destroyed sin's control over us by giving his Son as a sacrifice for our sins" (Romans 8:3). God himself entered the stage of human history in the person of Jesus Christ to atone for our sin and save us from the curse of eternal death.

Though we don't deserve it for a moment, "Yet now God in his gracious kindness declares us not guilty. He has done this through Christ Jesus. . . . For God sent Jesus to take the punishment for our sins" (Romans 3:24-25). The Incarnate One—Jesus Christ, who knew no sin and was undeserving of any punishment—became sin on our behalf.

That is what the Incarnation says to you—and to all of us. Despite your sin, Jesus *valued you enough* to die for you. His love for you is so great, he spread his arms the width of a cross and said, "I lay down my life for you." "Now, no one is likely to die for a good person, though someone might be willing to die for a person who is especially good. But God showed his great love for us by sending Christ to die for us while we were still sinners" (Romans 5:7-8).

> *The Incarnation says to you that despite your sin, Jesus valued you enough to die for you.*

Even in your sinful state, Jesus loved you with his life. "Greater love has no one than this," Jesus said, "that he lay down his life for his friends" (John 15:13, NIV). If you were to wear a price tag indicating your worth to God, it would read: "Jesus!" "He paid for you with the precious lifeblood of Christ, the sinless, spotless Lamb of God" (1 Peter 1:19). Jesus Christ became the atoning sacrifice for your sins and mine.

"*This* is real love, . . . that [God] loved us and sent his Son as a sacrifice to take away our sins" (1 John 4:10, emphasis mine). The truth of the Incarnation reveals that God so desires a relationship with you that he made the ultimate sacrifice . . . for you. *God loves you and longs to relate to you.* He proved it by becoming human himself and laying down his life for you.

3. God Understands You Intimately

One of the phrases often used by young people is, "They don't understand me." We all long for someone to understand and identify with us, especially when life seems hard or confusing or unfair. I certainly desired that as a young person.

Everyone knew everyone else in the small Michigan town in which I grew up, and that meant that everyone knew about my father and his drinking. My teenage buddies made jokes about him, and I laughed along with them, hoping my laughter would hide the pain and shame I felt.

My efforts to mask my feelings seemed to work. No one understood how deeply it hurt me that my dad was the town drunk. Other people didn't know how much his drunkenness embarrassed me. No one could understand how much it hurt me to see the pain he inflicted on my mother.

By the time I was fourteen I not only hated my father, I began to act on my hatred. Sometimes I would go out to the barn and find my mother lying in the manure behind the cows, beaten so badly by my father that she couldn't get up. To avenge my father's cruel treatment of my mother, I would do everything I could to humiliate or punish him. When he got drunk and threatened to beat my mother, or when he was drunk when my friends were planning to come over, I would drag him out to the barn, tie him to a stall, and leave him there to "sleep it off."

As I got older—and bigger and stronger—I did this more often. Sometimes I was so enraged that I tied my father's feet with a rope that ended in a noose around his neck. I hoped he would choke himself while trying to get free. On one occasion, when I found my father drunk—again—I flew into such a rage that I tried to sober him up by shoving him fully dressed into a bathtub full of water. In the struggle, I found myself holding my dad's head under water. If a deputy sheriff hadn't stopped me (to this day I'm not sure who it was), I probably would have drowned him. If I hadn't left home when I did, I fear I could have killed my own father.

Then, in my last year of high school, I returned home one night from a date around midnight. As I walked into the house, I saw my mother weeping bitterly.

"What's wrong? What happened?" I demanded, thinking that my father had beaten her again. After several sobs and a few agonizing minutes, she finally gained enough composure to speak.

"It's all too much . . . I can't take it anymore," she sobbed. "Your father . . . his drinking . . . his abuse. I've lost the will to live. I want to wait until you're on your own after graduation next month, then I just want to die."

This wasn't the first time my mother had talked this way. But this time I sensed something different. It was almost as if she was predicting her own death. Was she hinting about suicide? I couldn't tell for sure, but her outburst frightened me.

I graduated from high school, and a few months later my mother died. Can a person die of a broken heart? It may seem incredible and science might answer differently, but my mother's heart had been ripped apart by my father's treatment. Mentally and emotionally, she had lost the will to live.

When she died, I lost something, too. I lost the only person who ever seemed to understand me and be there for me. Before, no matter where I went or how late I came home, my mother had always been there. But suddenly she was gone, and I believed I had no one to turn to, no one who could possibly know what it was like to be me.

Even after becoming a Christian, I did not realize for years that the Incarnation—the truth that God had become human—meant that Christ wanted a relationship with me and that he understood me. Christ wants us to know that he understands everything we have ever endured—and more. The Incarnate One, Jesus Christ, experienced the ups and downs of life as a human baby, child, teenager, and man. He suffered embarrassment, humiliation, and rejection. As God, Christ understood his creation perfectly, but by becoming a human being, Jesus let us know how intimately and completely he understands us—and all we have experienced.

Yes, God loved us and sent his Son in the form of a human being to die for us so we can have a relationship with him. We all know that. But many of us focus so exclusively on that central truth that we miss the full significance of how deep he wants that relationship to be.

Because Christ took on human form, we can know that he truly understands our weaknesses and temptations. He wanted me to know that he identified with my humiliation as the son of the town drunk. He wants you—and your kids—to know that he identifies with your feelings of rejection when your child is not chosen for the basketball team or when you're overlooked for a job promotion. He understands how it feels to be teased cruelly by classmates or shunned by associates or "friends." He can identify with what it feels like to be betrayed by a girlfriend or boyfriend, a coworker, or a spouse.

Think of it: He is the all-sufficient Lord, yet he became as dependent as you were when you were a baby. He was the one who fashioned the human body, yet like you he had to learn to walk. He was the preexistent Word, yet he had to learn to speak, just as you did. He created clouds and rivers and lakes, yet he got thirsty. He endured the taunts of those who knew only part of his family's story. He must have felt the almost unbearable weight of grief when his earthly father, Joseph, died. He suffered not only the physical torture of the cross as he died for you but also the anguish of being rejected, humiliated, denied, abandoned, and even betrayed by his closest friends. Why did he willingly go through all that?

Because he wanted you to know that he understands. He wanted you to know that he understands what it means to suffer like a human being. The writer of Hebrews tells us that Christ "has gone through suffering and temptation, . . . [and] is able to help us when we are being tempted. . . . [He] understands our weaknesses, for he faced all of the same temptations we do, yet he did not sin. So let us come boldly . . . and we will find grace to help us when we need it" (Hebrews 2:18; 4:15-16).There is nothing you have experienced that God in Christ does not understand firsthand! He, like you, has experienced

- rejection—by his own people
- abandonment—by his own disciples
- misunderstanding—by his own followers
- ridicule—at his own trial
- betrayal—by a close friend
- criticism—by the religious leaders of his day

But that's not all. He has also experienced human achievement and victories. He knows what it's like to feel loved and accepted. He knows the joy of completing a job well done. He has heard the voice of his Father say, "This is My beloved Son, in whom I am well pleased" (Matthew 17:5, NKJV). He has also known the joy of fulfilling his Father's will and the victory of conquering what no one has ever conquered: death.

He has experienced all the ups—*and* downs—of human existence. He's "been there, done that," just like you. The Incarnation is Jesus' way of saying, "I understand." By means of the Incarnation *Jesus understands you and your child,* no matter what emotion you may be feeling, no matter what experience you may be enduring.

> **The Incarnation is Jesus' way of saying, "I understand."**

4. God Relates to You Continually

They didn't want him to go. When Jesus approached the conclusion of his three-year ministry on earth, his disciples—his closest friends on earth—struggled to understand his talk about leaving them.

"I will be with you only a little longer," he told them.

"Lord, where are you going?" Peter asked. "Why can't I follow you now?" (see John 13:36-37).

Peter was not alone. The other disciples also confessed their confusion. They had been his followers, his closest friends, his constant companions for much of the previous three years. They ate from the same bowl and slept in the same room much of the time. They walked everywhere together, enjoying intense conversations about important subjects. They had developed close relationships with each other. He knew them better than they knew themselves. And they felt as if they were finally growing in their knowledge and understanding of him.

So they couldn't understand why Jesus would talk about leaving them. They couldn't fathom what he was saying when he told them, "It is actually best for you that I go away" (John 16:7). They couldn't imagine how that could be true. But Jesus knew.

Jesus knew that by "going away"—dying a sacrificial death, rising again, and ascending into heaven—he could not only atone for their sin and deliver them from the curse of death but also take his relationship with them to a whole new level.

He explained, "I will ask the Father, and he will give you another Counselor, who will never leave you. He is the Holy Spirit, who leads into all truth. . . . He lives with you now and later will be in you. No, I will not abandon you as orphans—I will come to you. In just a little while the world will not see me again, but you will. For I will live again, and you will, too" (John 14:16-19).

By means of the Incarnation, God made it possible for his followers—and that includes you, me, and our kids—to experience a real relationship with God in Christ. By becoming human—and by dying, rising from the dead, and ascending into heaven again—God made all the affection, acceptance, and affirmation of Jesus available to us every moment of our lives through the constant, indwelling presence of the Comforter, his Holy Spirit. "For we know how dearly God loves us, because he has given us the Holy Spirit to fill our hearts with his love" (Romans 5:5).

That is how Jesus delivers on his promise to his first disciples and to his followers today: "I am with you always, even to the end of the age" (Matthew 28:20). Through the Incarnation *Jesus is available to us,* anywhere, anytime, and all the time.

You see, contrary to the way many of our kids have learned to think of him, Jesus Christ is not some distant historical figure who lived two thousand years ago. He's not a mythic hero who died on a cross. He is as real as your kids' heartbeat, as relevant as their closest friends, and as "right now" as the latest e-mail or Instant Message. He is able to literally take up residence within them by his Holy Spirit. He so deeply wants to connect with you and me and the young people in our lives that he enters our very being to become one with us. Now that's a close relationship!

God so deeply wants to connect with you and me and the young people in our lives that he enters our very being to become one with us.

WHO AM I?

The Incarnation is an important doctrine of the Christian church, but it is far more than something we should agree with intellectually. It is also something we must know emotionally and experientially. The fact that God became human, dwelt among us, and then died for us is the means God has used to reconnect us with his loving heart and restore our broken relationship with him.

And that relationship, in turn, results in something else. It solves one of our kids' deepest dilemmas. It answers one of the most pressing questions of life: Who am I?

To a large extent, we understand ourselves—our identity—in terms of our relationships. We perceive ourselves—and others around us—as this person's son or daughter, that person's husband or wife, and someone else's mother or father. We also distinguish ourselves as "the Rileys' neighbor," "Josie's friend," or "Richard's pastor."

Our relationships provide insight to our identity. But earthly relationships are limited. They cannot completely or exhaustively answer the question Who am I? Each of us longs for a better answer to that question than "Carol's friend" or "John's son."

That is why it's so important, so crucial, for our children, students, youth group members, and church members to understand what the Incarnation means to their lives—because the Incarnation sheds light on a person's true identity. Now that "God has sent the Spirit of his Son into your hearts, . . . you can call God your dear Father" (Galatians 4:6). As the apostle John said, "See how very much our heavenly Father loves us, for he allows us to be called his children, and we really are!" (1 John 3:1). Jesus, through the Holy Spirit, "speaks to us deep in our hearts and tells us that we are God's children" (Romans 8:16).

Because Jesus Christ entered our world to redeem us and make us God's children, we are connected and bonded to God's family. The means God used to reconnect with you is the means by which he defines your identity. Because of the Incarnation, you, your children, students, youth group members, or church members are now in God's family. You can realize your true identity as a son or daughter of your Father God, who relationally

- accepts you unconditionally
- loves you sacrificially
- understands you intimately
- relates to you continuously

And that is all possible because "God so loved the world that he gave his only Son" to be born supernaturally into the human family to relationally connect us to God's family (John 3:16). Thanks to the Incarnation, we can know "who we are" because we have experienced the connection of knowing God personally. And that is precisely what a disconnected generation needs. We are no longer adrift and alone; we become rooted and secure in a new relationship, for we now belong to God. We can say with confidence, "I know who I am: I'm a child of the King of the Universe!" And while that identifies who you and I—and our children—are in this world, that identity goes even deeper.

A SPECIAL, ONE-OF-A-KIND CHILD OF GOD

Born alienated and disconnected from God, we have all lost the sense of who we really are. But it is through this relational atmosphere of God's love, acceptance, understanding, and continuous involvement in our lives that we can discover the unique people God made us to be—that one-of-a-kind original children designed to relate to God and others.

Have you ever stepped outside on a winter's morning as the soft flakes of snow drifted slowly to the ground? If you could inspect the microscopic details of these tiny snowflakes landing on your sleeve, you would see, of course, that each has a distinct shape. You've probably seen a photograph or video that magnifies a snowflake; if so, you've certainly marveled at the intricate shape, structure, and beauty of that single flake. And undoubtedly you've heard scientists claim that no two snowflakes are alike. They are all one-of-a-kind originals.

You and I and the young people in your life are one-of-a-kind originals as well. We have been given distinct and special identities that make each of us unique. Coming into relationship with God through the miracle of redemption allows his Spirit to lead each one of us to discover the person he created each of us to be. He has placed deep within you special gifts, talents, passions, and a distinct personality that make you uniquely you. If you have a brother or sister, you can probably see the likeness that comes from being of the same family. Yet you also know that each of you is different. If you've raised children, you certainly realize that no two children are alike. Each of us, as a human child and as a child of God, has an original identity.

One of the indications that Scripture recognizes a child's originality is found in the familiar words penned by King Solomon: "Train up a child in the way he should go, even when he is old he will not depart from it" (Proverbs 22:6, NASB).

Unfortunately, this verse is often misunderstood, and misapplied, by those who are responsible for the training of young people. Many parents and youth leaders think it means, "Have family devotions, make sure kids attend church and youth group and a Christian school, and when they are grown up, they will not depart from the faith."

The real emphasis of this verse, however, centers on the phrase "the way he [or she] should go." The writer is referring to the *child's* way, his or her leaning or bent. The root meanings of these words suggest stimulating a desire for guidance according to each child's own uniqueness.

The same Hebrew word that is used in Proverbs 22 is translated "bend" in two psalms and refers to the bending of the archer's bow (see Psalm 11:2; 64:3). Today, with precision manufacturing, almost anyone can pick up a bow with a forty-five-pound draw weight and do a fair job of hitting the target. But in biblical days, nothing was standardized. All archers made their own bows and had to know the unique characteristics of that bow if they hoped to hit anything with it.

God's Word is telling us that you and your child have an inborn uniqueness that parents and caregivers need to identify and train accordingly. In the *Ryrie Study Bible*, a note for Proverbs 22:6 explains that "'the way he should go' really means 'according to his way; i.e., the child's habits and interests.' The instruction must take into account his individuality and inclinations, his personality, the unique way God created him, and must be in keeping with his physical and mental development."[5]

The apostle Paul explains that "God has given each of us the ability to do certain things well" (Romans 12:6). He goes on to enumerate those things and admonish us regarding the attitude and relationships in which we are to exercise the gifts and abilities God has given each of us. It is clear we all have been given gifts that are distinctive to us.

When God directed Moses to construct the tabernacle, he led him to Bezalel, son of Uri, grandson of Hur, of the tribe of Judah, to oversee the massive project. Why had God led him to this person in particular? Because "the Lord has filled Bezalel with the Spirit of God, giving him great wisdom, intelligence, and skill in all kinds of crafts. He is able to create beautiful objects from gold, silver, and bronze. He is skilled in cutting and setting gemstones and in carving wood. In fact, he has every necessary skill. And the Lord has given both him and Oholiab son of Ahisamach, of the tribe of Dan, the ability to teach their skills to others" (Exodus 35:31-34). God placed within these two men special gifts that others didn't have. They had skills designed by the great craftsman and creator God himself. God gave them gifts that no one else had to create and craft wood, gold, silver, and bronze into beautiful objects for his glory.

The Incarnate One came to provide a means to adopt you into the family of God. He has made you his special, one-of-a-kind child by giving you various skills, perhaps to craft objects or to teach others. He has given you certain talents as well. And he has also placed within you certain personal preferences with a distinct personality that makes you a one-of-a-kind individual—a person designed to do things in ways that only you can do. God has made you like a complex snowflake, a unique person to stand out to him as his special and original child.

God infused you with his life and made you his child, uniquely crafted as part of his family, for a relational purpose. God intends you to use your unique God-given characteristics to relate not only to him but to others as well. "Just as our bodies have many parts," Paul said, "and each part has a special function, so it is with Christ's body. We are all parts of his one body, and each of us has different work to do. And since we are all one body in Christ, we belong to each other, and each of us needs all the others" (Romans 12:4-5).

There will never be another you. God has specially gifted you to fill a role—a purpose—that no one else can fill. Our kids inwardly want to know their place in this world, as do each of us. God has crafted us specifically for that place that we—and only we—can fill.

You are a child of God by means of a new birth, with unique characteristics with which to love and live for God in a way that only you are empowered to do. You belong to Christ's body, God's family. That family needs you because there will never be another who can fill that place as you can. And God wants to exercise his love and life in and through you in a unique and original fashion. Yes, he wants all of us to love each other, but he wants you to do that in the unique and original fashion in which he has crafted the one-of-a-kind you. Again, Paul declares, "There are different ways God works in our lives, but it is the same God who does the work through all of us. A spiritual gift is given to each of us as a means of helping the entire church. . . . It is the one and only Holy Spirit who distributes these gifts. He alone decides which gift each person should have" (1 Corinthians 12:6-7, 11).

God wants to unleash his love and power through the special, one-of-a-kind child of God that you are. No one else can do it as you can. These are the means by which each of us loves and relates to him. These are the means by which we are to love and relate to each other. God redeemed us for his glory—so we could have a loving, personalized relationship with our Father and a loving relationship with our brothers and sisters in the family.

Who are you? You are God's chosen child to love him and others as only you can.

DISCOVERING YOUR UNIQUENESS

We all intuitively realize we are originals. Our personal identification is distinctly ours. Our fingerprints are unique; our retina scans are distinct; our faces and bodies are all slightly different. But it may be challenging to understand the distinctiveness with which God created us and what gifts the Holy Spirit has distributed to us.

God has chosen *special gifts* just for you to express his love for others in a special way. Are you aware of those gifts?

He has placed deep within you a natural bent; they are your *talents* and unique interests. He wants you to use them within his and your family as only you can. Do you know what those are?

God has given you built-in preferences: things like how you are energized, how you process information, how you make decisions. These things make up your *distinct personality*. God's love is to be distinctly expressed through this distinct personality, as only you can express it. Do you know your personality traits?

God has instilled within you certain *passions*: things you feel strongly about, things you're fervently interested in, things that give you a special sense of joy when you talk about them or pursue them. Those passions direct you to whom, where, and what God wants you to love in life . . . as only you can. Can you specifically identify your God-given passions in life?

If your parents understood you were a one-of-a-kind individual and sought to train you up in "the way you should go," you have no doubt come a long way in identifying your personality type, talents, special gifts, and passions in life. But if you are like most people, you have only a partial understanding of who you are. And if so, you are probably struggling to help your child or youth group unlock the secret to their true identities, too. That is why most of us could use some help in identifying who we really are.

Perhaps no other book and course can better help you and the young people in your life discover who they are than the book and workbook *Find Your Fit* by Jane Kise and Kevin Johnson. We have drawn much of what we have said here about what makes each of us unique from their book and workbook. Kevin has devoted his life to ministering to young people and helping youth workers and parents successfully guide their young people through a godless culture. Jane has an extensive background in career counseling both young people and adults.

The *Find Your Fit* course can be used by a youth group, small group, or by a parent and child. Through a series of exercises and self-tests, your youth will identify their God-given talents, spiritual gifts, personality types, and passions for life. A companion course for adults, called *LifeKeys* (by Jane Kise, David Stark, and Sandra Krebs Hirsh), is also available to help "older kids," like me, to better discover who we are (more about these courses is detailed in appendix B).

One final thought about our personal identities. Understanding that we are God's children who have a special place in his body doesn't mean that unbelievers don't have talents or natural gifts. It also doesn't mean that they can't come to understand themselves and their uniqueness to varying degrees. What it does mean, however, is that unless and until people come to know God as their Father through Christ, they will never understand their true place in this world as God designed. A non-Christian may exercise a talent or skill, but that expression will never be fully expressed as it was meant to be or will never bring maximum meaning to that life unless it is done for God and by his power.

The true thrill of forming a relationship with God through Christ is that you discover you really are God's chosen child to love him and others as only you can.

KNOWING IT BUT STILL NOT "GETTING IT"

Even though our family connection with God provides an answer to who we are, many Christian kids from fine Christian homes are still struggling with knowing who they are. Many more simply don't feel loved. Obviously, if someone hasn't guided them to discover their uniqueness, they will struggle. But even when young people do learn their unique gifts, talents, personality, and passions, they often still struggle. Why?

My life as a young Christian is a prime example. Although I had trusted Christ and become a true child of God as a university student, it still took time for me to comprehend who I was. It wasn't because I wasn't convinced of Christ's deity. It wasn't because I didn't believe I was a child of God. Rather, it was because I had very little—if any—experiential and emotional context in which to understand my newfound relationship with God and others.

God wanted me to discover my new sense of identity in him. I had felt disconnected emotionally as a young person, and I knew God wanted me to know experientially that I was a child of God with gifts, talents, personality, and passions that I needed to embrace for my sense of wholeness and for his glory. And he personally was providing all the love, acceptance, and understanding I could ever ask for. While I was able to grasp that truth on an intellectual level, my previous life experience provided very little context or point of reference that could give that truth deep meaning in my life.

Because my earthly father had never really accepted me, I struggled to emotionally understand what acceptance was. Because I had never seen unconditional acceptance modeled in real life, I wasn't fully equipped to comprehend it. Yes, God spoke to me by his Spirit to tell me that he accepted me, loved me, understood me, and would always be available to me. I completely believed that truth intellectually. But relationally and emotionally? That wasn't so clear.

Consequently, though I was a new believer and had been changed by the transforming power of God's Holy Spirit, I still felt somewhat disconnected. And, tragically, many of our fine young people today are in that same condition.

I am happy to say that something took place to enable me to emotionally and relationally comprehend what my mind had already believed. I knew the truth about Jesus Christ, who he was, and what he provided—a Father-child relationship. But it took something else to help me grasp that truth on a relational level. That "something else" is what our kids need in order to know experientially what they have come to believe intellectually. And that is what we'll discover in the next chapter, as we trace Lauren's spiritual and relational struggle.

CHAPTER 6

Relationally Connecting the Disconnected

Lauren Johnson sat at Duane and Liz Cunninghams's kitchen table. The trio had engaged in small talk until Duane and Liz had each place set with scrambled eggs and ham, toast, and coffee.

At first Lauren seemed to find it hard to express herself, but after some gentle probing from Liz, she said she needed to talk about her relationship with her parents.

"It's never been all that great at home anyway," Lauren said. "But it's just so much worse now."

Liz ignored her eggs. "How is it worse?"

"Well," Lauren said, "ever since I moved out of the house and into the dorm, it's like I'm not even part of the family anymore. Especially with Dad."

Duane stirred his coffee. "I thought things got better after your dad became a Christian last year."

Lauren nodded. "Yeah," she said. "They did. It was a big change in a lot of ways. I felt like, at least for a while, he noticed I was alive." She tilted her head as if she were thinking. "But . . . well, you guys know how my mom and dad feel about Stephanie. She's the perfect little daughter, you know? And I'm . . ." She lowered her gaze and seemed to study her plate. "I'm not."

Liz and Duane studied her face. They had known Lauren for most of her life, and they knew that she had seen more struggles than victories in her spiritual life and she had made more than her share of wrong choices. They knew, too, that her behavior—especially during her high school years—had strained her relationship with her parents.

Liz shook her head. "I don't think your parents love you any less than they do Stephanie." She hesitated, then continued. "I just think they struggle with your independent streak, you know?"

Duane nodded and started to speak, but Lauren spoke first.

"Yeah, I know," she said. "I'm not like them, and they hate that. They've never understood me or accepted me for being me . . . especially my dad. He's always compared me to Stephanie, but I'm just not like her, and I never will be."

"You don't feel that your parents accept you?" Liz asked.

"No!" Lauren said, her voice rising.

"Not even since your dad became a Christian?" Duane asked.

"Like I said, it's even worse now. I mean, now that he's a Christian, he's all concerned about me spiritually, especially now that I'm in college. He thinks I need to believe exactly like he does, and I don't anymore."

She paused, but Duane and Liz saw that she was mulling over her next words, so they waited. "It's like I'm not even part of the family," Lauren continued. "They've got their own little club—just Mom, Dad, and Stephanie—and I don't fit in. Like, I've been home for Christmas break for over a week now, and no one in my family has even asked me what's happening in my life at school, not even my mom."

"Well, Lauren," Liz said hesitantly. "You know you're still part of God's family, right?"

Lauren stared at Liz for a second, then dropped her gaze. It was clear she wasn't cheered by Liz's words. "Yeah, I guess," she said, her tone flat.

Liz exchanged a helpless look with Duane and sensed that her attempt to be encouraging had sounded trite. Lauren pushed her food around aimlessly with her fork. The conversation stalled. The couple was becoming aware that Lauren's relational problems with her parents—and her pain—went deeper than they had imagined.

● ● ● ● ●

Liz is right, of course. However disconnected Lauren may feel from her human family, she is still God's child. And she can still know she's connected to God in a father-child relationship, one that is characterized by unconditional acceptance, love, understanding, and constant availability. And she can even discover that she is a one-of-a-kind child of God as she understands her God-given gifts, talents, personality, and passions.

But Liz's reminder sounded woefully inadequate to Lauren. As real as Lauren's family connection to God may be, it's obviously not that meaningful in her heart and mind. And her relationship with God doesn't seem helpful with what she's going through right now. While she may understand intellectually that she's a part of God's family, that doesn't seem to mean much when she doesn't know through her own experience what a loving family feels like.

What we experience in our human relationships, especially during childhood, significantly affects how we perceive and experience our relationship with God.

What we experience in our human relationships, especially during childhood, significantly affects how we perceive and experience our relationship with God. We all tend to see God through the lens of our human experiences. For example, if you had an authoritarian father who seemed to be looking for you to make a wrong move so he could correct you, you may tend to see your heavenly Father as an authoritarian figure. If you experienced a permissive childhood environment, in which it seemed that your parents didn't much care what you did, you may view God as distant and uninvolved. If you felt relationally disconnected at home, you probably find it difficult to feel emotionally connected to God.

As I said in the last chapter, I also lacked an experiential context to fully grasp—emotionally and relationally—what it meant to be a member of God's family. But something happened to provide that context. During my seminary years, God led me to a married couple who modeled what a loving family looked, sounded, and felt like. Dick and Charlotte Day took me in and demonstrated what family was all about. In many ways, Dick became the father I never had. God used him to open up my heart and equip me to embrace the reality of my heavenly Father's love so that I could experience emotionally and relationally what I had already accepted intellectually.

Human relational connections and deepened convictions about God are intertwined. Thus, if we are going to deepen our young people's convictions about a God who is passionate about relationships, we need to form strong, positive relational connections with them. The more we relate to our youth in accepting, loving, and affirming ways, the more equipped they will be to emotionally embrace God's acceptance, love, and understanding. That, in turn, will create an atmosphere that's conducive to discovering who they really are.

If we fail to relationally connect with our children, students, youth group members, or church members, they will find it far more difficult to become rooted and grounded in the faith.

Of course, properly connecting to our kids will not provide an ironclad guarantee that they will move beyond belief to conviction and find the meaning to life. But this much is guaranteed: If we fail to relationally connect with our children, students, youth group members, or church members, they will find it far more difficult to become rooted and grounded in the faith.

That—as Duane and Liz have just discovered—is where Lauren is. Like Lauren, many of our kids are so emotionally disconnected from their families that they're ill-equipped to experience God and his love in a way that will produce convictions and answers to life. So, what can be done?

THE EMBODIMENT OF CHRIST: THE CHURCH

What if a few other people cared enough about Lauren to accept her, just as she is, so she could experience on a human level what it feels like to be accepted unconditionally? What if a group of her peers were to find ways to communicate to her—despite all her faults, failures, and doubts—that when they look at her, they like what they see? Lauren might then begin to develop an emotional and relational context in which to comprehend the truth behind the Incarnation—a truth that says, "I believe you're worth relating to, no matter what you've done."

As it so happens, that is exactly what God has planned. His intention all along has been for the relational meaning of the Incarnation to be translated into human relationships. Much as the infinite God entered a finite human body by means of the Incarnation, so today Jesus, the Incarnate One, inhabits an earthly body: the church, which is called the body of Christ. The church is literally the embodiment of Christ. As we have already mentioned, each new child of God has "been baptized into Christ's body," Paul says (1 Corinthians 12:13). "And since we are all one body in Christ, we belong to each other, and each of us needs all the others" (Romans 12:5).

What that means in practical terms is that if one person—for any reason—feels disconnected and alone, God intends for other members of the body to provide that missing connection and re-move that person's aloneness.[1] If someone is hurting, the rest of the body can bring comfort and healing. God's wise intention and fervent desire is "for harmony among the members, so that all the members care for each other equally. If one part suffers, all the parts suffer with it, and if one part is honored, all the parts are glad" (1 Corinthians 12:25-26).

That is what Lauren needs. That is what so many of our young people need. Because, when a member of Christ's body receives that kind of relational care and concern from others, he or she will begin to develop an emotional and relational context for receiving those things from God.

In addition, when you and I reach out and relationally connect with a young person, the Spirit of Christ actually ministers through us to that person, so that we're not just offering our own care and concern; we become a conduit of God's care. God has positioned each of us, as a member of his family, to express his love and acceptance as no one else can. When you "accept each other just as Christ has accepted you," you become a relay station of sorts to accept others with Godlike acceptance (Romans 15:7). That means the acceptance you receive from Christ is expressed through you to others. When you extend love to someone as God has uniquely gifted you to do, that love "comes from God . . . [For] if we love each other, God lives in us, and his love has been brought to full expression *through* us" (1 John 4:7, 12, emphasis mine). When we bring comfort to a hurting soul, it is "the God of all comfort, who comforts us in all our troubles, [who helps us to] comfort those in any trouble with the comfort we ourselves have received from God" (2 Corinthians 1:3-4, NIV).

Thus, when you as a unique child of God demonstrate a *sacrificial love* to others, you are allowing them to experience a sampling of God's love. When you encounter young people who feel lonely and discouraged, and you make yourself *available* to them, or when you say, *"I identify with you and understand you* in what you're going through," you are not only saying that they are valuable to you; you are also ministering God's love, availability, and understanding to them.

At such times, when you make yourself available to others and affirm, love, and accept them just as Christ has done for you, you are not only readying their hearts to relationally connect to God, but you are also becoming a one-of-a-kind living agent of the Incarnation. You are the means God uses to say to other members of his family, "I accept you without condition," "I love you sacrificially," "I understand you intimately," and "I'm here for you always."

And not only are you ministering God's love and care to *others* when you live like Christ in relationship to them; at such times you also, in a mysterious way, minister to *Christ himself.* Matthew 25 records the clear and wonderful teaching of Jesus about what really happens when you become an agent of the Incarnation:

When you make yourself available to others and affirm, love, and accept them just as Christ has done for you, you are not only readying their hearts to relationally connect to God, but you are also becoming a one-of-a-kind living agent of the Incarnation.

> When the Son of Man comes in his glory, . . . he will place the sheep at his right hand and the goats at his left. Then the King will say to those on the right, "Come, you who are blessed by my Father, inherit the Kingdom prepared for you from the foundation of the world. For I was hungry, and you fed me. I was thirsty, and you gave me a drink. I was a stranger, and you invited me into your home. I was naked, and you gave me clothing. I was sick, and you cared for me. I was in prison, and you visited me."
>
> Then these righteous ones will reply, "Lord, when did we ever see you hungry and feed you? Or thirsty and give you some-

thing to drink? Or a stranger and show you hospitality? Or naked and give you clothing? When did we ever see you sick or in prison, and visit you?" And the King will tell them, "I assure you, when you did it to one of the least of these my brothers and sisters, you were doing it to me!" (Matthew 25:31-40).

In other words, when you express loving care to your child, student, youth group member, or church member—or to anyone—you are also doing so to Christ himself. Which means, of course, that if we miss the opportunity to connect with our kids and convey the meaning of the Incarnation to them, we are rejecting the Incarnate One himself, for Jesus said, "I assure you, when you refused to help the least of these my brothers and sisters, you were refusing to help me" (Matthew 25:45). (Intimate Life Ministries has done extensive work in helping churches implement strategies for demonstrating Christ's love through effective personal relationships. For more information about resources and training, see appendix C.)

WHERE RELATIONAL CONNECTIONS BEGIN: THE FAMILY

God is pleased to use the body of Christ—the church—as a tool to translate the relational meaning of the Incarnation into human relationships. But it is not his only tool.

In fact, God's family, the church, is an extension of the first relationship God ordained—the human family—and the church can often contribute or supplement what is lacking in a young person's family relationships. But God never intended for the church to take the place of the family. I believe God's wise and loving design is for every newborn child to experience that relational connection— that intimate attachment that can make the difference between connection and disconnection, between conviction and confusion, between self-doubt and knowing who we are—first and fore-most from his or her mom and dad. The human family is the pre-ferred route for leading youth into the kind of relational connections with God and others that will anchor them in the faith and hold them steady in "a dark world full of crooked and perverse people" (Philippians 2:15).

But in my travels I see many parents who are struggling to know how to connect and stay connected with their kids. Believe me, I know that parents who want to connect with their kids face incredible obstacles today. It's never been easy, of course, but in many ways

The human family is the preferred route for leading youth into the kind of relational connections with God and others that will anchor them in the faith and hold them steady.

it's harder than ever. Both parents and kids contend with grueling schedules and unrealistic expectations. In many families, parents live in one world, and kids live in another world. It can be an enor-mous challenge to find ways to enter our students' sometimes complex and confusing world and make relational connections at a deep, emotional level so we can pass on our faith and values to our kids. But that's what I want for my own four kids and for the tens of thousands of kids I minister to around the world each year. And I'm sure that's what you want, too.

But if we are going to connect relationally with our kids—and stay connected—we must do it up close and personal. God's plan to relationally connect with us meant that he had to enter our world. "Because God's children are human beings—made of flesh and blood—Jesus also became flesh and blood by being born in human form" (Hebrews 2:14). If we hope to relationally connect and help our kids develop deepened convictions, we also must en-ter their world to truly understand and relate to them on their level.

When I talk about entering their world, I'm not talking about trying to live like preteens or teenagers—dressing like them, talking like them, listening to their music, and so on. I mean taking an interest and being aware of what's happening in their lives and then relationally connecting with them as Christ the Incarnate One models for us—*accepting* them without condition, *loving* them sacrificially, *affirming* them in their struggles and victories, and *being available* to them always. When you make that kind of connection with the young people in your life, you ready their hearts for the relational connection God wants to have with them through his Son Jesus Christ.

STARTING WITH THE RELATIONAL CONNECTING POINT OF ACCEPTANCE

Take Lauren, for example. She feels distant from God and has virtually no relational context to comprehend how Christ's coming to earth demonstrates that she is unconditionally accepted. A contributing factor to her sense of distance from God is her sense of disconnection from her human family, especially her father; the only acceptance she's ever known is a performance-based acceptance. She senses that she's been measured against her younger sister and has always come up short. By the time she started high school, her life had entered a cycle of behavior. Craving acceptance (and pessimistic about finding it at home), she would do things that were calculated to bring acceptance from her peers, only to experience further conflict and sense further rejection from her parents. Thus, all her efforts drove her further from experiencing the acceptance she wanted where she desired it the most: home.

Lauren's first year of college is only exacerbating the problem as she starts to form her own beliefs about God and the Bible, beliefs that do not please her parents. Of course, her parents want her to believe right and live right, and they're doing the best they know how, but Lauren is not feeling their care and concern; she's feeling further rejection and alienation. But if someone doesn't enter

Lauren's world and relationally connect with her, she will probably continue to struggle and may never develop the convictions and values that God knows are in her best interest.

Her parents don't realize it—in fact, Lauren probably doesn't realize it herself—but deep down inside, she is saying: "Please allow me to believe differently without rejecting me as a person. I may not be perfect, but please look beyond my failures and imperfections and accept me for who I am." She longs for a family relationship that says, "Even if nothing about you ever changes, I will love you anyway, just the way you are. We may not see eye-to-eye on a lot of things, but you are my daughter, and I will love you always and forever."

Unfortunately, Lauren's parents, like many others, have made the common mistake of attaching acceptance to behavior. Genuine acceptance attaches to the person, not to his or her behavior. Genuine acceptance loves people for who they are, "warts and all." Lauren is crying out for that kind of acceptance.

That is the kind of acceptance God expressed in Christ. When Jesus met a Samaritan woman on a trip through Samaria, he encountered a person who had three strikes against her socially:

1. She was a woman, considered to be inferior to men in that culture.
2. She was a Samaritan, despised by the Jews.
3. She was immoral, living with a man who was not her husband.

While Jesus did not condone her sin, he engaged her in conversation without judgment or condemnation. As a result, the woman welcomed the truth when Jesus shared it, and her life was changed.

In another encounter, a woman was dragged before Jesus while he was teaching; she had been caught in the act of adultery. After dealing with the vindictive spirit and political agenda of the woman's accusers, Jesus faced her. Only then did he speak to the woman, and his first words to her are revealing. There are many things he could have said and done. He could have flashed her a disgusted look and walked away. He could have said, "Shame on you." He could have turned to his disciples and said, "Do you see what sin does to a person?" But he did none of those things. Listen to the acceptance in his words, followed by a command intended to protect and provide for the woman: "Neither do I condemn you. . . . Go now and leave your life of sin" (John 8:11, NIV).

The Pharisees of Jesus' day criticized him for fraternizing with "tax collectors and many other notorious sinners." But Jesus replied, "Healthy people don't need a doctor—sick people do" (Matthew 9:10, 12). How does a doctor respond to someone with an illness or injury? Does the doctor condemn the poor patient for his or her ailments, saying something like, "How stupid! How disgusting! If you want me to help you, you're going to have to stop bleeding and hurting?" That would be ridiculous, of course, not to mention cruel. A good physician accepts the patient right where he or she is and focuses on providing the comfort and healing needed.

That is exactly how God connects with us when we are in pain, trouble, or crisis. He doesn't condemn us or criticize us, even though we may be in the wrong. He does not condone or overlook our sin; it must be dealt with on his terms. But he loves us for who we are and accepts us at the point of our failure.

God loves us for who we are and accepts us at the point of our failure.

That's what Paul means when he exhorts us to "accept each other just as Christ has accepted you; then God will be glorified" (Romans 15:7). Christ did not wait until we were believing right or living right before he invited us into a relationship with him; he died for us "while we were still sinners" (Romans 5:8). And if we are to relationally connect to our young people, we must learn to accept our children, students, youth group members, and church

116

members for who they are, no matter what. Then God will be glorified, and they will experience a relational connection that is reflective of Christ's connection to us. And it is that kind of connection that will help lead them to deepened convictions.

The Basis of Genuine Acceptance

Most adults will agree, of course, that the ideal is to accept kids without conditions. Our attitude must not be "acceptance *if*" or "acceptance *when*" but "acceptance, *period.*"

Young people—in fact, all of us—need to know that our value to others is not determined by what we believe or how well we perform. In actual practice, however, the acceptance adults offer young people is often conditional. As long as students are following the rules, staying out of trouble, and believing right and doing what is expected of them, they find their parents and other important adults in their lives to be generally accepting and agreeable. But when young people make a mistake, break a rule, or express a less-than-desirable attitude, they sometimes can be made to feel like second-class citizens. Adults sometimes talk to them differently, become cool and distant, or withhold affection. Adults can withdraw their acceptance very subtly, even without realizing it themselves. But kids sense the change instantly.

Genuine acceptance is a full-time job that requires divine help. It's not something that comes easily, much less automatically. If you hope to convey genuine acceptance to your kids, you must take every opportunity to let them know that they are totally accepted by you, whether they win or lose life's daily battles and challenges. You must enter their world, identify with what they're dealing with, and commit to making sure they sense your acceptance every day.

Your son or daughter is always your son or daughter, a unique gift from God and worthy of your love and acceptance. The kids in your youth group are always individuals for whom Christ died, worthy of your love and acceptance. Totally accepting kids doesn't mean approving of everything they do. But we must go to great lengths to let them know we accept them as being one-of-a-kind and deal separately with their behavior whenever necessary.

Remember, acceptance is based on who a person is—a unique human being made in God's image with infinite value, dignity, and worth. On the other hand, conditional acceptance focuses on performance; it is given only when a person obeys, achieves, or performs well. When acceptance is conditional and the young person's attitude or performance falls short of the standard, feelings of rejection are almost sure to result. And such rejection can lead to a diminished sense of value, dignity, and worth.

The more firmly we grasp this principle, the more intimately we can bond with young people. We must accept kids where they are—apart from their behavior. This is what makes kids feel secure in relationships. And if they don't feel secure in their relationships with us, our efforts to alter their behavior or lead them to convictions about Christ and his Word will be much more difficult and much less fruitful.

Acceptance by Comparison

Lauren is feeling rejected not only because of her unacceptable beliefs and past behavior but also because she isn't like her sister, Stephanie. She senses that she's being compared to her sister and that she's always coming up short.

What the Johnson family is forgetting is that Lauren is not Stephanie and never will be, because she is Lauren—a one-of-a-kind original. As we have said, God has created each of us uniquely different, and Lauren is no exception. In all probability, Lauren's parents haven't discovered who she is as an original child of God, and consequently they haven't raised her up according to her "way" or "bent" (see Proverbs 22:6, NIV).

Even though parents know instinctively that each of their kids is different, they still often make the mistake of training and disciplining them all in essentially the same way. Perhaps this comes from having the same expectations for all of them. I agree that families need standards by which to operate, but there is no standard way to treat all kids because each one responds differently to how he or she is treated. In fact, "standardized" training and discipline is one of the best ways to disconnect from your young people.

As a youth worker, you may find that different kids respond in different ways to you. Take, for example, your attempt to settle down a rowdy youth-group meeting. Some will respond immediately to a gentle, "Okay, let's settle down now." Others seem to need a hammerlock to quiet them. I know that as a parent, I couldn't discipline my daughter, Kelly, in the same way I disciplined my son Sean. Why? Because God created each of them as an original. And unless we understand their distinctives, we will be much less likely to make a connection with them.

Acceptance Fosters a Secure Connection

It is so important for parents—and all those who deal with youth—to learn and practice acceptance of their young people. If we want our students to feel secure in our relationships with them, they need to feel that they are accepted for who they are. That doesn't, however, mean we must condone wrong behavior. Yet when young people feel unaccepted and insecure, they live in fear—the fear that "I'll be rejected if I don't toe the line and live up to expectations."

As you seek to nurture a relational connection with your young people based on Christlike acceptance, you will most likely get a positive response. It may not always be as obedient and sweet as you would like, but it will be a response made in trust, not fear, because the young people will know that whatever happens and whatever they do, you love them for who they are. Period. And when your children, students, or young people receive that kind of acceptance from you, they will develop a relational context in which to grasp their worth in God's eyes. And that, in turn, can bring them to fully know and identify with the original person God has adopted as his child.

MORE ABOUT RELATIONALLY CONNECTING

You may be thinking right now that the challenge to connect and stay connected to your child, youth group, or students in order to help them develop deepened Christian convictions and to know themselves is significant enough to require an entire set of resources. And you would be right. The last number of pages you have been reading have been drawn from my book *The Disconnected Generation*, which provides practical guidance on how to relationally connect and stay connected to your youth by not only *accepting them without condition* but also *affirming* them, *being available* to them, *giving loving affection* to them, *showing appreciation* to them, and *providing loving accountability* to them.

That book is part of several resources in the Beyond Belief family of products designed to assist your efforts to move young people to live out their convictions. Beyond Belief helps you and young people develop convictions, knowing why you believe what you believe. Yet we have created an additional set of resources to help you provide a relational context for young people to live out those deepened convictions. It provides practical ways to develop relational connections and guidance in how to live out what you believe in relationship with others. (See appendix A.)

LAUREN'S STORY: MAKING A CONNECTION

Lauren has adopted a distorted belief about God, truth, and reality, and her situation is not at all uncommon among youth, even those from solid Christian homes. But many parents don't even realize what their kids believe. Lauren's parents are just now finding out what she believes, and they're becoming concerned.

So what should parents do when they're troubled about what their kids are believing? What should youth workers do when one of their young people feels disconnected from his or her parents? What should pastors or Christian educators do when they discover that their kids are struggling with questions about their faith or personal identity?

These are the questions that Duane and Liz must confront as they continue their efforts to help Lauren.

• • • • •

Liz wiped her face with a napkin and then leaned closer to Lauren. "You say your dad wants you to believe the same things he does," she said. "What do you mean?"

"I don't know," Lauren said. "We've had some arguments because I . . . I think they're too dogmatic about some things, you know? Like about Jesus' being the only way to God, stuff like that. But we can't even talk about it without them foaming at the mouth and acting like I've totally rejected God and I'm going to shave my head and become a Buddhist monk or something."

Duane smiled sympathetically. "Well, how *is* your relationship with God?"

Lauren took a few moments to answer. "I don't know," she said again, this time with a shrug. "I mean, I guess I am sorta questioning the things I believed before, and I don't have everything figured out." She stopped and swallowed, and her eyes began to fill with tears. "But even if I'm not as close to God as I used to be, my dad shouldn't hate me like he does."

"Oh, why would you say he hates you, Lauren?" Duane asked.

She quickly wiped her tears. "He said he wished I'd never been born."

"He told you that?" Liz asked, her mouth hanging open.

Lauren shook her head. "Not me. He told my mom. I told Mom a few nights ago that I wasn't in the mood to hear her read Scripture to me, and I guess it hurt her feelings. So later I was walking past their bedroom door, and I heard Dad say, 'If that's the case, I wish she'd never been born.'"

"Are you sure?" Liz asked. "Maybe he was talking about something else."

"No," she said, shaking her head. "I know they were talking about me." She bit her lower lip.

Liz laid a hand on her chest, and her own eyes filled with tears. Lauren lowered her head, and a tear dropped from her cheek onto the kitchen table. She grabbed her napkin, wiped her face again, and looked up.

Liz reached out and touched Lauren's arm. "I'm so sorry, Lauren," she said. "I know that has to hurt you deeply." Lauren dropped her head as tears gently trickled down her cheeks.

Getting up from her side of the table, Liz slid her chair next to Lauren. She squeezed Lauren in a hug and leaned close to her. "It hurts me so much that you had to hear your dad say that. I'm so sorry. I'm so sorry," she repeated, her voice just a whisper. "But I want you to know that no matter what anyone else says or thinks, Duane and I are so glad you were born. You're a precious child of God, and you mean so much to us. We love you, Lauren. We love you, and we always will, no matter what. Okay?"

Lauren watched the tears flow down Liz's face, and then she faced Duane and saw that there were tears in his eyes, too. She suddenly began to sob quietly, resting her face against Liz's shoulder. Duane reached across the table and touched Lauren's and Liz's arms and began to pray softly.

"Lord," he said, "we're hurting right now for Lauren. And we know you're hurting for her, too. We know that you know what it's like to feel rejected and abandoned by those closest to you. And while Lauren may not feel the acceptance of her earthly father right now, please let her feel the healing love of her heavenly Father. God, wrap your arms around her, and let her feel them this very moment. Let her feel you touch her as we touch her. Let her feel your acceptance—and ours—and remind her that she's not alone. In Jesus' name, amen."

When Duane finished praying, the three of them sat for a few moments while Liz hugged Lauren and Duane's arms stretched across the table. After a few moments, Lauren lifted her napkin to her face again.

"You guys are great," she said. "I've never had friends like you."

"Well, now you do," Duane said.

Lauren finished wiping her tears. "I've just got so many questions."

"All you have to do is ask," Liz said.

"I don't even know where to start. I feel like I'm all messed up."

"Why don't we do this," Liz offered. "Why don't we get together a few mornings each week—while you're home from school for the holidays—and just talk things through and try to answer all your questions."

"Thanks," Lauren said, looking from Liz to Duane and back again. "That would be great."

"All right," Liz said. "It's a deal."

Lauren searched their faces again, a question in her eyes.

"What?" Duane asked. "Is there something else?"

Lauren nodded. "I don't know," she said. "I'm just wondering . . ."

"What is it?" Liz asked, her right arm still around Lauren's shoulders.

"Well, do you think you could talk to my parents for me? I don't know, maybe just my dad. I just think maybe . . ."

Liz patted Lauren's arm with her left hand. "Yes," she said. "We'd be glad to." She stretched both arms around Lauren's shoulders then and exchanged a nervous glance with Duane, wondering what they had gotten themselves into.

CHAPTER 7

The Incarnation Celebration

Gary Johnson, Lauren's father, shifted in his chair and leaned forward, propping his elbows on his knees and gazing intensely at the Cunninghams. He and his wife, Cheryl, sat in their family room with Duane and Liz. They had exchanged small talk since the Cunninghams had arrived moments earlier, but Gary's posture now made it clear that he was about to get down to business.

"I guess we're together here because we both want to talk about Lauren," he said. "We're really concerned about her, and we don't know what to do."

Liz nodded as she searched Gary and Cheryl's faces. "We've been wanting to get together and talk with you, too," she said, her voice tentative. "We've met with her lately, and we can sense that she's struggling right now, questioning a lot of things."

"It's more than questioning things," Cheryl injected.

"In what way?" asked Duane.

"Well," Cheryl began. She looked to her husband, who flashed her a comforting smile. "It's like the other evening . . . Lauren came into the family room while I was reading the Bible to prepare for my care group. I had just gotten this fresh insight into the passage I was reading, so when she came in, I was all excited, and I said to her, 'Listen to this verse honey, it's really amazing.'" Cheryl's voice quivered slightly. "And before I could even read it, Lauren got a really stubborn look on her face and said, 'Please, Mom, I don't want to hear it.' When I asked why, she started carrying on about—about me pushing *my* religion on her."

"She says that kind of stuff more and more these days," Gary added.

"She's getting it from that college," Cheryl said. "It's like she's throwing away everything we ever taught her, everything she ever believed as she was growing up."

Gary nodded. "We've been worried for a while now. Whenever she calls home—which isn't often anymore—it's like she always manages to get offended by something we say. It's like she's rejecting us, as a family."

Gary paused, and cast a quick glance in Cheryl's direction. His voice dropped. "Rejecting me mostly, I guess. I'm the one she has the biggest problem with."

"It's not just you, Gary," Cheryl offered.

"Maybe not," he continued. They all fell silent for a few minutes. "I'm—I'm just afraid she's going to walk away from everything we've taught her."

Liz nodded, took a deep breath, and began. "You know, it's interesting that you said you feel like Lauren's rejecting you guys as a family because she used the same words the other night—only she feels like it's the other way around."

"She thinks *we're* rejecting *her*?" Gary asked.

Liz nodded slowly. "That seems to be the way she feels."

"Well, she's got it wrong on that one," Gary retorted. "Just because we can't go along with all these new ideas of hers doesn't mean we're rejecting her."

"You're right, Gary," Duane interjected, his tone conciliatory. "But I think what Lauren may be wanting to feel emotionally from you right now is that you still love and accept her regardless of what she believes. And I'm sure you do."

"Of course I do," Gary answered emphatically, then hesitated. "I may not express it the way she wants. Emotional stuff isn't easy for me—especially with Lauren."

"They're so much alike," Cheryl offered. "You know, both of them are opinionated, and they can clash so easily if they're not careful."

"Well," Liz began. "Lauren seems to think she's really not wanted anymore. She told us she overheard you two talking, and something was said about wishing she'd never been born or something."

"She said what?" Gary asked, a sharp edge in his voice.

"We're not saying you said it," Duane jumped in, fearing that Liz had been a bit too forthright. "It's just that Lauren was telling us about that exchange with you, Cheryl, about the Scripture reading, and later that evening she overheard you guys talking. She . . . she thought she heard Gary say something like you wished she'd never been born."

"I said no such thing," Gary quickly responded.

"I think I know where the misunderstanding is," Cheryl said softly. All eyes went to her as she continued.

"Remember, Gary, when you and I were talking in the bedroom about how it seems Lauren is walking away from everything we have taught her?"

Gary nodded.

"Well," Cheryl continued, "I said I hated to think of living in heaven without all of our family and how I couldn't bear the thought of Lauren's not being there with us." She turned to Gary. "That's when you said, 'If that's the case, I wish she'd never been born.'"

"You're right, that is what I said," Gary responded. His eyes were wide, and his voice was suddenly quiet. "But I was talking about what it would be like not to have my Lauren—my own daughter—with me in eternity." He looked from Duane to Liz, then back again. "That was what I was talking about. I said it because I don't ever want her to suffer, not because I don't love and accept her. I do."

"We know you do, Gary," Duane said. "But it's not us you need to convince. It's Lauren who needs to get a better sense of it."

Gary slumped back in his chair. "But how? What am I supposed to do?"

"First," Cheryl suggested, "we've got to explain to Lauren what you really meant."

Gary nodded. "But how do we get through to her that we're not rejecting her as part of our family? Just tell her?"

"I think it's going to take more than words," Liz responded. "Lauren needs to feel your heart, Gary. You need to emotionally connect with her so she senses what you really feel for her down deep."

Gary nodded slowly and took a deep breath. "I know, but for some reason that is so hard for me." Cheryl reached over and touched Gary's arm. He went on. "I love Lauren so much. Cheryl and I have wept together for her so many times. But it's hard for me to let those feelings out in front of Lauren—but I do love her and . . ." Gary paused. "And I really do miss my little girl."

Gary looked from Duane to Liz, his eyes rimmed with tears. Cheryl looked at her husband and tenderly rubbed her hand on his arm. The two couples sat in silence for a few moments.

Finally Duane spoke. "I have an idea. Liz and I have been working together on a special dinner at our place for the youth group. I think it's the kind of thing that may help you with Lauren if you'll join in on it with us."

Liz jumped in. "We're calling it an 'Incarnation Celebration.' We're hoping it will help our kids develop a greater understanding of the meaning of Christmas. We want to help them deepen their convictions by showing them how the fact of Christ's deity—and his incarnation—really does relate to them."

"How's that going to help us with Lauren?" Cheryl asked.

"Well," Duane said, "if we could get together—the four of us—a couple of times in the next few weeks, I'd like for the two of you to help us with the readings. There's one reading in particular that I think might really help you, Gary, express your heart—directly to Lauren."

"In front of the whole youth group?" Gary asked.

"I think it could be really meaningful," Duane responded.

"I don't know . . ." Gary said slowly.

Cheryl laid a hand on Gary's arm. "At this point," she said, "we're willing to try anything." She looked to Gary for confirmation.

He gave her a small shrug. "If you think it might help," he said.

"I think it might," Duane said, as he reached for his calendar. "It's definitely worth trying."

Several days later, the Johnsons and the Cunninghams met at Duane and Liz's house to begin their preparations for an Incarnation Celebration. As they sat down together around the kitchen table, Duane turned to Gary.

"I'm so anxious to find out how it went," he said. "With Lauren."

Gary and Cheryl exchanged expressive glances.

"You have talked to her about what she heard you say, haven't you?" Liz asked.

"Yeah," Gary answered unenthusiastically. He and Cheryl nodded together.

"It didn't go too well," Cheryl added.

"What do you mean?" Liz probed. "You told her that she just heard a part of the conversation, right?"

Gary shrugged. "Yeah, but . . ." He hesitated, shooting a pleading glance at Cheryl, who jumped in to explain.

"She understands that Gary didn't say what she thought he said. But she says that doesn't change how we treat her or how she thinks we feel about her."

Gary nodded unsmilingly. "She said that knowing what I

meant doesn't change the fact that she can't do anything right in our eyes. She thinks we'll love her only if she does certain things or believes certain things."

"We tried to tell her that's not true, but—"

Gary interrupted. "She got really angry with us, and I . . . I got a little upset, too, and . . . well, the whole thing just kind of blew up in our faces."

They sat in silence for a few moments, disappointment and sadness filling the space between them. Then Duane sighed and spoke.

"I'm so sorry," he said.

"I am, too," Liz added. "I guess I should have expected something like that."

"Well," Cheryl said, "at least she's talking to *you*. That's something."

Liz answered slowly. "Yeah," she said. "I think it is."

The two couples continued to work together over the next couple of weeks and devised a promising plan for their Incarnation Celebration. But at their third meeting, Gary shook his head gloomily. "I just don't know if I can pull this off," he said.

"What do you mean?" Liz asked.

Gary shuffled the pieces of paper he had in his hand and stared at them without looking up. "This," he said, pointing to the script. "This won't be easy to read to Lauren." Gary stopped talking, but no one interrupted. They waited for a few moments, until Gary found his voice again. "I'm not sure how to read it. This is pretty emotional, and I'm not very good at expressing myself this way to Lauren—especially in front of others."

"You just have to speak from your heart, honey," Cheryl offered.

"Right," he agreed. "It's easy to say what I *think*. But publicly expressing what's in my heart, that's a different story."

Duane and Liz nodded sympathetically. No one was surprised by what Gary had revealed about himself.

"Why don't you try taking the reading into a room," Duane

suggested, "where you can practice it and get used to reading it aloud, as if Lauren were there?"

"I did," Gary answered. "I've done that a couple times, and it really got to me. I had to stop reading several times, it choked me up so much. I just don't know if I can do it with Lauren in the room. I'm just not good at that kind of stuff." He dropped his gaze to the papers in his trembling hands.

"We understand, Gary," Liz said. "I can see how this would be quite a stretch for you."

"But," Cheryl said, "I think Lauren really needs to hear it from Gary."

"I know," Gary said. He smiled nervously. "I'll just need you to really pray for me."

Just over a week later, the Johnsons—including Lauren—gathered at Duane and Liz's house with seven other teenagers from the Westcastle Community Church youth group. Gary and Cheryl grew excited as they watched Lauren mingle so naturally among her old youth group friends. Perhaps their daughter's times alone with Liz and Duane discussing spiritual things would pay off tonight. At least they were praying they would.

"It's time for our celebration meal," Duane announced. "Let's all have a seat at the table and listen as Megan reads something for us."

Megan Wagner, Lauren's close friend, stood and read from the second chapter of Luke's Gospel, the account of the angels' announcing the birth of Jesus to shepherds in a field near Bethlehem. When the reading was over, Liz stood as Megan sat down.

"Thanks, Megan," Liz said. "I know we've all heard that Christmas story before. But I want to ask this: How did the shepherds know where to find Jesus?"

Allen Franklin answered quickly. "The angels told them."

"Right, Allen," Liz said. "The angels gave the shepherds specific directions—kind of an address—for where they could find Jesus: in a manger in Bethlehem. And how do you think the shepherds knew that this baby was actually the Son of God, the Messiah?"

After a slight hesitation, Janelle Iverson spoke up. "Well, when an angel says so, most people are gonna listen up. And besides, when everything the angels said turned out to be true, they had no reason to doubt it, right?"

"Right," Liz said again. "And God has done the same kind of thing for us. He wanted us to be able to know for sure that the Jesus who was born in a manger in Bethlehem really is the Christ, the Son of God. So he gave us a sort of 'address' for Christ, so it would be unmistakably clear to us that he was the one true God born into the human race. And how did he do that?"

Liz's question met blank looks all around the table. She waited a moment, then smiled reassuringly and continued. "You see, more than four hundred years before Christ was born, God had his prophets foretell a lot of very specific things about how the Messiah would come.

"Each and every one of those things the prophets predicted," Liz explained, "had to be fulfilled by the Messiah. If any person fulfilled *some* of the prophecies but not *all* of them, well, that wasn't the right address. It would be like looking for an address, and if you find a house with three out of four numbers right, you keep looking, because you know you haven't yet found the right house number. It was the same with the prophecies God gave his people about the Messiah. They were so numerous and specific that if all those prophecies were fulfilled in one person, we could be sure he was the true Messiah, God in the flesh, the Son of God and Savior of the world."

Duane rose from the table and reached for a small tree that had been standing in the corner of the room. On the branches were fastened rolled slips of paper tied with ribbon. As Liz concluded, he placed the tree in the center of the large table.

"This," Duane began, "is something called a 'Prophet Tree,' a different kind of Christmas tree. We'd like you all to take turns untying the slips of paper from the tree and reading what each one says. What you will be reading are some of the specific prophecies that give us an 'address' by which to recognize and identify the true Son of God, the Messiah."

Duane looked at sixteen-year-old Sarah, Pastor Milford's daughter. "Sarah, why don't you go first?"

Sarah took one of the rolls, untied it, and unrolled it. "It says, 'According to Genesis 22:18, the Messiah will be among the descendants of Abraham.'" She looked up at Duane. "Do you want me to read the verse?"

Duane nodded, smiling.

She read: "'This is a record of the ancestors of Jesus the Messiah, a descendant . . . of Abraham,' Matthew 1:1."

"Thank you, Sarah," Duane said. "Allen, why don't you go next, and we'll just go around the table."

"According to Isaiah 11:1," Allen read, "the Messiah will be born in the lineage of Jesse. And then it says, 'This is a record of the ancestors of Jesus the Messiah, a descendant of King David . . . [and] Jesse was the father of King David,' Matthew 1:1 and 6."

Duane continued to pass each small scroll from the Prophet Tree to each of the students until eight prophecies had been read. Then Gary Johnson rose to his feet and read from a sheet of paper Duane had given him earlier. "Those are eight prophecies that were fulfilled in one person, Jesus, who was born over two thousand years ago," he said. "But do you know how amazing that is? You might say, 'Well, it could all be coincidental, right? That doesn't really prove for certain that the man we call Jesus of Nazareth was—and is—God in the flesh.'"

Lauren's father looked around at the faces of the young people seated at the table. He explained how the odds of just *eight* prophecies about Jesus being fulfilled by one person were the same as picking a marked silver dollar out of a pile two feet deep—a two-foot-deep pile big enough to cover the state of Texas, that is. He went on to describe how there are *sixty* major Old Testament prophecies that have all been fulfilled in that one person, Jesus Christ. "That is convincing evidence that Jesus is truly God coming to us in human form," Gary said.

Gary stopped reading and looked around the table. Every eye was on him; the kids seemed to be genuinely amazed by what he had just said.

"Now," Duane said, standing up as Gary sat down, "to celebrate Christ's coming, let's read together a prayer of thanks before we eat." He passed another sheet of paper around the table, adding, "And then at the close of our time together, we will discuss the meaning of the Incarnation to us personally."

The group read the prayer in unison and then dug into the meal that Gary, Cheryl, Duane, and Liz had prepared. The conversation around the table was often light, sometimes serious, but always enjoyable. Everyone seemed to be having a good time.

Just as everyone finished the meal, Lauren slid back her chair from the table and leaned toward her parents.

"I've got to do some stuff," she said in a low voice. She glanced only briefly at her mother before standing.

"Oh, but Lauren," said Liz, who sat beside Lauren, "I'd love for you to stay for this next part. It's really—"

"Yeah," Lauren interrupted. "I'm really sorry." She backed away from the table and tossed a lighthearted wave at the rest of the group.

"Wait a minute—," Gary began, but his wife laid her hand gently on his hand. His face flushed red, and he pursed his lips tightly as he watched his daughter leave the room.

An awkward silence descended on the room until Duane rose to his feet and cleared his throat. "Well, wasn't this a great meal?"

Several of the kids voiced their agreement, and Allen Franklin started clapping, which prompted a round of applause for Cheryl and Liz, who had done most of the cooking and food preparation.

"Now," Duane continued, "we want to celebrate God's taking on human form—the Incarnation—by understanding the reason he came to earth. And this will explain to us the very meaning of Christmas. So, to begin, I've asked Gary if he would read something to us. It's entitled, 'The Saddest Story That Could Ever Be Told: The Great Separation.'"

Gary hesitated, his face still flushed. "Do you think I still need to read this?" he asked, his gaze flitting from Cheryl to Duane to Liz.

"I think so," Cheryl said softly.

"But . . . but she's not here."

Cheryl laid her hand on Gary's knee. "Read it as if she were here."

Gary stood and cleared his throat. "I, um . . . ," he started, then paused again. "I . . . I was going to read this directly to Lauren but she . . . well, she had to leave early. But I'll still read it as if she were here." He glanced around the room, his gaze landing on Duane, who nodded reassurance. Gary returned his gaze to the pages in his hands. "Okay," he said. "Here goes."

THE SADDEST STORY THAT COULD EVER BE TOLD: THE GREAT SEPARATION

"I want you to imagine with me," Gary began, "that once upon a time, in a land far away, I was the happiest king in all the world . . . the happiest king, in fact, in all the history of all the kings in all the world.

"This happiness was not because I was a great king. It was not because I had a grand castle. It was not because I ruled a glorious kingdom. It was because on one special day in the month of June, I became something even better than a great king. On June 3, you, Princess Lauren, were born . . . and I became your father."

Gary paused briefly in his reading and looked up at the attentive faces around the table. He smiled slightly and returned his gaze to the page.

"For nine months," he continued, "my queen and I had awaited your arrival. At the miraculous moment when your life first started, you were only one tiny cell; yet you were already, undeniably, a part of us. You already possessed a complete set of chromosomes—half of which came from me, your father, and the other half came from your mother, Queen Cheryl. And as you grew rapidly from a single cell into a fully functioning human body of more than sixty trillion cells, we experienced a powerful connection to you. We charted your development and thrilled every time you moved. And you—even from inside your mother's womb—you responded to the sounds of our voices.

"When you finally came into the world, you were truly a Johnson. Yet you were a new, unique, one-of-a-kind Johnson . . . one that had never been seen before. Never in the history of mortal time would there be another you—so special and distinct, so original, yet so connected to me.

"I'll never forget looking at you for the first time—your tiny fingernails, your sparkling eyes, your soft hair, pudgy nose, and fat cheeks. Oh, what a wonder you were! You had been created from me, formed in your mother, yet unmistakably you.

"From the first time I scooped you up in my arms and held you close, I wanted nothing more in all the world than to love you, be close to you, and watch you grow to experience all the joys of being you. You were my special child, after all, and I was your father. And I wanted nothing to ever come between us.

"But then . . . a horrible thing happened. The wicked prince of the Unhappy Kingdom tried to overpower me and take control of my kingdom. But he failed because I was too strong. So in anger and hatred, he chose to strike where he knew it would hurt me most. He cast an evil spell over you, my princess. It was a great, terrible, and powerful spell.

"The evil prince's spell caused a dreadful glass wall to surround you wherever you went and whatever you did. I could still see you and hear you—for I was still the great king—but it trapped you without your knowing it. It kept you from seeing me, hearing me, touching me, or even sensing that I was there.

"Thus it was, that unless the spell could be broken, the king and his precious, darling princess—" Gary's voice quivered, and he paused before reading on—"would . . . would never again experience the pleasure, the joy, the closeness of being father and daughter."

As Gary read, a movement in the next room caught Cheryl's eye, and she stole a glance through the open doorway. Lauren stood, just inside the next room, folding and refolding a lap rug, out of sight of everyone at the table except Cheryl.

"That wicked spell," Gary read, "caused me great anguish, Princess. A father may be a great warrior, a great man, even a king, but if his prize—his princess—is taken from him, he is a poor man no matter what else he may own—or rule.

"Oh, what anguish it was for your king, your father. I could see you, but you could not see me. I saw your first steps, but you could not hear me cheering you on. I heard your first words, but they weren't spoken to me. I watched everything . . ." Gary paused as tears caused the page to blur. He blinked quickly and went on. "I watched everything you did and followed everywhere you went. But the dreadful glass wall kept you from feeling my ever-present love for you. I wanted to share everything with you—the thrill of learning to ride your bike, the relief of passing a test in school, the excitement of winning a game—but the evil spell took all that away from me."

Megan raised a napkin to her cheeks and wiped her eyes. Several others followed suit, as occasional sniffles from those around the table now punctuated Gary's words.

"I was there, too, when you were hurt. When you cried, I reached out to wipe your tears away, but you never felt the touch of my hand. When you skinned your knee, I wanted to kiss it and make it better, but you didn't even know I was there. And on those nights when you would cry yourself to sleep, I heard you, Princess. I heard you cry, 'Where is my daddy? I want my daddy,' but you couldn't hear my sobs for you."

Lauren, still standing just out of sight, held her breath. She heard rather than saw her father's vulnerability, and for the first time in as long as she could remember, she sensed her father's love for her coming through his voice.

Gary continued, his voice faltering and occasionally failing him. "Oh, what a wicked spell! I would have given my kingdom— my life!—if it would have broken the spell and restored my princess to me. But it could not be. No human king could break this spell. I could only watch with broken heart, weep for my princess, and wait for the Spellbreaker who could reunite this king who had become a father with the princess, his daughter . . . and bring to an end The Saddest Story That Could Ever Be Told."

Gary finished reading. His head remained bowed as if he were still looking at the page, though his clouded eyes could no longer see the words.

No one spoke or moved for a few moments until Gary spoke again, in a whisper this time.

"Lauren," he said, "if you were here right now, there's so much I would like to say to you. I . . . I know this is just a make-believe story I've read tonight, but it's what's in my heart for you. It kills me to think that you can't feel my love for you, that you can't know how precious and special you are to me.

"I know you haven't felt that from me, but it's true. I'm not as good at expressing myself as I'd like to be, but I know it's not just that. I, uh . . . I've done a terrible job at showing you, even if you do things I don't understand or approve of, I still love you and accept you just the way you are. That's the kind of dad I *want* to be, I just don't know how most of the time, and I'm so sorry for that. You *are* my princess—" he hesitated and Cheryl laid a reassuring hand on his arm— "and you're such a part of me. I wish you could know that no matter what, I want to accept you and love you and be there for you . . . just the way you are."

He finished, clearing his throat, still maintaining his composure. He stared through tears at the tablecloth, too embarrassed to look up to see what reaction his display of emotion had caused.

Suddenly a pair of arms wrapped around his neck, and Lauren laid her cheek on the top of his head. She held him, and they stood silently together for a few moments until Lauren choked out the words, "Oh, Daddy . . ."

Gary inhaled sharply and fought to control his voice. "I'm sorry," he said. "I'm so, so sorry . . . I—"

"It's okay," she answered, tears streaming down her face.

He turned his head and leaned backward into her embrace. "I really do love you, Lauren . . . so much."

"I know," she said, the tone of her voice communicating that, perhaps for the first time, she *felt* the truth of her father's love—and acceptance.

Cheryl joined the embrace, then, and the others in the room watched the scene through their own tears. After a few more minutes, Lauren straightened and seemed to hesitate, until Liz caught Lauren's eye and touched the chair where Lauren had been sitting. Lauren drew a deep breath and returned to her seat beside Liz.

Duane and Liz nodded to each other, and Liz stood.

"The story that Gary just read," she said, "shows how sad our lives would be if we couldn't feel each other's love. But, while that's just a fable, it actually parallels a real situation, a story that's absolutely true . . . for every one of us. And Cheryl's going to read that story for us."

THE GREATEST STORY EVER TOLD: THE GREAT RECONNECTION

As Liz sat down, Cheryl Johnson stood to her feet. She paused for a moment and looked at all the expectant faces around the table. Even Lauren watched her with apparent interest.

"In a Middle Eastern land many years ago," she began, "where a beautiful river branched out to form four other rivers, there was a pristine garden. Lush tropical trees and plants grew delicious fruit of every taste and texture. A paradise of grasses and flowers under a canopy of clouds and sky painted a breathtaking canvas. Musical birds and sparkling waterfalls produced a sound track of sheer delight. It was perfection itself, the Garden of Eden, where the first man and the first woman lived in perfect harmony with each other and with their Creator, the trinity of God the Father, God the Son, and God the Holy Spirit."

Cheryl's hands shook slightly with the awareness that her daughter was listening now. "From the first moments of their existence, this first couple—Adam and Eve—enjoyed a close relationship with their Creator. They talked to him just as they talked to each other. They walked with him in the Garden. They laughed together, sharing the delights of Paradise—reveling in the gazelle's grace, the eagle's soaring strength, the sparrow's playfulness.

"They communed with God as a dear Friend and loving Father, for they were a family. And through this relationship they had everything they needed. They had love because their love came from God. They had joy because their joy came from God. They had peace because their peace came from God. There was no hunger, greed, fear, or pain because God's holy presence was felt all throughout the wonderful garden.

"And God told Adam and Eve that the world was theirs to keep and that they were to fill it with a human family of their own. For the God of love, their Father, wanted to shower his love on even more children and enjoy their company. He wanted them to know him as their God and to love him as their Father."

Cheryl paused and looked up from the paper, speaking the next sentence from memory. "But then something terrible happened." She looked back to the page and continued. "A rebellious angel named Lucifer plotted in hatred to ruin the perfect family and world God had created. Lucifer, who had been cast out of heaven because he wanted to rule his own kingdom without God, persuaded the first human couple that they, too, should rule their own world without God. So he deceived them into believing that they knew better than God. He convinced them to selfishly and sinfully choose their own ways rather than trusting in God's ways. He persuaded them to eat the fruit God had forbidden them to eat. And so they sinned. And their sin brought about a devastating effect on them . . . and on the world around them."

Cheryl's voice slowed now; she wanted her listeners to feel the full emotional impact of what she read next. "Adam and Eve's sinful choice to reject God and his ways formed a dreadful wall—a wall of death—that separated them from their loving Creator and Father God. *Gone,*" she said, emphasizing the word, "were their shared moments of intimacy and happiness. *Gone* were the trills of laughter they enjoyed together. *Gone* was their close relationship.

"From that point on, God watched in grief and sadness as children—his children—came into the world he created without knowing him and feeling his love. He watched them every moment of the day, but they could not feel his interest. He saw them follow the sinful path of Adam and Eve that would keep every child, teenager, and adult from knowing and feeling his love."

Silence gripped the room except for Cheryl's voice. Lauren blinked. She realized with a start that she had already stopped listening as if this were a *story;* she was listening as if what her mother was saying was the *truth.*

"The perfect and holy Creator, who knew no sin, watched as his sinful children separated from his very presence. They were now disconnected from the only source that could sustain life and love and joy and peace. He watched as his children had to suffer the agony of war and hunger, disease and heartache, which would last forever and ever. The sin separated God from the cherished family he had created, and it broke his heart. And at that moment when his heart broke for his children, he already knew how he would respond."

Cheryl looked up again and said, "And this—though it is miraculous—is no fairy tale. It is absolutely true."

Lauren braved a quick glance at her father, her face contorted with emotion. Suddenly she saw it. She realized the titanic effort it had taken for her dad to say those things he had said to her a few moments ago, how desperately he wanted to reach her with his love. She saw, too, how fervently her heavenly Father loved her and what lengths *he* had gone to in order to show his love. And just as she had that night—for the first time—felt the impact of her father's love, she was now, even as her mother read, beginning to feel the depth and breadth of the love of God in Christ . . . for her. She inhaled sharply and tried to stifle the emotion that was welling up in her.

Cheryl returned her gaze to the page and found her place again. "God wanted so much to reconnect to his children and restore a relationship with them—with *you*—but God, being holy, could not relate to sin. So he devised a plan. He sent his Son into our world to became one of us—a child himself, a human baby—for you. He who was God came to earth—in a virgin's womb, as the prophets foretold, as the shepherds learned—to cancel the curse so you could know, so you could *feel* his love for you."

She paused briefly and then continued to read. "The sin of the first couple and your sin caused death, and the prince of darkness, Satan himself, held the power of death over you. And there was only one thing that could cancel the curse of sin: A sinless human had to be willing to sacrifice himself for you. So God's Son, perfect and sinless in every way, became human. As the Bible records, 'Only as a human being could he die, and only by dying could he break the power of the Devil, who had the power of death,'" she said, quoting from Hebrews 2:14.

"He did it all for you." Cheryl's voice was a whisper now. "Though you sinned against him, he loved and accepted you. That is the meaning of the Incarnation. It shows you how much he wants a relationship with you."

Suddenly Lauren's head dropped into her hands as her mother read on, unaware of what was happening to her daughter.

"And that kind of relationship," Cheryl continued, "is available to anyone who responds to his offer of a never-ending, always-with-you love relationship by believing and trusting in Christ as the Son of God, your Savior, Redeemer, 'reconnector,' and friend.

"Not the end," Cheryl intoned, "but the beginning, if you trust in the Incarnate One." Cheryl then sat down.

Liz, who had noticed Lauren's change in posture, slipped slowly out of her chair and knelt beside her. Lauren was sobbing softly, and it took several minutes of soft whispers and reassuring words from Liz before Lauren spoke.

"I . . . I always thought I knew God, but I never . . ." She reached for a napkin and wiped the tears from her face. She spoke softly to Liz so the others could not hear, "I never before sensed how much my . . . my sin . . . hurt him." She exhaled a gasp and cried softly again for a few moments. "Oh," she said finally. "Oh, I'm so sorry. I'm so sorry I've gone my own way and not his."

Liz squeezed Lauren's shoulder. "Lauren," she said quietly, but firmly. "Are you saying that you're ready, like we've been talking about these past couple weeks? Are you wanting to turn your life over to God . . . right now . . . tonight?"

Lauren nodded vigorously. "If I do that, he'll accept me, right?"

"Oh," Liz said, "he already *does*. He always *has*."

Lauren gazed through tear-filled eyes at Liz, as if searching her face for the truth. Finally, she buried her face in Liz's shoulder and cried, "Yes."

For the next few moments, Liz led Lauren in a quiet prayer, while others in the room bowed their heads and prayed silently. When they had finished, Liz lifted her head and located Gary and Cheryl with her eyes. She nodded meaningfully to them, and they quickly rose from their chairs and joined Liz and Lauren.

Through tears, then, Lauren shared how she had just trusted in the Incarnate One—Jesus Christ—as her Savior and Lord. She shared how she had never before really given up her way of living and turned her life over to God. She told how what she was hearing at college caused her to question so much about what she'd been taught. She explained how that over these past few weeks she and Liz had dealt with many questions and squarely addressed the main issue: Was she going to reject God's way to live her own way?

With that, Lauren looked around the room, stood up, and stated, "I'm part of a whole new family tonight." Soon everyone in the room surrounded her in a laughing, crying, hugging celebration of her new life in Christ and her fresh start with her family.

After the celebration had abated a bit, Duane stood and smiled broadly at the group. "I can't think of a better way to celebrate the Incarnation than to see somebody I love connect with God and enter that never-ending love relationship with him.

"And as we finish the evening together," he continued, holding four large index cards in his hand, "I want a few of you to help me share some really wonderful things that the truth of the Incarnation communicates to you about how much God wants to have a relationship with you.

"I'd like to ask some of you to read from these cards," Duane said, handing cards to Megan, Allen, Brent, and Lauren. "I'd like each of you to read these," Duane continued, "and as you do, I want everyone else to keep in mind that what they're reading applies to you in just the same way it applies to them. Megan?"

Megan smiled nervously, and read without rising from her seat. *"God accepts me unconditionally."* She licked her lips. "Like every other human being, I suffered the curse of death. I was born in sin, disconnected from God, and that broke his heart. And even though I sinned against him—" she paused, and her voice got softer—"he accepted me without condition. He wanted so much to have a love relationship with me that he was willing to set aside his glory, humble himself, and even go through a torturous death on a cross for me even though I didn't deserve it." Her voice tightened. "His incarnation shows how passionate God is about enjoying a relationship . . . with me."

Megan finished, and Duane let a moment pass before nodding to Allen.

Allen, a high school senior, cleared his throat nervously and gripped the card as if it were a steering wheel. *"God loves me sacrificially."* He cleared his throat again, then continued. "Even though I was born with a sinful nature—and added to my guilt many times by sinning myself—God solved the problem of my sin in a way that satisfied his mercy *and* his justice. 'He sent his own Son in a human body . . . [and] destroyed sin's control over [me] by giving his Son as a sacrifice for [my] sins.' Romans 8:3. In spite of my sin, God loved me enough to sacrifice himself, and he proved it by laying down his life for me."

As Allen finished, Brent glanced at Duane, who nodded for him to begin reading. *"God understands me intimately,"* he began. "When God took on human flesh to be born, grow up, and live as a human being, he endured everything I could ever endure and more: every trial and every joy. And he did it all for *me*. Because he wants me to know that he understands what it's like to be me. The Incarnation means that Jesus, my Lord and my God, understands me like no one else and identifies with me . . . whatever I go through . . . whenever I go through it."

Duane nodded, then turned to Lauren. Their eyes met. She smiled warmly, then dropped her gaze to the card she held in both hands.

"God relates to me continuously," she read. "Jesus isn't some distant mythical-type figure of a baby in a manger, and he's not just a historical figure on an old rugged cross. He wants . . . " She stopped.

Everyone in the room sat watching Lauren. She stared at the card. She seemed to freeze in position. They waited.

Lauren seemed to be reading the whole card, unconscious of everyone's stares. Only her eyes moved, scanning the words on the card's surface. Then, unmistakably, color flooded her face, reddening her cheeks.

"He wants," she continued, her voice thick with emotion, "to do more than save me by his incarnation and crucifixion. He wants to spend time—and eternity—with . . . *me!* He wants to share the joy of being in my company. He wants me to know the joy of being in his company. He wants to be there for me wherever I am, whatever I'm doing, to go through it with me and never leave me because he loves me . . . always . . . and forever."

Lauren set the card on the table in front of her, and her eyes widened with emotion. "I just don't know what to say," she whispered. "I've learned this week that I didn't deserve Christ's dying for me and I couldn't do anything to make him love me. And in spite of my self-will . . ." Lauren paused to regain her composure. "God loved and accepted me, and because of Christ, I now *know* I have a relationship with him—and with Mom and Dad, too!"

The room erupted then with clapping and shouts of joy as if they were at a high school basketball game. Lauren slipped over to Gary and Cheryl, and all three embraced tearfully. After a few moments, they were all standing around the table, and Duane told them all to join hands.

"Let's close in prayer and thank God during this Christmas season for sending us his Son to earth as our sacrifice. Without that act of love and mercy we could not be rejoicing with Lauren tonight."

$$\bullet \ \bullet \ \bullet \ \bullet \ \bullet$$

Teachable Moments

Something exceptional has just happened in Westcastle. A connection has been made, not only between Lauren, her heavenly Father, and her earthly father, but also between the youth group and the truth of the deity of Christ. Such connections will quite naturally—and supernaturally—result in deepened convictions.

But an Incarnation Celebration isn't the only way to encourage young people to understand why Christ's deity is objectively true and relationally meaningful. There are additional ways—even in the midst of our busy lives and daily routines—to help kids believe with confidence. The following Teachable Moments section is designed to provide practical examples of how to use the Christmas season as a way to reinforce that Jesus Christ is truly the Son of God, who wants a relationship with us.

Keep Christmas Focused

The Christmas season provides rich opportunities each year to freshly focus on the awesome truth of the Incarnation—"God wants to have a relationship with you!" Here are some practical ways to accomplish that.

WHILE TRIMMING THE TREE

Some people say that the Christmas tree tradition began when Martin Luther, struck by the beauty of a forest of starlit fir trees, brought one indoors and decorated it with candles to remind his children of God's creation. When you and your children are trimming your Christmas tree, you can have this conversation:

Ask, "What can the lights on the tree tell us about the meaning of Christmas?" After fielding questions, turn off the Christmas lights on the tree and say, "This represents that all of us are like empty bulbs without light or life." Turn on the lights and say, "This represents all those who make a relational connection to God because God is the one who gives life and light to all those who believe in Christ as their Savior. When you see the Christmas tree lit up, think of the true meaning of Christmas—that God sent his Son to earth because he wants so very much to have a relationship with you."

Ask, "What can the evergreen tree tell us about the meaning of Christmas?" After some discussion say, "Before Christ was in our lives, we could never live forever. But because of Christ we have the promise of eternal life. When you see the evergreen tree, remember that Christ came so that you can have an everlasting relationship with him."

WHEN OBSERVING A MANGER SCENE

When you and your children see a manger scene, you can have this conversation: Ask, "How can we be sure that the baby Jesus born in a manger was really the Son of God?" After interaction you can say, "There are a number of ways we can be sure Jesus was truly the Son of God. For example, more than four hundred years before Jesus was born, prophets foretold just where Christ would be born, where he would grow up, what he would be like, very specific things he would do, how people would respond to him, what they would do to him, etc. More than sixty prophecies were fulfilled perfectly in Christ, and that enables us to be confident that the Jesus born of the Virgin Mary in a stable in Bethlehem was the Son of the one true God!"

BEFORE OR AFTER SINGING OR HEARING CHRISTMAS MUSIC

Christmas music is an excellent tool to reinforce the meaning of the Incarnation. When the word *Immanuel* is used in a song, ask what the word means. Explain that Christ was called Immanuel, meaning "God is with us," because Jesus was God coming to live with us. And why did Christ come to earth? Jesus came to offer himself as a sacrifice so that we could have a relationship with God.

When hearing "Away in a Manger," ask, "What does it mean that Jesus was a 'holy infant so tender and mild'?" This gives you the opportunity to point out that Jesus was the "holy infant" because his birth father was not Joseph but rather the Holy God of the universe. Thus, Jesus was born of a virgin, with God as his birth father.

When hearing "Angels We Have Heard on High," ask, "Why did the angels sing 'Gloria in excelsis deo'?" The angels sang, "Glory to God in the highest" because it was a most glorious day when God took on human flesh as part of his wonderful plan to restore us to a relationship with him.

WHEN DECKING THE HALLS

Young people may not relate to the garland, tinsel, and Christmas decorations as a celebration. But use the time of decorating your home or youth group meeting place or church to say, "We celebrate with these decorations to express how very thankful we are that God did what he did in sending Christ to earth so we can enjoy a relationship with God."

Write a Christmas Card to Jesus

Christmas cards are used primarily to express holiday wishes and sentiments to one another. But you can also use cards to teach young people the relational meaning of Christmas. Ask them to write a card to Jesus, expressing their thankfulness for Christ's becoming human and for what he says to them through the Incarnation:

1. "Thank You for Accepting Me Unconditionally." This would be a card expressing how they feel about God's unconditional acceptance. Suggest, "First, tell Jesus that you know that he sees and knows everything you do and think (good or bad), yet he accepts you just the way you are. And then tell Jesus how that makes you feel. Thank him for accepting you without any conditions."

2. "Thank You for Loving Me Sacrificially." This would be a card expressing how they feel about the great sacrifice Christ made to purchase our salvation. Suggest, "Write to Jesus, and tell him you understand he left a wonderful place in heaven to come to earth to suffer and die a terrible death. And why? Because he loved you that much. He felt you were that valuable to him. Tell him how that makes you feel, and thank him for loving you so sacrificially."

3. "Thank You for Understanding Me Intimately." This would be a card expressing how grateful they are that Christ identifies with everything they go through. Say, "This is a card that first tells Jesus that you realize he was born and grew up facing the same struggles you have faced, yet he never did wrong. And because he lived a human life, he understands what it's like to be you. That means he identifies with everything you go through and is there to comfort you and go through it with you. Tell him how that makes you feel. And thank him for understanding you so intimately."

4. *"Thank You for Relating to Me Continually."* This is a card expressing how they feel about a God who will never leave them no matter what. Say, "This is a card where you tell Jesus you know he has given you his Holy Spirit to be with you for every minute of every day so that you can know and feel his love. Let him know how it makes you feel that he is always there to help you and live his life in you. Thank him for being there for you always."

Explain Where the Power Originates

Make a habit of entering your child's world to demonstrate an unconditional acceptance for who he or she is, a love that is willing to sacrifice, an understanding of what he or she is going through, and an availability that says, "I'll be there for you no matter what." And whenever you sense that the young person appreciates or actually acknowledges your acceptance, affection, understanding, or availability, take the opportunity to tell him or her where all of that actually originates. Our model for acceptance, affection, understanding, and availability is not only the Incarnate One, Jesus Christ, but also God's Holy Spirit, who empowers each of us to demonstrate those relational qualities. Honor God by letting your kids know it is because of Jesus and your trust in him that you are able to become more and more relational, a better mother, father, grandparent, youth worker, etc.

● ● ● ● ●

Now, let's go back to the story to set up the next section.

BUT IF THE BIBLICAL DOCUMENTS ARE NOT ACCURATE, THEN WHAT?

After Duane prayed, the group began to break up, and several people dashed out while others made their way to the door. As the last of the group was leaving, Megan and Lauren hung back and got Liz and Duane's attention.

"Could we talk to you guys for a minute?" Lauren asked.

"Sure," Duane responded, and they all made their way to the family room and sat down.

"This was great tonight," Megan began. "I've got a whole new understanding about the meaning of Christmas, why Christ came, and all that stuff. And the way you guys presented everything, it really helped me to see that Jesus really is God's Son." Megan hesitated briefly. "But something has bothered me ever since Lauren spent a weekend at my place two weeks ago." She glanced at Lauren.

Duane and Liz leaned forward in anticipation of what was coming next.

"I should never have shared that stuff with Megan," Lauren began. "But I guess I wanted to explain all the things I was learning."

"Share what stuff?" Liz interrupted. "Learning about what?"

"Well . . . ," Lauren began hesitantly.

"Lauren told me about what she's learning about the Bible in college," Megan interrupted. "She told me that many of the stories found in the Bible either never happened or were really exaggerated. And she said that a book that old is full of all kinds of mistakes, and she could prove it to me."

Duane nodded soberly. He studied the troubled look on Megan's face.

"I'm really sorry," Lauren said. "I should never have talked to Megan and gotten her all confused. But I was just telling her what my professor was saying, and it's got me confused now, too."

Liz slid forward in her chair. "You know, girls, a lot of people have attacked the Bible before, but I can tell you this—what the Bible says is true."

"It's not that I don't believe you guys," Megan responded. "I still believe the Bible . . . I guess. But if Lauren's professors are right, it's just that . . . I don't know . . ." She dropped her gaze and shrugged her shoulders.

"That if the Bible isn't true," Duane injected to complete Megan's thought, "then how can we know the prophecies of Christ really came true? Or that any of what we read in the Bible is real?"

Megan and Lauren exchanged glances, as if Duane had read their minds.

"I'll tell you what I'd like to do," Duane continued. "Rather than try to give you a quick answer tonight, I'd like to bring this up with the entire youth group so we can examine together just how reliable the Bible is and why Liz can say what she said. How does that sound?"

Megan smiled. "Thanks, you guys. I knew you'd have an answer."

"And Lauren," Liz interjected, "I can go over it all with you when you're home from school."

Lauren agreed, and a few minutes later, the foursome concluded their meeting. As they said good-bye to the girls and closed the door behind them, Liz turned to Duane.

"I think we've got our work cut out for us this week," she said.

• • • • •

Duane and Liz may have their work cut out for them, but there is an abundance of evidence to share with their young people, and that information will give them remarkable confidence that the Bible is very reliable. And Duane is right. If we can't trust that we have a reliable record of what happened two thousand years ago, how can we be convinced that Jesus was the Messiah? Practically everything we know about Jesus—the messianic prophecies, his virgin birth, and his miracles—are recorded in an historical document. If the historical record is in question, then the historical evidences of Christ's deity are in doubt. So just how reliable is that historical record? Let's find out in the next section.

PART THREE

THE BIBLE: GOD WANTS US TO KNOW HIM AND BE LIKE HIM

CHAPTER 8

The Bible: Relational and Reliable

Duane pulled up a stool and perched on it as he addressed the Westcastle youth group.

"Okay, let's get started," he said. "I think all of you know that some exciting things have happened the last few weeks, and a few of us have begun to ask some really good questions about the Bible and whether or not we can really trust it. So I've decided to talk tonight about why we really can trust the Bible.

"Let me start by asking this question: How would you describe the Bible?" He looked around the room at his students' expectant faces. "What is the Bible? How would you describe what it is and what it does for us?"

A few moments passed. A few in the group seemed to be thinking.

Finally Allen raised his hand. Duane nodded and called Allen's name.

"It's God's truth," Allen said. "It's the inspired Word of God."

Duane nodded. "Okay," he said. "Good. Who else has an answer?"

"It's . . . it's the book of Christian teachings," Karen offered.

"It's the teachings of the Jewish religion, too," Megan added. "The Old Testament is, anyway."

Several others in the group spoke at once, offering other answers.

"All right," Duane said, nodding his approval. "Those are all good responses. But let me give you a little different description of the Bible and see what you think." He glanced down at his notes as he read, "The Bible is God's instruction manual for living. It is our road map to heaven. It is God's love letter to us. It's the means we use to get to know him." He allowed the words to sink in for a moment, then held up his Bible in one hand and continued. "So if people don't read this book, they can't very well know him."

"Wait a minute," Karen said, her brow furrowed in thought. "There are some countries that don't even have the Bible. You're saying they can't know God because of that?"

"Well—," Duane began, setting his Bible down on the table.

"What if we don't have all of the Bible?" Allen interrupted. "What if there's, like, missing books or chapters? Does that mean we can't know God?"

"Yeah," Karen interjected, sliding forward to perch on the edge of the couch. "What if God really gave fifteen commandments, but we have only ten of them?"

"Now, slow down," Duane said, holding his hand in the air as if trying to stop traffic. "Let's not get carried away."

"But Karen and Allen are right," Megan protested. "What if the people writing the Bible didn't put down everything God said . . . or like, maybe they got it all wrong or something. Does that mean we're all out of luck? Is that what you're saying?"

Duane sighed deeply and stared at the group, his expression frozen. Finally he turned and cast a helpless glance at his wife. "Tell you what," he said. "Maybe this is a good time for pizza." He looked back to the curious faces around the room. "I'll, uh . . . we'll come back to these questions some other time, okay?"

• • • • •

We can hardly blame Duane for being caught a little off guard. The questions the youth group is asking might overwhelm even the most seasoned parent, pastor, or youth leader. But they're good questions—ones that must be answered if our young people are ever going to develop deep, solid, and lasting Christian convictions. And they are questions that will inevitably confront our young people as they grow up in a postmodern society that considers truth something that can be determined subjectively.

If the Bible is just a helpful collection of nice thoughts, then it doesn't matter too much if parts have disappeared or been mistranslated over the years. If the Bible is merely another version of truth, then it makes little difference if it is accurate. But if the Bible is what Duane claims—God's instruction manual for living, our road map to heaven, and the main means by which we can know God—then it becomes extremely important to know whether it's reliable, whether it was recorded exactly as God gave it, and whether it's been accurately passed down to us. If we truly understand what the Bible is—that is, if we understand how important it is to each of our lives—then questions about its reliability become suddenly and critically important.

> *If the Bible is God's instruction manual for living, our road map to heaven, and the main means by which we can know God, then it becomes extremely important to know whether it's reliable.*

THE RELATIONAL MEANING OF THE BIBLE

Duane's question elicited some decent answers from his youth group. The Bible *is* God's truth. It *is* the inspired Word of God. It is the assembled teachings of the Christian church, and, of course, the first thirty-nine books are also important to Judaism.

And, as Duane said, the Bible is certainly a road map to heaven.

Additionally, it is God's instruction manual for living. The apostle Paul explains that "all Scripture is inspired by God and is useful to teach us what is true and to make us realize what is wrong in our lives. It straightens us out and teaches us to do what is right. It is God's way of preparing us in every way, fully equipped for every good thing God wants us to do" (2 Timothy 3:16-17).

All the teachings of Scripture then—whether in the form of an instruction, parable, admonition, precept, ordinance, or command—are intended to show us the right way. And when God's Word says, "Follow this way," "Avoid those places," "Abstain from those actions," or "embrace those thoughts," it is not trying to restrict us or bully us. God always has our best interests at heart, and his Word is intended to protect us and provide for us. As Moses told the nation of Israel, "Obey the Lord's commands and laws that I am giving you today *for your own good.* . . . I am giving you the choice between a blessing and a curse! You will be blessed if you obey the commands of the Lord your God that I am giving you today. You will receive a curse if you reject the commands of the Lord your God and turn from his way" (Deuteronomy 10:13; 11:26-28, emphasis mine).

But the fundamental purpose of the Bible goes even deeper than providing us with rules and guidelines that can bless our lives.

We all, no doubt, accept the proposition that obedience brings blessing. But how? How can adherence to a certain code or set of laws or various commands protect us from harm or provide for our good? Does the Book have the power to bless or curse us?

If I told you the Bible, with all its instructions for right living, had no power to protect us or provide for us, you might label me a heretic. But the truth is, there is no authority in the words of Scripture in and of themselves. The authority and the power of Scripture to protect us and provide for us derive from the author of the Book—God himself. The power to bless and curse resides not in the written words but in the One who inspired them. God is the power behind the Book.

The reason that obedience to God's Word protects us from harm and provides for us is because when we obey God's commands, we are acting in accordance with his ways. You see, God, by his very nature and character, defines all that is perfect, right, good, and blessed. "Whatever is good and perfect," the writer of the book of James says, "comes to us from God above" (James 1:17). So when we act according to God's ways, we enjoy blessing because God's ways reflect who he is—the ultimate good and perfect God. Being honest brings blessing because God is true. Staying sexually pure brings blessing because God is holy. Treating others justly brings blessing because God is just. God's commands for us to act in certain ways flow out of who he is and how he himself acts. His ways simply reflect who he is—perfectly right—and that way of living brings blessing. The psalmist David said:

> The law of the Lord is *perfect,*
>> reviving the soul.
> The decrees of the Lord are *trustworthy,*
>> making wise the simple.
> The commandments of the Lord are *right,*
>> bringing joy to the heart.
> The commands of the Lord are *clear,*
>> giving insight to life.
> Reverence for the Lord is *pure,*
>> lasting forever.
> The laws of the Lord are *true;*
>> each one is fair. (Psalm 19:7-9, emphasis mine)

The laws and commands of God's Word are perfect, trustworthy, right, clear, and true because those are qualities of the Lawgiver—God—himself. The Word of God doesn't possess those qualities or powers in and of itself; it derives them from God.

And living according to God's ways simply reflects the way God is, which, in turn, brings clear and certain benefits. As David said, the law of the Lord revives our soul, makes us wise, brings us joy, and gives us insight for living. Knowing the Word of God—and obeying it—can provide us with the benefits of knowing God (for example, peace of mind, a clear conscience, strong relationships, a healthy self-esteem, and so on) and protects us from the curses of life apart from him (guilt, emotional distress, shame, loneliness, disrupted relationships, for example).

Thus, we can say we believe the Bible is a perfectly right set of laws and guidelines that flows out of a perfectly right God. To put it more accurately, we might say that the Bible is God's revelation of himself to us, which in turn declares his ways. It reveals a personal God, the God who "would speak to Moses face to face, as a man speaks to his friend" (Exodus 33:11). It is the revelation of "a God who is passionate about his relationship with you" (Exodus 34:14). And it is a revelation that, from the first words Moses penned in the book of Genesis to the last word John wrote in Revelation, reflects the loving heart of a God who wants us to be in right relationship with him so that we can enjoy all the benefits that relationship offers.

Scripture is the means by which God has chosen to introduce and reveal himself to you so that he can enjoy a relationship with you. Moses understood this, of course; he begged God, "If you are pleased with me, teach me your ways *so I may know you*" (Exodus 33:13, NIV, emphasis mine). God's Word—the record of all his ways—is given to us for a very relational purpose: so we may know him and enjoy all the blessings of a relationship with our loving Creator. When we approach the Scriptures in order to know God and have a relationship with him, it not only brings a temporal blessing but also results in eternal life. Jesus prayed to his Father, "And this is the way to have eternal life—to know you, the only true God, and Jesus Christ, the one you sent to earth" (John 17:3).

Scripture is the means by which God has chosen to introduce and reveal himself to you so that he can enjoy a relationship with you.

That is what our young people need, of course. They need to see God's Word as the revelation of the one true God who desires to have a relationship with them, a relationship that brings blessing now and for eternity. But that presumes that the Bible—as we possess it—is accurate and reliable. In fact, the more our kids realize how important the Bible is to their lives, the more they will want to know that it can be trusted. As Megan asked, "What if the people writing the Bible didn't put down everything God said . . . or like, maybe they got it all wrong or something. Does that mean we're all out of luck?"

As it happens, Megan's question has already been answered in the Bible itself, in an incident that's recorded in the Old Testament.

WHEN THE BOOK OF THE LAW WAS LOST

The incident took place in Judah, during a period when a young man named Josiah reigned as king. At that time, the people of Judah had been worshiping idols for many years, and many of the old ways had been neglected or lost. But Josiah "began to seek the God of his ancestor David" (2 Chronicles 34:3). He decreed the destruction of the pagan idols and altars that dotted the land and began an effort to repair, restore, and reconsecrate the temple in Jerusalem.

But one day, as Hilkiah the high priest was working amid the flurry of the temple restoration efforts, a long and ancient scroll was discovered. The priest's hands must have trembled as he rolled through the scroll, reading words that had been lost many years earlier. Recognizing its importance, Hilkiah conveyed the scroll to a man named Shaphan, the king's private secretary.

As Shaphan read from the scroll to Josiah, the king no doubt recognized the words—even though he had never heard them before—because much of what Shaphan read had been circulated for years by word of mouth, from parent to child and sage to student. Josiah, like Shaphan and Hilkiah, recognized this as "the Book of the Law of the Lord as it had been given through Moses" (2 Chronicles 34:14).

But soon Josiah's fascination turned to worry and then quickly to horror as Shaphan read:

> If you fully obey the Lord your God by keeping all the commands I am giving you today, the Lord your God will exalt you above all the nations of the world. You will experience all these blessings if you obey the Lord your God. . . .
>
> *But* if you refuse to listen to the Lord your God and *do not obey* all the commands and laws I am giving you today, . . .
>
> You will be cursed wherever you go, . . .
>
> [with] curses, confusion, and disillusionment in everything you do, until at last you are completely destroyed" (Deuteronomy 28:1-20, emphasis mine).

When the King heard those words, he tore his clothes with his bare hands. "We have not been doing what this scroll says we must do" (2 Chronicles 34:21). He understood that, regardless of his good intentions, God had not been revealed to his people because they had been without the written revelation of God.

Fearful for himself and his people, Josiah gathered the people together. He read to them from the lost scroll, and together they pledged to obey the Lord and his Word.

A DISTORTED REVELATION
PRODUCES DISTORTED RESULTS

The story of King Josiah emphasizes how dangerous it would be if God's Word were lost . . . or distorted, altered, or misrepresented to us through inaccurate copying over hundreds or thousands of years. Before the written word, God spoke directly to Moses, Abraham, and the prophets. God also revealed himself in the flesh and spoke to us through his Son, Jesus (see Hebrews 1:1-2). Now these revelations of God have been recorded in written form and preserved in the pages of Scripture. But if the facts and events of the Bible weren't carefully and truthfully recorded, then the Bible we have today is a distorted reflection of God's nature and character.

So knowing God and living in relationship with him are dependent on us receiving and possessing an accurate revelation of him. Without a reliable Word, we have no assurance that what we follow and obey is true at all. Imagine, for example, that God really did give Moses fifteen commandments and some scribe along the way decided to eliminate five of them. We would—at best—possess an incomplete picture of what God is like and what he requires of us. And at worst, as Josiah realized, we would be courting disaster, inviting "curses, confusion, and disillusionment in everything [we] do" (Deuteronomy 28:20).

Without a reliable Word, we have no assurance that what we follow and obey is true at all.

Or what if, during the copying of Mark's Gospel some hundred years after he wrote it, someone added five chapters? Imagine a person's adding to or twisting around the things Jesus said or did. As Peter confessed to Jesus, "Lord, to whom would we go? You alone have the words that give eternal life" (John 6:68). What if the things Jesus said—the words of eternal life that he spoke—were changed or exaggerated down through the years? If the words God gave to Moses, David, Matthew, and Peter were later changed or carelessly copied, how could we be sure we are coming to know the one true God? How could we be confident that the commands we're obeying are a true reflection of God's nature and character?

If we hope to enjoy the benefits of knowing God, we must be sure that we have a Bible that accurately represents what God inspired people to write on his behalf. Because if we don't—if the Word of God was not accurately recorded and relayed to us—then we and our children, like Josiah and the nation of Judah, will be cheated in our efforts to know God and may be exposed to "curses, confusion, and disillusionment."

WHAT THE BIBLE REFLECTS

God doesn't want his people to miss knowing him or his ways. That is why he miraculously intervened during the time of Josiah and why he led Hilkiah to discover the lost Book of the Law in the temple. God has a redemptive, relational purpose in giving us his inspired Word, and he has declared that he will not allow the Bible—the relational revelation of himself—to be lost, twisted, or distorted. As Jesus said, "I assure you, until heaven and earth disappear, even the smallest detail of God's law will remain until its purpose is achieved" (Matthew 5:18). He will permit nothing to impede his purpose. "Heaven and earth will disappear," Jesus said, "but my words will remain forever" (Matthew 24:35).

God is so passionate about his relationship with you and your kids that he has personally—and miraculously—provided the inspiration of his Word, supervised its transmission, and repeatedly reinforced its reliability so that all those who have open eyes and open hearts may believe it with assurance and conviction.

God is so passionate about his relationship with us and our kids that he has personally—and miraculously—provided the inspiration of his Word, supervised its transmission, and repeatedly reinforced its reliability so that all those who have open eyes and open hearts may believe it with assurance and conviction. Nations may have rejected it, tyrants may have tried to stamp it out, heretics may have tried to distort it, but the evidence for the Bible's reliability is sufficient to assure us and our kids that it has remained a true reflection of reality—of who God is—and that "it is stronger and more permanent than heaven and earth" (Luke 16:17). Moreover, an examination of how God has meticulously and miraculously protected the integrity of his Word will impress us and move us with the depth of God's love for us and his faithfulness toward us (see Psalm 36:5).

God's Word Has Been Recorded Exactly

Long before the invention of human language, God spoke. He who is pure *existence* ("I Am") is also pure *expression* ("the Word"), and at his word the universe blazed into being. And then he created humanity, and the Infinite One made himself known to the finite. He whose language is heavenly, whose every word is eternal, condescended to express himself within the crude limitations of human language, like a master architect stacking building blocks on the floor with a child.

That is but one miracle of God's Word, the first of many. He whose words generated light and heat at the creation of the world, spoke through forty ordinary human beings—shepherds, soldiers, prophets, poets, monarchs, scholars, statesmen, musicians, masters, servants, tax collectors, and tentmakers—to reveal himself to us and our children. But it's not just that he chose human language and human scribes to record his words that should impress us; he also took great care to ensure that those words were recorded exactly as he intended.

You see, many ancient writings adhered only loosely to the facts of the events they reported. Some highly regarded authors of the ancient world, for example, report events that took place many years before they were born . . . in countries they had never visited! And while their writing may be largely factual, historians admit that greater credibility must be granted to writers who were both geographically and chronologically close to the events they report.

With that in mind, look at the loving care God took when he inspired the writing of the New Testament, for example! The overwhelming weight of scholarship confirms that the accounts of Jesus' life, the history of the early church, and the letters that form the bulk of the New Testament were all written by men who were either eyewitnesses of the events they recorded or contemporaries of eyewitnesses. He selected Matthew, Mark, and John to write the Gospels. These were men who could say such things as, "This report is from an eyewitness giving an accurate account" (John 19:35). He spoke through Luke the physician to record the third Gospel and the book of Acts, using as "source material the reports . . . from the early disciples and other eyewitnesses of what God [did] in fulfillment of his promises" (Luke 1:2).

God could have spoken through anyone, from anywhere, to write his words about Christ. But he worked through eyewitnesses such as John, who said, "We are telling you about what we ourselves have actually seen and heard" (1 John 1:3). He worked through Peter, who stated, "For we did not follow cunningly devised fables when we made known to you the power and coming of our Lord Jesus Christ, but were eyewitnesses of His majesty" (2 Peter 1:16, NKJV). And whom did he choose as his most prolific writer? The apostle Paul, whose dramatic conversion from persecutor of Christians to planter of churches made him perhaps the most credible witness of all!

But God didn't stop there. He also transmitted his inspired Word through his apostles to appeal to the firsthand knowledge of their contemporaries, even their most severe opponents (see Acts 2:32; 3:15; 13:31; 1 Corinthians 15:3-8). They not only said, "Look, we saw this," or "We heard that," but they were also so confident as to say in effect, "Check it out," "Ask around," and "You know it as well as I do!" Such challenges demonstrate a supreme confidence that the "God-breathed" Word was recorded exactly as God spoke it to them (2 Timothy 3:16, NIV).

Such careful inspiration and supervision of the Bible underlines God's loving purpose, that not a single piece of this relational revelation of himself be left to chance or recorded incorrectly, so as to deprive us of his protection and provision. Ample evidence exists to suggest that God was very selective in the people he chose to record his words—people who for the most part had firsthand knowledge of key events and who were credible channels to record exactly those truths he wanted us to know. (More on this area of evidence, known as the internal evidence test of the New and Old Testaments, is documented in appendix D, which is drawn from chapters 3, 4, and 21 of my book *The New Evidence That Demands a Verdict*. A comprehensive treatment of the internal evidence test is covered in those chapters.)

God's Word Has Been Relayed Accurately

It's not difficult to see the superintending work of God in the composition of the Old and New Testaments alike. But still, only the original manuscripts—called autographs—were inspired by God, and none of those is in existence today. What we read now are printed copies based on ancient handwritten copies of yet other copies of the original.

The Bible was composed and transmitted in an era before e-mail or even printing presses. If a document was to be preserved and passed down to the next generation, the manuscript had to be written by hand. Over time, the ink would fade, and the material it was written on would deteriorate, so new copies would have to be hand copied or the document would be lost forever.

But doesn't the making of hand-copied reproductions open up the whole process to error? After all, who's to say that a copier didn't omit some of God's words? What if years later someone who was not inspired by God decided to add some new idea to the Bible? How do we know that a weary copier, blurry-eyed from lack of sleep, didn't skip whole sections or misquote some key verses? What if it's true, as Lauren has been hearing at the university, that the Bible is a collection of outdated writings that are riddled with inaccuracies and distortions?

In other words, even if the Bible's human authors recorded exactly what God inspired them to write, how can we believe that what we read today is what they originally wrote? How can we be sure that the manuscripts available to us today are an accurate transmission of the originals?

God has not left us to wonder. Just as he went to great lengths to ensure that his Word was recorded exactly, so he miraculously supervised its transmission to ensure that his Word was also relayed accurately from one generation to another.

THE CASE OF THE METICULOUS SCRIBES

How did God preserve his Word through centuries of copying and distribution . . . even before the invention of the printing press? He did it through a string of painstaking providences that underscore his determination that no child of his would miss knowing and loving him or the provision and protection that comes with living according to his ways.

One of the ways he ensured that his Word was relayed accurately was by choosing, calling, and cultivating a nation of men and women who took the Book of the Law very seriously. God commanded and instilled in the Jewish people a great reverence for his Word. From their very first days as a nation, God told them, "Listen closely, Israel, to everything I say. . . . Commit yourselves wholeheartedly to these commands I am giving you today. Repeat them again and again to your children. Talk about them when you are at home and when you are away on a journey, when you are lying down and when you are getting up again. Tie them to your hands as a reminder, and wear them on your forehead. Write them on the doorposts of your house and on your gates" (Deuteronomy 6:3, 6-9).

That attitude toward the commands of God became such a part

of the Jewish identity that a class of Jewish scholars called the Sopherim, from a Hebrew word meaning "scribes," arose between the fifth and third centuries B.C. These custodians of the Hebrew Scriptures dedicated themselves to carefully preserving the ancient manuscripts and producing new copies when necessary.

The Sopherim were eclipsed by the Talmudic scribes, who guarded, interpreted, and commented on the sacred texts from A.D. 100–500. In turn, the Talmudic scribes were followed by the better-known Masoretic scribes (A.D. 500–900).

The zeal of the Masoretes surpassed that of even their most dedicated predecessors. They established detailed and stringent disciplines for copying a manuscript. Their rules were so rigorous that when a new copy was complete, they would give the reproduction equal authority to that of its parent because they were thoroughly convinced that they had an exact duplicate.

This was the class of people who, in the providence of God, were chosen to preserve the Old Testament text for centuries. A scribe would begin his day of transcribing by ceremonially washing his entire body. He would then garb himself in full Jewish dress before sitting at his desk. As he wrote, if he came to the Hebrew name of God, he could not begin writing the name with a quill newly dipped in ink for fear it would smear the page. Once he began writing the name of God, he could not stop or allow himself to be distracted; even if a king was to enter the room, the scribe was obligated to continue without interruption until he finished penning the holy name of the one true God.

The Masoretic guidelines for copying manuscripts also required the following:

- The scroll must be written on the skin of a clean animal.
- Each skin must contain a specified number of columns, equal throughout the entire book.

- The length of each column must extend no less than forty-eight lines or more than sixty lines.
- The column breadth must consist of exactly thirty letters.
- The space of a thread must appear between every consonant.
- The breadth of nine consonants had to be inserted between each section.
- A space of three lines had to appear between each book.
- The fifth book of Moses (Deuteronomy) had to conclude exactly with a full line.
- Nothing—not even the shortest word—could be copied from memory; it had to be copied letter by letter.
- The scribe must count the number of times each letter of the alphabet occurred in each book and compare it to the original.
- If a manuscript was found to contain even one mistake, it was discarded.[1]

God instilled in the Masoretes such a painstaking reverence for the Hebrew Scriptures to ensure the amazingly accurate transmission of the Book of the Law so that you and I—and our children—would have an accurate revelation of God.

Until recently, however, we had no way of knowing just how amazing the preservation of the Old Testament has been. Before 1947, the oldest complete Hebrew manuscript dated to A.D. 900. But with the discovery of 223 manuscripts in caves on the west side of the Dead Sea, we now have Old Testament manuscripts that have been dated by paleographers at around 125 B.C. These Dead Sea Scrolls, as they are called, are a thousand years older than any previously known manuscripts.[2]

But here's the exciting part: Once the Dead Sea Scrolls were translated and compared with modern versions, the Hebrew Bible proved to be identical, word for word, in more than 95 percent of the text. (The variation of 5 percent consisted mainly of spelling variations. For example, of the 166 words in Isaiah 53, only 17 letters were in question. Of those, 10 letters were a matter of spelling, and 4 were stylistic changes; the remaining 3 letters comprised the word "light," which was added in verse 11).[3]

In other words, the greatest manuscript discovery of all time revealed that a thousand years of copying the Old Testament produced only excruciatingly minor variations, none of which altered the clear meaning of the text or brought the manuscript's fundamental integrity into question.

The critics will make their pronouncements in opposition to the evidence. However, the overwhelming weight of evidence affirms that God has preserved his Word and accurately relayed it through the centuries so that when you pick up an Old Testament today, you can be utterly confident that you are holding a well-preserved, fully reliable document.

THE CASE OF THE NEW TESTAMENT TEXT

As you know, the Hebrew scribes did not copy the manuscripts of the New Testament. Thus, the same disciplines were not followed in its transmission from one generation to another. However, God simply chose a different means to produce a similarly overwhelming result so that we might be confident that the New Testament has been accurately transmitted from the first century until now. In the case of the New Testament, God did a new thing to ensure that the blessing of his Word would be preserved for us and our children.

Historians evaluate the textual reliability of ancient literature according to two standards: (1) what the time interval is between the original and the earliest copy; and (2) how many manuscripts are available.

So, for example, virtually everything we know today about Julius Caesar's exploits in the Gallic Wars is derived from ten manuscript copies, the earliest of which dates to within 1,000 years of the time *The Gallic Wars* was written. Our modern text of Livy's *History of Rome* relies on one partial manuscript and nineteen much later copies that are dated from 400 to 1,000 years *after* the original writing. (See chart of "Textual Reliability Standards Applied to Classical Literature.")[4]

		DATE WRITTEN	EARLIEST COPIES	TIME GAP	NO. OF COPIES
AUTHOR	**BOOK**				
Homer	*Iliad*	800 B.C.	c. 400 B.C.	c. 400 yrs.	643
Herodotus	*History*	480–425 B.C.	C. A.D. 900	c. 1,350 yrs.	8
Thucydides	*History*	460–400 B.C.	C. A.D. 900	c. 1,300 yrs.	8
Plato		400 B.C.	C. A.D. 900	c. 1,300 yrs.	7
Demosthenes		300 B.C.	C. A.D. 1100	c. 1,400 yrs.	200
Caesar	*Gallic Wars*	100–44 B.C.	C. A.D. 900	c. 1,000 yrs.	10
Livy	*History of Rome*	59 B.C.– A.D. 17	4TH CENT. (PARTIAL) MOSTLY 10TH CENT.	C. 400 YRS. C. 1000 YRS.	1 PARTIAL 19 COPIES
Tacitus	*Annals*	A.D. 100	C. A.D. 1100	C. 1,000 YRS.	20
Pliny Secundus	*Natural History*	A.D. 61–113	C. A.D. 850	C. 750 YRS.	7

TEXTUAL RELIABILITY STANDARDS APPLIED TO CLASSICAL LITERATURE

By comparison, the text of Homer's *Iliad* is much more reliable. It is supported by 643 manuscript copies in existence today, with a mere 400-year time gap between the date of composition and the earliest copies we have available for examination today.

But the textual evidence for Livy and Homer pale in comparison to what God performed in the case of the New Testament text.

THE NEW TESTAMENT HAS NO EQUAL

Using the accepted standard for evaluating the textual reliability of ancient texts, the New Testament stands alone. It has no equal. No other book of the ancient world can even approach the reliability of the New Testament. (See chart of "Textual Reliability Standards Applied to the Bible.")[5]

Nearly *25,000* manuscripts of the New Testament repose in the libraries and universities of the world. The earliest of these is a fragment of John's Gospel currently located in the John Rylands Library of Manchester, England; it has been dated to within *50 years* of the date when the apostle John penned the original![6] (More extensive details of when many of these manuscripts were written can be found in *The New Evidence That Demands a Verdict,* explained in appendix D.)

TEXTUAL RELIABILITY STANDARDS APPLIED TO THE BIBLE

AUTHOR	BOOK	DATE WRITTEN	EARLIEST COPIES	TIME GAP	NO. OF COPIES
John	New Testament	A.D. 50–100	C. A.D. 130	+50 YRS.	Fragments
The rest of the New Testament authors			C. A.D. 200 (BOOKS)	100 YRS.	
			C. A.D. 250 (MOST OF N.T.)	150 YRS.	
			C. A.D. 325 (COMPLETE N.T.)	225 YRS.	+5,600 Greek mss.
			C. A.D. 366–384 (LATIN VULGATE TRANS.)	284 YRS.	
			C. A.D. 400–500 (OTHER trans.)	400 YRS.	+19,000 TRANS. MSS.
			TOTALS	50–400 YRS.	+24,900 MSS.

Since the time the original manuscripts were written—more than eighteen hundred years—skeptics have tried to refute the Bible, infidels have tried to stamp it out, and dictators have tried to burn it. However, God's Word has not only prevailed but also proliferated. Voltaire, the noted eighteenth-century French skeptic, predicted that within a hundred years of his time Christianity would be but a footnote in history. Ironically, in 1828, fifty years after Voltaire's death, the Geneva Bible Society moved into his house and used his printing press to produce thousands of Bibles to distribute worldwide. "People are like grass that dies away, . . ." Peter stated, quoting Isaiah the prophet, "but the word of the Lord will last forever" (1 Peter 1:24-25).

No other book in history has been so widely distributed in so many languages. Distribution of the Bible reaches into the billions! According to the United Bible Society's 1998 *Scripture Distribution Report*, in that year alone, member organizations had distributed 20.8 million complete Bibles and another 20.1 million New Testaments.[7] They also report that the Bible or portions of the Bible have been translated into more than 2,200 languages. And, amazingly, these languages represent the primary vehicle of communication for well over 90 percent of the world's population![8]

The evidence for the reliability of the Old and New Testaments is not only convincing and compelling but also a clear and praiseworthy indication of how God lovingly supervised its accurate transmission so that he might preserve for us—and our children—all the blessings that come from knowing him and obeying his Word.

God's Word Has Been Reinforced Externally

God did not stop working when he compiled the massive textual evidence for the reliability of his Word; he has since worked to reinforce the evidence through external means.

A routine criterion in examining the reliability of an historical document is whether *other* historical material confirms or denies the internal testimony of the document itself. Historians ask, "What sources, apart from the literature under examination, substantiate its accuracy and reliability?"

In the case of the Bible, this external evidence adds a coda to the masterpiece God has composed in creating, conveying, and confirming the Scriptures that reveal him to us.

In all of history, the Bible is by far the most widely referenced and quoted book. For example, the New Testament alone is so extensively quoted in the ancient manuscripts of nonbiblical authors that all twenty-seven books from Matthew through Revelation could be reconstructed virtually word for word from those sources.

The writings of early Christians like Eusebius (A.D. 339) in his *Ecclesiastical History 111.39* and Irenaeus (A.D. 180) in his *Against Heresies 111* reinforce the text of the apostle John's writings. Clement of Rome (A.D. 95), Ignatius (A.D. 70–110), Polycarp (A.D. 70–156), and Titian (A.D. 170) offer external confirmation of other New Testament accounts. Non-Christian historians such as the first-century Roman historian Tacitus (A.D. 55–117) and the Jewish historian Josephus (A.D. 37–100) confirm the substance of some scriptural accounts. These and other outside sources substantiate the accuracy of the biblical record like that of no other book in history.[9] (For more information on the confirmation of the Bible's reliability in extrabiblical sources, see chapters 3 and 4 of *The New Evidence That Demands a Verdict.*)

However, ancient literature's extrabiblical references are not the only external evidences that support the Bible's reliability. The very stones cry out that God's Word is true. Over and over again through the centuries, the reliability of the Bible has been regularly and consistently supported by archaeology. Consider the following proofs:

- At one time "scholars" argued that Moses couldn't have written the Pentateuch because writing didn't exist in his lifetime. Then the "black stele" was discovered, containing writing that predated Moses by at least three centuries.
- Some radical scholars once suggested that David, the shepherd-king of Israel, was a mythical figure . . . until a 1993 ex-

cavation unearthed a ninth-century-B.C. tablet referring to the "house of David."

- Daniel's mention of the last Babylonian king, Belshazzar (Daniel 5), was once thought to be an embarrassing mistake (since a clay tablet named Nabonidus, not Belshazzar, as the last king of Babylon). However, later discoveries confirmed that Belshazzar, the son of Nabonidus, ruled as coregent with his father.

- Until 1961 there existed no archaeological evidence for Pontius Pilate. That year two Italian archaeologists uncovered a Latin inscription referring to the Roman governor.

- An inscription dated between A.D. 14 and 29 was found near Damascus, confirming the existence of a first-century "Lysanias the tetrarch" (Luke 3:1, KJV), which some had formerly thought to be an inaccuracy on Luke's part since the only Lysanias previously known had been killed in 36 B.C.[10]

Repeatedly throughout history, the astounding accuracy of God's Word has been confirmed externally, giving us and our children every reason to revere it, trust it, obey it, and thus to enjoy the blessings of its protection and provision.

GOD'S ETERNAL THEME AND ENDLESS QUEST

This God-inspired book called the Bible was written during a 1,500-year span through more than forty generations by more than forty different authors from every walk of life. Its God-breathed words were written in a variety of places: in the wilderness, in a palace, in a dungeon, on a hillside, in a prison, and in exile. It was penned on the continents of Asia, Africa, and Europe and was written in three languages: Hebrew, Aramaic, and Greek. It tells hundreds of stories and songs, and addresses hundreds of controversial subjects. Yet through it all it achieves a miraculous continuity of theme.

From Genesis through Revelation, one recurring master theme wends through its pages. From God's loving laws and commands to the sacrifice of lambs and goats, one purpose stands out. From a sinless babe in a manger to a holy sacrifice on Calvary, a single plan is clear. From Christ's humiliation before Pilate to the universal acknowledgment of the King of kings and Lord of lords, every verse of Scripture shouts God's passion for his relationship with the human race, crying out with one voice his relational theme: *redemption.* God has gone to extraordinary lengths to reclaim the intimate relationship with men and women he first created and enjoyed in the Garden of Eden. And the Bible is the means he has chosen to reach out in human language, reveal the essence of his relational heart, and relate the Good News of his redemptive plan.

It is overwhelming to realize that the God of the universe has superintended the writing and passing down of his words from generation to generation so that you and I can have an accurate revelation of him. It is truly amazing to hold in your hand a book you can confidently believe is an accurate transmission of God-breathed (inspired) words. And it is thrilling to know that God gives us his Word so that by following his ways we can count on his protection and provision.

The Bible is the means God has chosen to reach out in human language, reveal the essence of his relational heart, and relate the Good News of his redemptive plan.

But still more astounding is the fact that the Word of God also reveals our true purpose in life. All of us, and our kids as well, long to know our purpose for living. Whether consciously or subconsciously, we want the answer to the question, "Why am I here?" And God's Word provides that answer. And in the next chapter, we are going to discover how our young people's convictions about Christ and God's Word can lead them to live the joyous and blessed—and purpose-filled—life they were meant to live.

CHAPTER 9

The Meaning of God's Word to Our Lives

"I'm really sorry, Megan," Duane began. He and Liz sat in their family room with Megan, Lauren, and Allen. "I wasn't prepared at all for what happened in youth group last week. I know you were at school, Lauren, but—"

"Megan told me," Lauren said.

Megan shrugged and smiled. "It's not a big deal," she said.

"Maybe not," Duane answered, "but I was caught off guard, and I didn't respond to Karen's and Allen's questions the way I should have. I feel like I let the group down. But we've got some answers now. And a big part of it has been due to Allen's hard work." Duane glanced over and winked at Allen.

"Well, it's really helped me to do all this research," Allen said. "And it's helped me to get my mind off other things."

Liz suddenly turned to Lauren, her eyes wide. "Oh, Lauren," she whispered, her voice heavy with sadness. "It just dawned on me that you may not have heard."

"Heard what?" Lauren whispered back, although everyone was politely listening to the exchange.

"Allen's eight-year-old sister passed away last week from

Fanconi anemia, a rare disease that shuts down the internal organs."

Lauren's gaze went immediately to Allen, who studied the floor at his feet. "Angie? Angie died?" she gasped. "Oh, I'm so sorry, Allen. I didn't know." A solemn silence interrupted the conversation, as if someone had asked for a moment of silence. "I hope all this research stuff didn't . . . didn't interfere with . . ."

"No," Allen answered quickly, "I think it's been a good thing, as I said. It's given me something else to think about. It's been hard, you know, but it was good to get lost in the research. And I really do think this research has got some real answers for us."

Lauren's eyes brightened. "I'm glad to hear that. I mean, I've heard some things at school that have raised some serious questions, you know? And I've tried to talk them over with Megan, so she's as confused as I am now." She scooted forward in her seat, leaned her elbows on her knees, and looked at Duane and Liz. "And I'm afraid . . . I don't know," she said, her voice trailing off.

"What?" Liz said, her voice soft and encouraging. "What are you afraid of?"

Lauren pursed her lips. "I don't know," she said. "It's just that . . . well, something happened to me that night the youth group met here. I . . . I really saw the way I'd been living, how selfish I'd been, and how wrong it was. And when I prayed, I really sensed God forgave me. Something happened to me. I mean, I really felt different inside."

"You *are* different," Megan added.

"I just don't want to ruin everything," Lauren said.

"What makes you think you'll ruin it?" Duane asked.

She shrugged. "I just want it to stay real. I really want to hold onto what I've been feeling inside."

Duane nodded. "That's pretty much why I wanted to talk about the Bible in youth group." He smiled weakly. "I just didn't start off as strong as I wanted to."

"But," Liz interjected, "we think with your help—all three of you—we can make up for that. And Allen's going to get us started off right." She smiled, leaned forward, and slapped Allen on the knee. "He's been doing all this in-depth research that will answer all our questions. Right, Allen?"

He smiled back and shrugged. "Well, I don't know about *all* the questions." He patted a stack of books and papers he had brought in with him. "But there should be enough here to convince just about anybody that the Bible is the most reliable document ever written."

"What have you got?" Duane asked. He pulled his chair beside Allen's to look at the research he had gathered. Lauren, Megan, and Liz also leaned forward as Allen started to lift pages from the stack and pass them around as he explained what he had discovered.

More than an hour later, Lauren leaned back in her chair. "Wow," she said. "I had no idea."

"You've done some *excellent* work, Allen," Duane said.

Allen leaned back, smiling, clearly pleased.

"Yeah," Lauren said. "It's pretty . . . amazing."

Liz looked at Lauren. "What's wrong, Lauren?" she asked. "You sound like something's still bothering you."

Lauren cocked her head. "I don't know," she said slowly. "I mean, I can see that the Bible's really reliable." She paused. "But there's something about all this that doesn't feel right."

"What do you mean by 'doesn't feel right'?" Liz asked.

"We-e-ll," Lauren said, drawing the word out slowly. "I mean, I can see that the Bible's really reliable." She paused. "But it almost sounds like you're saying that the Bible is true . . . for everyone."

"Yeah," Duane said, "we are saying that."

Lauren blinked a few times. "Oh," she said softly.

"You sound disappointed," Liz suggested.

"Well, yeah," Lauren replied. "It just sounds so . . . exclusive. Because if it's true for everyone, then you're pretty much saying that

Jesus is the only way for the whole world . . . and, for some reason, that just doesn't feel right."

AN EXCLUSIVE BOOK PROCLAIMING AN EXCLUSIVE TRUTH

Lauren is like the majority of our young people. Many of them have been conditioned to believe that their beliefs are very personal and subjective. Remember that while most of our kids (61 percent) believe the Bible provides "a clear and totally accurate description of moral truth," they don't believe that means the Bible is authoritatively true for everyone.[1] The vast majority—81 percent of our youth—claims that "all truth is relative to the individual and his/her circumstance."[2]

Therefore, having been taught that it's up to them to *create* their own truth, to decide whatever is true *for them*, they're uncomfortable with any suggestion that a particular viewpoint is true for everyone. So when the Bible is shown to be a historically accurate and objectively trustworthy source (especially when its evidences support the conclusion that Jesus Christ is the Son of the one true God), it "feels" too exclusive to them.

With such a mind-set, most of our kids view the Bible—if they read it at all—*not* as a universally true revelation of the one true God but as a mere resource, a set of inspirational stories and helpful insights that might offer guidance in creating their own "truth."

That helps to explain why many good Christian kids adhere to some biblical standards but violate others. I've talked to thousands of Christian kids who can say that adultery is wrong but premarital sex is okay. I've heard kids insist that lying to a friend is wrong but cheating on a test—especially if they had a good reason for not studying—is all right. Many of them honestly think that when they choose to believe something, *it becomes true for them* simply because they believe it. Thus, they go to the Bible *not to discover the truth* but to use it as sort of a self-help book to help them concoct their own version of what's true and false, good and evil, right and wrong.

But when young people encounter the historical accuracy of the Bible, they inevitably come face-to-face with the claims of Christ. That is when our young people, like Lauren, are faced with an inescapable conclusion: Scripture accurately reveals Jesus Christ as the only way to the one true God. And that, of course, flies in the face of their cultural conditioning, which makes it difficult for them to embrace the implications of the Bible's reliability. That was the case for me as a university student.

When I set out to refute Christianity, I sought to disprove the Bible's historical reliability. I knew that Christ, with his claims to be God, was the linchpin of Christianity. So I reasoned that if the historical document containing the evidence of Christ's virgin birth, his miracles, and the messianic prophecies could be exposed as inaccurate, then that foundation would surely crumble. If I could show that the Bible was historically unreliable, I could invalidate the claims of Christ.

I failed in that quest, of course, because the evidences convinced me that the Bible is historically reliable—unquestionably so. And that is when I came face-to-face with the awesome truth that God really wanted a relationship with me through Christ, his Son.

The Bible isn't a mere resource, a set of inspirational stories and helpful guidelines from which we can form "our own truth," as so many of our kids believe.

The Bible isn't a mere resource, a set of inspirational stories and helpful guidelines from which we can form "our own truth," as so many of our kids believe. It is the means by which the one true God has chosen to reveal details of himself to you and me. When you hold a Bible in your hand, you are cradling a holy book to be reverenced and hungered after because its very words reveal the God who gives your life its true purpose.

WHY AM I HERE?

Picture the Hebrew scribe—one of the Sopherim, the ancients who copied and preserved the sacred writings of the Jews—as he enters his small workroom. Since the fall of Jerusalem and the destruction of the temple by the Babylonians in 586 B.C., the Book of the Law was all the Jews had left, their only connection with the God of Abraham, Isaac, and Jacob. The Torah scrolls the scribe kept in clay jars in his workroom contained the very words God gave to Moses and the prophets, and told of God's passion for relationship with them (see Exodus 34:14). Those words written on animal skins revealed the universal dilemma shared by the whole human race, the sin that separated them from God, and his merciful intention to solve that dilemma. Those stylus marks detailed God's special relationship with his chosen people and told of his promise to lead them back to him—a promise that included restoring them again as a nation in relationship with him as their king and loving Lord, where all things would one day be as they were in the pristine Garden of Eden.

Therefore, this scribe—like *all* the Sopherim—treated those words, those books, with the utmost care and attention. He washed ceremonially, meticulously, before picking up a stylus. He copied every word, every letter, with painstaking care. And, lest anyone misunderstand what God had said through his misreading or miscopying of a fading, crumbling, or stained scroll, he carefully buried those that were old or marred. He did all these things (and more) because he believed an awesome, universal truth, one that had been proclaimed by God to Hosea. "I don't want your sacrifices," he says. *"I want you to know God"* (Hosea 6:6, emphasis mine).

Yahweh, the almighty God of the universe, has revealed himself in human language so that we will come to know him intimately— so intimately, in fact, that we become like him. And that awesome, universal truth answers our pressing question "Why are we here?" Our purpose in life—your purpose and your children's purpose—is to know God and become more and more like him (see Romans 8:29; 2 Corinthians 3:18; Ephesians 1:4-5; 2 Peter 1:3).

"God knew his people in advance," Paul declared, "and he chose them to become like his Son" (Romans 8:29). Even though sin broke our relationship with God and tarnished the image of God in us beyond recognition, because of Christ—and our adoption into his

Our purpose in life is to know God and become more and more like him.

family (see Ephesians 1:4-5)—our Godlikeness can be restored, as "we, who with unveiled faces all reflect the Lord's glory, are being transformed into his likeness with ever-increasing glory, which comes from the Lord, who is the Spirit" (2 Corinthians 3:18, NIV).

When we become more and more like God, we glorify him because we reflect positively on him—on his character and nature. We also gratify him because seeing us reflect his nature gives him great pleasure. The apostle Paul said, "Long ago, even before he made the world, God loved us and chose us in Christ to be holy and without fault in his eyes. His unchanging plan has always been to adopt us into his own family by bringing us to himself through Jesus Christ. And this gave him great pleasure" (Ephesians 1:4-5).

Just as a human father swells with pride when his child follows in his footsteps and just as a human mother takes pleasure in her youngster living out the values she's instilled, so our heavenly Father exults to see us become more and more like him.

THE WRITTEN REVELATION

God's taking on human form through the Incarnation reveals God's relational heart, which says to each of us, "I want a relationship with you. And in that relationship I want you to know me and be like me." Yet it is the written revelation of himself in his Word that gives us a description of his image. God's written Word is the picture-perfect lens of his image. It is as if God is saying to you and me and our children, "I have preserved for you my written Word, as a perfect lens to see me for who I am. Read its pages to know me, so you can reflect what you see of me. Become intimate with me and through our close relationship together you will enjoy the true meaning in living, for you will bear the fruit of my nature—love, joy, peace, patience, kindness, goodness, faithfulness, gentleness and self-control" (see Galatians 5:22-23).

God's heart says, "I want a relationship with you. And in that relationship I want you to know me and be like me."

When you and I and our children begin to fulfill our purpose (of knowing God and becoming more and more like him), we begin to live out the truly meaningful life that God originally designed for us. God created us in his likeness and image so that we could relate to him and enjoy all the blessings that come from being godly. As we said before, acting according to God's ways brings blessing because all that is defined as perfectly right and good is derived from his nature (see James 1:17).

We were created to live happy, fulfilled lives. We were made to know the gratifying joy of being accepted, approved of, and appreciated, with the ability to freely love and be loved. We were designed to experience a fulfillment and satisfaction beyond measure, a contentment and peace beyond understanding, and an abundant life beyond belief. And that kind of meaningful life comes only from living in fellowship with God and conforming to his likeness. Sin all but destroyed God's design, but because of Christ we can now be adopted into God's family and begin the transformation process, allowing the divine nature of God to permeate our lives. And without God's Word, we would be without the handbook on living an abundant life, we would be without direc-

God's Word is the perfect lens to see— and then reflect—the divine nature of God.

tion, and most important, we would be without an accurate revelation of God, unable to know him for who he is. That is the significance of the Bible to each one of us and to our everyday lives. God's Word is the perfect lens to see—and then reflect—the divine nature of God.

EMPOWERED BY THE SPIRIT AND THE WORD

God has revealed himself to us in written form. But he has done more: He has also given us his Spirit to explain those words to us. Paul says, "No one can know God's thoughts except God's own Spirit. . . . We speak words given to us by the Spirit, using the Spirit's words to explain spiritual truths. . . . We who have the Spirit understand these things" (1 Corinthians 2:11-15). Jesus said he abides in us; "He is the Holy Spirit, who leads into all truth. . . . He will teach [us] everything and will remind [us] of everything I myself have told you" (John 14:17, 26). But if we don't hide the words of God away in our hearts, how can his Spirit remind us of what Christ said? If we don't learn what God is like through his picture-perfect Word, then how can we cooperate with the Spirit as he replicates that image in our lives?

Imagine this scene. You are seated alone in your living room. A large family Bible is open on the coffee table. Suddenly a radiant light appears; when it subsides, Christ is seated in front of you. Immediately, you drop to your knees and press your face to the floor. His holiness seems to permeate the room and expose your humanity, your sinfulness in such stark relief that you cry out, "Lord, have mercy on me, a sinner!"

In the next moment, you feel a warm hand cup your chin, and he gently lifts your head to meet his tender gaze.

"Beloved," he says, "truly, you were born in sin. You are lost and alienated from me. You had no life, only a lonely, empty existence. Disconnected from my Father—and yours—you didn't know who you were. You felt as if you didn't belong. You were inwardly afraid you would never know who you were or why you were here.

"Then you learned of me, and you believed in me. And now, because of me, you are God's child. You belong to me, and I belong to you. You are no longer a child of this world; you are the child of the King."

You gain the courage to smile and look deep into his eyes, for you sense he really means it; you belong to him.

He continues. "But when I say you are a child of the King, I don't speak figuratively. You really are one with my Father, and with me. You are being transformed more and more into the likeness of God. By my Spirit, who lives in you, I am becoming more and more at home in your heart. And you are beginning to live as you were meant to live—a godly, Christlike life. You are beginning to experience the abundant, fulfilled life of happiness and meaning. And that pleases your Father and brings joy to my heart."

Tears trickle down your face and drop onto the open Bible on the coffee table. "Please, Lord," you say, your voice trembling. "I do want that. I want to be more and more like you. I want to please you. Won't you stay with me and teach me to be like you? I want to see and hear you every day. I want to have you with me. If you're with me each day, I can see your example, and maybe then I can be like you."

He smiles and extends a nail-scarred hand to your face, brushing the tears from your cheek. "I have been with you. All along." He points to your chest. "I have given you my Spirit, who lives within you. But I have given you my Word, too. And I have been waiting to be seen and heard here." He points to the open Bible.

A shadow seems to cross his face, and a single tear escapes his eye and rolls down his cheek.

"Lord, please don't cry," you say.

He looks at you through tear-rimmed eyes. "I know you and love you so very much, just for who you are. I know every thought and motive, every desire of your heart. I even took on human flesh and tasted firsthand all the joys and pains of the life you lead. But . . ." He stops.

"Go on. Please go on."

"I want *you* to know *me*. I never intended for our relationship to be one-sided. I long for you to know me for who I really am—to experience my love, my patience, my joy—all that I am. I want to become more and more at home in your life until you and I are so intimate and you become so much like me that my life is inseparable from yours. That's what I meant when I said this." He points to a spot on the page of the open Bible. You pull it closer to you and read. "These things I have spoken to you, that My joy may be in you, and that your joy may be made full" (John 15:11, NASB).

A flash of brilliant light blinds you momentarily as you realize what you've been missing, what you've neglected, and what you must do now.

• • • • •

Though you may not see Jesus in the room with you, he is there nonetheless. And he wants *you* to know *him* intimately, so intimately that his patience will replace your impatience, his peace will replace your anxiety, his love will replace your self-centeredness—his life will become your life. He longs to become "more and more at home in your [heart] as you trust in him" (Ephesians 3:17). But in order for that to happen, you must first know him through the picture-perfect lens of his Word and then allow him to live his life in and through you. "He died for everyone so that those who receive his new life will no longer live to please themselves. Instead, they will live to please Christ" (2 Corinthians 5:15).

God doesn't want you to go to his Word to simply learn the

rules of the Christian life. He doesn't want you to read the Bible only to gain inspiration to live better. He wants you to see his Word as an open door to his heart, a way to know him for who he is. And his invitation to know him brings with it the power for him to live his life through you. "As we know Jesus better," the Bible says, "his divine power gives us everything we need for living a godly life. He has called us to receive his own glory and goodness! And by that same mighty power, he has given us all of his rich and wonderful promises. He has promised that you will escape the decadence all around you caused by evil desires and that you will share in his divine nature" (2 Peter 1:3-4).

God wants you to see his Word as an open door to his heart, a way to know him for who he is.

That is what we want for our young people, isn't it? And all that is possible as you and I—and our young people—come to know Christ better by making the reliable Word a centerpiece of our lives. Not by using the Scripture as a "suggestion manual" or self-help book to create our own brand of truth. Not even by trying to obey a set of rules or trying to live a good life. Intimacy with God and living like Christ happens supernaturally as we gain a clear, true vision of God and his ways, make his Son at home in our hearts, and thus receive "his divine power [that] gives us everything we need for living a godly life" (2 Peter 1:3-4).

That's what our kids need. That's what God wants to give them.

LIVING WHAT WE BELIEVE

"So, let me see if I've got this right," Lauren said when Duane and Liz had finished explaining things to her. "The Bible is reliable and . . . so we can be sure that Christ is God. . . ."

"Go on," Duane urged.

"But that isn't being narrow-minded because, uh . . . because . . ." She looked to Duane and Liz for help.

"Because," Duane said, "the Bible wasn't given to exclude anyone but to lead as many people as possible to the knowledge of God."

"And," Liz added, "only the God who made us in his image could transform us back into his image. Other religions or our own efforts to do good couldn't. Only the God who made us in his likeness could."

"And," Duane added quickly, as Lauren glanced from Liz to Duane like a spectator at a tennis match, "being transformed more and more into Christlikeness is accomplished through the power of the Holy Spirit as we—"

"Wait," Lauren interrupted. "I know this. It happens through the power of the Holy Spirit, as . . . as we come to know Jesus and his ways better and make him more at home in our lives, right? And the way we know Jesus better is through the Bible, which we know is reliable."

"You've got it!" Duane said, smiling broadly and holding his hand in the air for Lauren to give him a high five.

Just then Megan, who, like Allen, had been listening intently, spoke. "May I ask a question?" she said.

They all turned their attention to Megan.

"Well," she said, "maybe Lauren's getting it right, but I feel like I'm still confused."

"About what?" Duane asked.

"Well," Megan began, "it's not so much what you've just been talking about, but some of the things you said earlier. I mean, I can see that God wants all of us to be more like him. But—"

"What?" Liz asked. "What's wrong?"

"I don't know . . . it's just that . . . to be honest, I'm not very much like Christ sometimes. In fact, most of the time, I feel like I'm nothing like him."

"Well," Duane responded, "none of us is angelic yet. But we can become more and more like Christ. Here, look at what the apostle Paul said." He handed Megan his Bible. "Read Philippians 3, verse 12 to us."

Megan turned to the passage. "I don't mean to say that I have already achieved these things," she read, "or that I have already reached perfection! But I keep working toward that day when I will finally be all that Christ Jesus saved me for and wants me to be."

"You see," Duane said, "as the Holy Spirit shows us in his Word what Jesus is like, he leads us into a deeper love relationship with him and a process of being made more and more like him. We 'are being transformed into his likeness with ever-increasing glory,' as Paul says in Second Corinthians. In fact, before Paul told the Philippians that he wasn't angelic yet, he began his letter to them by saying—" Duane reached for the Bible that Megan held and turned to Philippians 1:6—"'I am sure that God, who began the good work within you, will continue his work until it is finally finished on that day when Christ Jesus comes back again.'" Duane looked up at Megan and then turned his gaze to take in everyone in the room. "It's a process," Duane said, "a process that God will keep doing in you until Christ returns."

"But what if the process isn't working very well?" Megan said, to no one in particular.

"Things been a little tough lately?" Liz asked.

Megan nodded. "More than a little," she said. "I've . . . I've been really blowing it, like a lot. And I know God's disappointed with me."

"Well," Duane stepped in. "One of the first steps in this process is to get to know God's Word so you will fall in love with the God of the Word. Knowing his Word can help us keep from blowing it. Here let me read to you what David said in Psalm 119." Liz turned the pages of her Bible and shared it with Lauren and Megan. Allen looked over Duane's shoulder as Duane read verses 4 through 11.

You have charged us
>to keep your commandments
>carefully.
Oh, that my actions would consistently
>reflect your principles!
Then I will not be disgraced
>when I compare my life with your
>commands.
When I learn your righteous laws,
>I will thank you by living as I
>should!
I will obey your principles.
>Please don't give up on me!
How can a young person stay pure?
>By obeying your word and
>following its rules.
I have tried my best to find you—
>don't let me wander from your
>commands.
I have hidden your word in my heart,
>that I might not sin against you.

"I can't believe what you just read," Megan said softly. Her eyes remained fixed on the pages of the Bible. Choking back emotion, she whispered, as if no one else was listening to her but God. "I wish I could say I have obeyed your Word and followed your rules, but I haven't. Not at all." She looked at Liz's Bible as she continued praying. "I feel like I *have* been disgraced, and I . . . I know I haven't tried my best to find you. But please don't give up on me. Don't let me wander from you anymore." Megan paused. Liz gently rubbed Megan's back in a circular motion. "I'm so sorry I've hurt you. I'm sorry I have sinned against you. Please forgive me. And let me get to know you as I read your Word. And right now I'm going to start to hide your Word in my heart that I might not sin against you. I want you to live your life in me."

For the next few moments, the rest of the group prayed silently as Liz helped Megan complete her confession to God. When they finished, Megan cleared her throat and spoke, tentatively at first, but gradually gaining confidence and volume. "I guess I can see now how God has been using these past few weeks to bring me to this point. Lauren, seeing the change in your life did something to me. I've been a Christian for a while, but I've pretty much taken the Bible as a suggestion book, you know? I guess I've always thought I had to determine what was best for me . . . like, I even knew what that was. I thought God would sorta help me make good choices, but I guess I thought it was all pretty much my call. But I'm starting to realize that it's not about me anymore. It's about him and his Word. It's about knowing him and making him at home in my life."

Megan tapped on the open Bible sitting in Liz's lap. "Something's happened tonight to make me really hungry to know God more. When you read that one verse, Duane, about knowing Jesus better, I said to myself, *That's it. I want to know him better.* That's what I've been missing, and I know I need to do that through his Word. I need to know the Bible better so I can know what he's like, right?"

"Right," Duane answered enthusiastically. "That is what being convinced about the reliability and accuracy of this book can do. You can know it's a true picture of what he's like *and* what he wants to transform you into."

"And as you do, as you go to the Bible with a heart to know God better, God will do the rest. He'll draw you closer into a relationship with Christ and transform you more and more into Christ's image." Liz added, "Especially if you quit *trying* to live the Christian life."

"What?" Allen asked. They all flashed surprised looks at Liz.

"Well," Liz answered, "you've all been influenced to believe what's right for you and then try to make that work in your life. But that's not the way God works."

"Instead of *trying* to live the Christian life," Duane interjected, "and believing in your own efforts, you need to get to know God, to have such a close relationship with him that his life is lived through your life."

Megan stared blankly at Duane. "I gotta agree with Allen. I don't know what you mean."

"Maybe I can help out with an example," Duane said, glancing around the room for a moment. "Let's say you believed in this coffee table to get you to school every morning. I mean, you believed it so much that you sat on it every morning to see if it would take you there. Would the coffee table get you to school?"

Megan rolled her eyes. "Of course not," she said.

Duane reached in his pocket. "But what if I gave you these?" He pulled out a set of keys and dangled them in front of her. "These are the keys to my Honda 750. Let's say you believed in my cycle to get you to school. Would that be different?"

"Yeah," Megan said. "I'll show you." She snatched the keys from Duane's hand.

"Okay," Duane said, smiling. "So what's the difference? Why would your belief in the cycle get you to school but your belief in the coffee table wouldn't?"

"For one thing," Megan said with a teasing tone, "I could never start a coffee table, but I could your 750."

"Exactly," Duane said. "That's my point. The coffee table doesn't have what it takes. There is no power in it to take anyone anywhere. But my cycle is different. When you put yourself in the seat of that Honda, it'll get you where you want to go."

"That makes sense," Allen said. "I think I see what you're saying. It's like, it doesn't matter how sincere our personal beliefs are or how hard we believe them. They won't do us much good if we're not believing in something that can come through for us."

Liz nodded. "That's why it's so important that we put our trust in Christ's ability to live in us because that's where the power is."

"And being convinced of the Bible's reliability is important," Lauren said, "because that's our key source for knowing about Christ and his work in our lives."

"Wow," Megan said. "I see now that I've been really missing it. Maybe that's why I've had so many problems. I've been depending on myself instead of relying on God."

Duane smiled broadly. "I think you're right. And the Bible—the reliable Word of God—is the perfect lens to see God for who he is: a God who wants us to know him and trust in him so we can be like him."

DO WE SEE HIM AS HE IS?

We can be confident that when we read the Bible, we are getting a reliable revelation of God. It is a perfect lens that allows us to see God for who he is and his ways for what they are. But does that mean if our young people go to the Bible to know Jesus better, we can be confident they will come away with a correct understanding of God and how to follow his ways? If the Holy Spirit is there to guide them into all truth, they can't go wrong—right?

Well, not exactly. A note of caution is in order.

Paul warned the church at Corinth of false teachers who "have fooled you by disguising themselves as apostles of Christ. But I am not surprised! Even Satan can disguise himself as an angel of light" (2 Corinthians 11:13-14). The enemy will do everything possible to keep the truth about Christ from being clearly seen. Just because he failed to thwart the accurate transmission of God's Word doesn't mean he's stopped trying.

Our adversary, the devil, may not be able to destroy the Word of God, but he still works to twist and abuse Scripture as he did when he tempted Christ in the wilderness (see Isaiah 40:8; Matthew 4:1-11; 5:18). He cannot change the words already written down in Scripture, but he still tries hard to cloud our minds and hearts, and cause us to ignore, misunderstand, or misinterpret God's Word. He cannot change the reliability of the Bible, but if he can prompt its disuse or misuse, he can still achieve many of his deceptive ends.

That is why it is crucial for us—and our young people—to heed the challenge of Paul to "be diligent [in] . . . handling accurately the word of truth" (2 Timothy 2:15, NASB). Our Christian young people, as hungry for the Word and well intentioned as they might be, can misinterpret what the Bible says and means. Though their hearts may be in the right place, they can nonetheless cause themselves—and others—great harm unless they learn and follow some fundamental guidelines to biblical interpretation.

I know this firsthand because I have fallen victim to it myself. I failed to properly understand several key, liberating teachings of Scripture. The result was a continued personal struggle that caused behavior unpleasing to God, disruption to my family, and diminished effectiveness in my ministry to others.

The "word of God is full of living power," the writer to the Hebrews said. "It is sharper than the sharpest knife, cutting deep into our innermost thoughts and desires. It exposes us for what we really are" (Hebrews 4:12). Something that powerful deserves special care to ensure that our young people are prepared to handle it correctly.

CHAPTER 10

Interpreting the Words of God

In my second year of college, my primary interest in the Bible was to disprove it. As I said before, I considered Christianity to be an intellectual joke, and I intended to discredit it. My plan was to prove that the document proclaiming Jesus Christ as the Incarnate God and Savior of the world was an unreliable source, thus demonstrating that Christianity was nothing but a fable. Of course, the joke was on me because the incredible reliability of Scripture brought me face-to-face with Jesus, the true Son of God.

But that experience did not complete my journey of discovering the reliability and applicability of the Bible. Even after I began a ministry of sharing the reliability of Scripture with others, I still had much to learn. I was committed to biblical truth. I had a growing ministry to youth. Yet I was not "handling accurately the word of truth" in one particular part of my life.[1]

In this area, I was like many of our young people today, who assume they know what the Bible says and even try to apply what it says to their lives but suffer immeasurably because they're dealing with mistaken or misguided ideas of what a Bible passage means. Similarly, for years I was misinterpreting and misapplying a specific truth in Scripture, a mistake for which I paid dearly—and one that illustrates the importance of teaching our kids sound, solid principles for interpreting and applying what the Bible says.

Let me be specific. I knew that Scripture repeatedly and specifically commanded me to love others:

Just as I have loved you, you should love each other. (John 13:34)

I command you to love each other in the same way that I love you. (John 15:12)

Live a life filled with love for others, following the example of Christ, who loved you. (Ephesians 5:2)

And God himself has commanded that we must love not only him but our Christian brothers and sisters, too. (1 John 4:21)

So I did my best to apply those scriptural commands to my life and love others as Christ loved me. But even as I did so, I operated from a basic misunderstanding of what biblical Christlike love looks like, sounds like, and acts like. When I read about Christ's loving sinners and people who hurt, all I saw was a sacrificial love that gave people its all. I never realized that I was dealing with a definition of love that was colored more by my past than by God's eternal Word.

And my failure to recognize that flawed definition of love resulted in years of pain and frustration for me, my family, and my ministry. It was only by God's grace and the help of a few wise men that I learned the fundamental guidelines to biblical interpretation, guidelines that have since allowed me to see how I was misinterpreting Scripture. Only then was I able to apply Scripture to the big question in my life: How do I love others as Christ does?

Allow me to be transparent and share my personal journey as a sincere but frustrated young man who came to understand what truly loving others meant *only* when he understood how to accurately interpret the Word of God.

MY HATRED WAS CHANGED TO LOVE

When I was confronted with the claims of Christ, I placed my trust in Christ as my Savior. But, in contrast to Lauren's experience in our story, nothing seemed to happen . . . at least nothing dramatic. If anything, I felt worse—almost physically sick—after I prayed.

But something *had* happened, and changes began to take place in my life. One of the earliest and most significant changes involved my resentment and hatred toward my father.

I confessed my sins to God that night, including my attitudes and actions toward my father, and invited Christ to live his life in me. And a miraculous transformation occurred. When God graciously forgave me because of Christ's atoning death, his forgiving love became my forgiving love. The Holy Spirit took up residence and began to live out his love through me. Where there once had been bitterness and hatred toward my dad, there was now love. Within a very short time, I found myself apologizing to my father for resenting him so. I recall looking him in the eye and saying something I never would have thought possible: "Dad, I love you."

Then six months after I became a Christian, I was seriously injured in a car accident, the victim of a drunk driver. I was moved home from the hospital to recover, and my father came to see me (remarkably, he was sober that day). He seemed uneasy, pacing in my room. Then he suddenly stopped. "How can you love a father like me?" he blurted out.

"Dad," I said, "six months ago I hated you. I despised you. But I have put my trust in Jesus Christ, and he has changed my life. I can't explain how, Dad, but God has taken away my hatred for you and replaced it with his love."

We talked for nearly an hour, and then he said, "Son, if God can do in my life what I've seen him do in yours, then I want to give him the opportunity." Right then, my father prayed and trusted in Jesus Christ as his Savior and Lord. Hearing my dad pray from his heart and place his trust in Christ was one of the greatest joys of my life.

I HEARD GOD'S CALL TO MINISTRY

I transferred to a Christian college and went on to seminary. But I really wanted to be in law school. God had so far led my body and mind to seminary to prepare for ministry, but my heart was still set on being an attorney.

One day I left class in frustration and started walking. A block away from the seminary campus, I heard a bell ring. It was exactly 11:45 A.M.—lunchtime at the local junior high. The sound of the bell startled me, and I stopped. The doors of the school burst open, and young people came flooding out. I backed up against a telephone pole on the sidewalk as kids rushed past me in every direction. I felt momentarily paralyzed. It was as if time had stopped for me and I was watching a sea of young people move in slow motion. And in that moment, my mind went to the book of Isaiah, when God asked the prophet, "Whom shall I send? And who will go for us?" (6:8, NIV). In my mind, however, those words possessed a new context. It was as if God said to me: "These young people are in crisis; they are a hurting generation, and they need help. Whom shall I send, and who will go for us?"

Instantly, my struggle to have my own career in law ended. I saw the faces of a generation in need. I sensed God's call to reach them, and I felt an overwhelming love for them. I prayed, "God if you can use me in ministry to kids like these, then pour out your love for them through me."

COMPULSION NOT COMPASSION

As sincere as my prayer was, I knew very little about real love at that moment. I thought I did, of course, but I would soon learn that I really didn't know how to love a hurting generation with a Christ-like love. My understanding of love was derived only partly from Scripture; much of it, I came to discover, was based on my past and the pain I and others around me had experienced.

I thought love meant saying *yes* to people in pain by doing whatever I could to fix the problem, remove the obstacle, and stop the pain. That's what I had always longed to do for the hurting people in my life. That, it seemed to me, was what the Bible showed Jesus doing when he was on earth. And when I responded that way to people in pain, most saw me as a compassionate, loving person. Thus, on the surface, it looked as if I were following John 15:12 and Ephesians 5:2 and loving others as Christ had loved me. But I eventually came to discover that my love was not based on Christlike compassion but was driven by compulsion.

Because my ministry was largely focused on the many crises faced by today's youth, I found myself surrounded by hurting people, people who needed help of one kind or another. However, when I found myself personally confronted with someone who was hurting, I responded irrationally to that person's need. I felt that love compelled me to meet that need. It wasn't that I was simply touched by that particular person's plight and wanted to help; I felt an emotional urge to solve the problem and to do it quickly. It was as if I was driven to somehow eradicate that person's pain.

I couldn't seem to say no to hurting people. Someone would say, "I'm really hurting, and I need your help." Another would say, "Can I just have five minutes with you, Josh? I really need your help." Or, "You've got to speak to our group. We really need it." And I seemed powerless to say no.

But as you can imagine, this caused increasing frustration, not only for me but also for my wife, Dottie. She would watch as, in the midst of an overflowing schedule, someone would call and ask me for something—for my time, help, counsel, money—and she never heard me say no. While it was troubling to Dottie and my family, it eventually began to kill me, not only with exhaustion but also with resentment. I was saying *yes* on the outside but frequently resenting it on the inside. And that is when I began to realize something was wrong. I thought I was loving hurting people, yet I was being controlled by their hurts. It became a vicious cycle. People would share their hurts with me, and I'd try to solve their painful situations so they could regain control of their lives. But the more I did, the more I'd feel their pain was controlling me. So I'd work harder and faster to remove their pain. But it just brought more pain and frustration to me.

So, to compensate, I developed an aloofness, a personal distance from people. Many people found it hard to get to know me, and I was often criticized for not being more personable. I didn't have any trouble talking to people on a ministry level, talking to them about what God was helping us accomplish, but I began to avoid talking to others on a personal level. If someone began to share some problem or mentioned a painful experience, I steered the conversation elsewhere or indicated I had to leave. I simply didn't want another problem I felt I had to solve or another hurt I felt responsible to fix.

Looking back on it now, it would be funny if it were not so unhealthy. Most people want to keep conversations on a surface level so other people don't learn too much about them. But for me, it was the opposite. I had no problem sharing what I was feeling. In fact, when I shared my testimony in public, I spoke openly of my difficult childhood, my hatred for my father, and my past and current struggles to be a good husband and father. I didn't care what anyone learned about my problems; I was an open book. I simply didn't want to learn about someone else's problems. Because if I let down my guard, that person might share a hurt or a need, and my brand of "love," one that I thought was biblical, just couldn't say no.

AT A LOSS FOR ANSWERS

This situation, of course, produced a personal crisis for me. God had called me to reach out to young people, and my response to his call had placed me in contact with many thousands of kids and their parents and pastors. And hundreds of young people and adults had confided in me, sometimes in person and sometimes by phone or in writing. I heard constantly the cries of people's hearts as they told me of the deep pain they had suffered as a result of broken homes or unhealthy family situations. Scores told me stories of emotional, physical, or sexual abuse from their past. And all of them were desperately seeking answers.

Because I hadn't yet learned what I'm going to share with you in this chapter about interpreting God's Word, I didn't quite know how to respond to hurting people. By this time in my ministry, I was repeatedly called on to give answers, but I had only partial answers for them. I could give textbook answers from a distance, but I feared becoming too emotionally involved. I could tell them Jesus loved them, but I could no longer tell them how I could love them. I cared, but for some reason that was yet unknown to me, I had to care from afar or I would end up feeling controlled by the problems and pain of others.

One day I received this letter:

Dear Josh,

I am twenty-one years old, and I have never heard my daddy say, "I love you." I was horrified as I heard the cries of my heart being read in the letters you shared during your talk of other young people with similar backgrounds. It opened up old wounds that I thought had scarred over. They ripped open to bleed again. At the end of the meeting one friend . . . saw tears in my eyes and gave me a quick hug and asked if I was all right. I couldn't answer. The wounds of a lonely heart are things I don't share, so I had to run off somewhere and just cry.

Now I am alone, been through a couple tissues, and felt the need to write you. You said that you came from a broken home. I always cry when I hear the story of your mother's broken heart. My own father and mother verbally abuse each other all the time, and they try to drag me down in their battles. Rather than join in, I have emotionally run away from both of them.

How can I overcome my brokenness? I have forgiven my parents for the hurt they have caused me over the years, but . . . I tremble at the thought of starting a family, bringing my broken heart into a relationship, and building a future generation. But you raised a family like a godly man. How? I scramble desperately for answers. If you have any, it would be an honor to hear from you.

A daughter of the King,

Sara

This young woman had prayed and with God's help had even forgiven her parents, yet the wounds of her past left her with a broken, lonely heart. I was sure that God and his Word held the answer for Sara (not her real name). But I had come to the place of admitting that I struggled to provide those answers.

It took me years to learn where I had gone wrong, that I had been misunderstanding and misapplying what the Bible taught me about loving others. And I am indebted to many people who patiently loved me and offered biblical guidance. A process that began with my seminary training was supplemented by three men who deserve special note for the insights I'm about to share: Dick Day, Dr. Henry Cloud, and Dr. David Ferguson. These godly men and students of the Word not only took time to answer my questions and address my unhealthy responses to hurting people, but their biblical insights also led me to a freedom in Christ to love people "up close and personal," in a way I had never imagined possible.

THE BIBLE IS NOT OPEN TO PRIVATE INTERPRETATION

We learned from the last chapter that God has miraculously preserved the written Word as a perfect picture of God and his righteous ways. We explored together how our purpose was to become more and more like Christ, whose image is reflected in the pages of Scripture. And, as we come to know him more intimately and welcome him to express his likeness in us, we bear the fruits of Christlike love, joy, peace, kindness, and all those qualities that are called good. But to bear Christlike qualities takes more than knowing what the Bible *says* about Jesus and then trying to apply it to our lives. We must also understand what Scripture *means*. We must realize what God really meant when he said what he did.

Peter tells us that "no prophecy of Scripture is a matter of one's own interpretation" (2 Peter 1:20, NASB). Yet if we don't seek to learn the objective meaning of each verse or passage in Scripture, we are effectively giving it our own interpretation. That is why we need clear guidelines for interpreting and applying what the Bible says, guidelines that will ensure that the image we see reflected in the pages of Scripture is an accurate image of the God who wants us to know him. If we can do that, we spare ourselves—and our kids—the kind of heartache and difficulty I experienced.

Allow me to share with you three fundamental guidelines for interpreting the Bible, after which I'll share the story of how I was changed by a sound biblical understanding of what it means to love as Christ does.

Ask "What Does It Say?"

Whenever we read the Bible, we need to "see it" for what it says. We need to understand what is in a passage. We do this by running Scripture through a six-part grid represented by these questions: Who? What? When? Where? Why? and How?

1. *Who?* This question helps us determine who the personalities are in the passage. Who is talking? Who is the passage talking about?

2. *What?* This question helps us determine the subject or message or atmosphere of a passage. What is happening in the passage? What did the people in the passage do? What caused that? What theme is the writer talking about?

3. *When?* This question helps us determine time elements of a passage. When did it happen? When will it happen? When can it happen?

4. *Where?* This question helps us determine the location in which a passage happens. Where did it happen? Where are the people going? Where will it take place?

5. *Why?* This question helps us determine the underlying message or reasons outlined in a passage. Why did the writer say that? Why did the character do that? Why did the character go there? Why will this happen?

6. *How?* This question helps us determine the process involved in a passage. How did it happen? How was it supposed to happen? How will it happen? Under what circumstances will the message or promise of the passage come true?

We may not be able to answer all six questions in every passage, but by asking and answering as many as possible, we will come to understand what the Word of God is saying to us.

Ask "What Does It Mean?"

Whenever we read God's Word, we need to "know it" for what it means. This is where many—young people and adults alike—fail. This is where I stumbled, assuming I already knew the answer. I failed to fully understand God's answer to these questions: What does "loving others as Christ loves me" mean? What does that kind of love look like, sound like, and act like?

Understanding the significance of a portion of Scripture *is not* the same as asking, "What does it *mean to me or you?*" Understanding Scripture is not "a matter of one's own interpretation." The words of the Bible have an objective meaning of their own—the meaning God intended. When we read a passage of the Bible, we need to ask, "What is the objective meaning or significance of this passage?" and then let the Scripture interpret that for us. This is where Bible study tools and techniques, such as the following, are helpful:

1. *Study the context.* Scripture must be understood in context. Giving careful consideration to the verses and chapters that precede and follow a particular portion of Scripture is necessary to understand the objective meaning of the passage. Understanding the cultural context of a passage is also crucial. Many teachings and commands of Scripture are cryptic or confusing unless one understands the cultural setting in which they were spoken or written. Answering the detail questions—*who? what? when? where? why?* and *how?*—of a passage will go a long way in helping us understand the cultural context of a passage. Reference books such as study Bibles, Bible commentaries, encyclopedias, and atlases are helpful in discovering the cultural context of a passage.

2. *Study the words and phrases.* Scripture is rich in meaning when we look at individual words and phrases that are used in specific

ways. Several reference tools can help you understand what words and phrases mean:

- *Concordances.* Use a concordance—an alphabetized list of words used in the Bible—to help you find where the word or phrase is used in Scripture. This will allow you to compare how the specific word or phrase is used in various contexts. Many concordances include the original Hebrew and Greek words for the English translation, and some understanding of the original meanings of words and phrases in a text often sheds light on a passage's meaning.
- *Cross-references.* Many Bibles have marginal cross-references that allow you to go from one verse to another that is similar or that contains the same word or phrase. Comparing cross-references can help you understand the objective, original meaning of a word or phrase.
- *Study Bibles.* Study Bibles are a rich source of background information about words, phrases, characters, prophecies, historical context, diagrams, and other valuable information that will help you understand the meaning of a passage.
- *Bible dictionaries.* Bible dictionaries can help even the novice Bible student understand the meaning of words used in Scripture.
- *Other Bible translations and paraphrases.* A dynamic way of understanding a passage better is reading it in a variety of translations or paraphrases. As you do this, take care to identify which Bibles are true translations (translated from the original languages) and which are paraphrases (based on English translations, for example, *The Living Bible* and *The Message*). Translations are more accurate for word study; paraphrases are often used for devotional purposes.

3. Read what scholars have written about the passage. Reading what Bible scholars have written in commentaries about various passages can illumine even the most straightforward verses. You can benefit from the exhaustive study many of the commentators have made of the Scripture passage. It is also helpful to compare the writings of the church fathers and great Christian commentators of the past with the analyses of more modern scholars.

By making use of sound Bible-study techniques and the excellent study tools available to us today, every Christian can search out the objective meaning of the biblical text. Of course, there is diversity within the church on various points of theology, forms of worship, and church standards and practices, but there are only a few scriptural passages that are not clearly comprehensible.

Ask "How Does It Apply?"

Whenever we encounter the truth of God's Word, we need to also "experience it." This is where David Ferguson and his book *The Never Alone Church* is so helpful because it helps a body of believers understand how to experience Scripture in relationship to God and one another. Once we grasp what the Scriptures say in a specific area and know what it means, we can experience that objective meaning in our own lives and relationships.

At least three categories of questions can help us to experience the truth:

1. *Identify the truth.* How is this truth of Scripture to be experienced in my relationship with God and/or others? What is this truth supposed to look like, sound like, and act like in my life?

2. *Know the hindrances to the truth.* What hinders me from trusting Christ to live out this truth in my life? What sins, self-centered attitudes, expressions of self-reliance, or other things might hinder me from experiencing this truth? What will I do with these hindrances?

3. *Commit to experiencing the truth.* What practical steps can I take to know God more and make Christ more and more at home

in my heart? How can I put the truth of Scripture into practice? How can I allow Christ to live his life through me? What is the first step I must take? Whom will I ask to pray with me about making the truth of Scripture an experienced reality in my life?

Again, it's important to emphasize the goal of reading and studying the Bible. We shouldn't study the Bible simply to know what Scripture says. We should read God's words for a relational purpose—to know him, to understand his ways, and to allow him to live his life in and through our lives.

Without that perspective—and the above guidelines for interpreting and understanding Scripture—I would never have understood where I went wrong . . . and what it really means to love others as Christ loves me.

SEEING CHRISTLIKE LOVE THROUGH THE LENS OF SCRIPTURE

One day after giving my testimony at a conference, two couples approached me.

"Could we have a minute with you?" one of them asked.

I reluctantly agreed. They introduced themselves as adult children of alcoholics and began sharing a few things they had learned, things that resonated in my heart and mind. I recognized that many of the things they shared from their experience had been going on inside me, too.

When they left, I went to God's Word. I prayed the psalmist David's prayer: "Search me, O God, and know my heart; try me and know my anxious thoughts; and see if there be any hurtful way in me, and lead me in the everlasting way" (Psalm 139:23-24, NASB). I knew something was wrong inside me. I knew something had to change. It was killing me. I was a driven man. I was running day and night, and I had few answers for people struggling with unresolved hurts. So I prayed, "God, show me the hurt that lives inside me and the whys of it."

God began almost immediately to answer that prayer. With the help of others, I began to understand where my unhealthy responses to hurting people came from. As I've said before, when I was growing up, I hated my father, especially for what he did to my mother. Once I was old enough and strong enough to do something about my father's abuse of my mother, I did. Each time I saw him try to hurt my mom, I would step in and try to rescue her. I loved my mother, and I tried over and over to prevent her from being hurt. When I saw her in pain, I was willing to do anything to make it better. That process, I discovered, had developed into an emotional pattern. I became a "rescuer," driven to try to rescue hurting, struggling people.

Many years after my mother died and even after forgiving my father for his abusive behavior, I was still not free of my past. While I was free of hatred toward my dad, I was in bondage to the hurts of others. I thought I was free; I thought I was doing the Christlike thing when I tried to rescue people from their hurts and problems. I had convinced myself that I was exhibiting Christlike love.

But God wanted something better for me. As I applied the guidelines of scriptural interpretation I described earlier to this specific area of my life, I discovered that God wanted me to love in a way that accurately reflected the image of Jesus Christ as revealed in his Word, not according to my own definition, filtered through my past experiences.

God *is* our rescuer. He saw the hurts of an entire human race separated from him because of sin, and it "broke his heart" (Genesis 6:6). Out of compassion, he freely gave his only Son. No one took Christ's life from him; he willingly and freely laid it down. He wasn't driven to act. He acted on the basis of his nature—which is a willful, giving love (see 1 John 4:8). It is that kind of love that purchased our salvation.

God's Word went on to tell me that God's Spirit lived in me to transform me more and more into Christlike love. And, as part of the body of Christ, I was to participate in his ministry of love to others. I was to be a conduit, a relay station of sorts, of God's ministry of love to others. When I extend love and care to someone, that love and care "comes from God . . . [for] if we love each other, God lives in us, and his love has been brought to full expression *through us*" (1 John 4:7-12, emphasis mine).

Yet I wasn't seeing Scripture clearly. I wasn't seeing what that "full expression" of his love looked like to someone who is hurting. However, the Bible gives us a view of how Jesus responded to Mary and Martha when their brother, Lazarus, died (see John 11). When Jesus arrived at their home, he wept with them. From my perspective that seemed to be a strange response. After all, Jesus certainly knew what he was about to do. He knew that he had the power to raise Lazarus from the dead. He knew that he would soon correct the cause of their grief. He knew, as he told Martha, that Lazarus would live again. But none of that changed the fact that at that moment, his friends were hurting. Instead of saying, "Cheer up, a new day will dawn," or "Don't be sad, I'll fix everything for you," he *identified with their hurt*, wept with them, and provided comfort. That's how Christ responded to people's hurts, and it was quite different from my typical response. But I also discovered that Christ's love and care were not only my example but also my empowerment to love with his kind of love.

Jesus had taught his followers, "God blesses those who mourn, for they will be comforted" (Matthew 5:4). And where does the comfort come from? It comes from "the God and Father of our Lord Jesus Christ, the Father of compassion and the God of all comfort, who comforts us in all our troubles" (2 Corinthians 1:3-4, NIV). God cares that we hurt, and he compassionately reaches his arms around us to comfort us. And then one day the rest of the verse stood out to me: "[God] comforts us in all our troubles *so that* we can comfort others. When others are troubled, we will be able to give them the same comfort God has given us"(v. 4, emphasis mine).

God wanted me to respond to the hurts of people just as he does, by sharing in their hurt. "If they are sad," his Word says, "share their sorrow" (Romans 12:15). And when I do that, I am ministering God's living Word to people who hurt. When I tenderly embrace a hurting young man, God's comforting arms become experientially real to him. My empathetic words to a hurting young woman allow her to hear God's comforting words to her. To young people who lacked the emotional context to know what real love sounds like or looks like, God uses my tears, my words, or my warm embrace to share his comfort, too. And it wasn't even up to me to manufacture or generate this love; God would be doing the comforting himself, involving me in his ministry to others.

By God's grace—and the careful interpretation and application of Scripture, along with the patient and godly advice of others—I began to feel hope that I could begin to respond to hurting people in ways that would please God.

God's Word admonished me, "Let each one do just as he has purposed in his heart; not grudgingly or under compulsion; for God loves a cheerful giver" (2 Corinthians 9:7, NASB). I didn't believe this verse applied only to my giving of money. I also needed to cheerfully give of my time, my energy, and myself to people. Doing good deeds and helping people were important, for the Scripture points out that our faith without good deeds is dead (see James 2). But I hadn't been a cheerful giver. The "loving" things I had been doing came out of an unhealthy compulsion, not from a giving heart.

For years, when I read verses like "Mourn with those who mourn" (Romans 12:15, NIV) and "Bear one another's burdens" (Galatians 6:2, NASB), they sounded to me like "The Rescuer's Great Commission": Feel bad about someone's problem and take it on yourself to eliminate the problem. But, of course, that's not what those passages mean.

First, Scripture taught me that comfort isn't fixing people's problems. It's not about giving a pep talk, providing wise counsel, or even teaching a lesson. As a rescuer, however, I had a skewed perspective of these verses. When my wife was hurting—for example, when someone said something critical of our kids—I'd say, "Well, Dottie, don't let it get to you," or "Why didn't you say this?" or "Here are three things to always remember." I was constantly reaching for a solution, trying to fix my wife's problem. But most often that was the last thing Dottie needed when she was struggling with a troubling situation.

What she needed was to know I identified with her hurt and was there to hurt with her. For the longest time I couldn't figure out how that would really help—until I tried it. I remember the first time Dottie shared a hurt and I actually comforted her rather than tried to fix it.

"Honey," I said, "I know that must have really hurt. I'm so sorry you had to go through that."

I offered no advice, no pep talk, no solutions. I just identified with her hurt and grieved with her. At first, I think she must have wondered who this man was wearing my clothes and speaking my voice because that reaction was so unlike me. And, in effect, I wasn't doing the talking; it was God ministering some of his comfort to her through me. And it worked. It was exactly what she needed. And, interestingly, she came back to me a few days later and asked, "Honey, what would you have done in that situation? How would you have responded?" Once her hurt was comforted, she was ready to tackle her own problem, aided by a little advice.

Second, I learned that bearing another person's burden doesn't mean taking responsibility for that person's problem or hurt. It means coming alongside and gently helping a person lift the load. In the past, I felt responsible for solving everybody's problems. But comforting others or bearing their burdens doesn't mean taking responsibility *for* their problem; it means being responsible *to* them—to comfort, encourage, and support them in their pain or difficulties.

In fact, I came to understand that when I stepped in to rescue people, I was often doing them a disservice. Once again, it was God's Word that brought light. I discovered that just three verses after Galatians 6:2, where we are commanded to "bear one another's burdens," verse 5 declares, "For each one shall bear his own load" (NASB).

Now, this may sound confusing at first. But, as we mentioned earlier, a few reliable Bible-study techniques and tools help lead us to greater understanding. In this case, I discovered an important difference between a "burden" and a "load." The Greek word for *burden* is a word that means "boulder," a large rock that is too heavy to carry alone. We all face situations that at times bear down heavily on us, and we need someone to come alongside and share our load. The situation could be an injury, an illness, the death of a loved one, or the loss of a job through no fault of our own, for example.

The Greek word for a "load" is different, however; it refers to a military knapsack, the supply pack a soldier would carry into the field. It represents something each of us is responsible to carry. It's what Paul meant when he said, "Each of us will have to give a personal account to God" (Romans 14:12).

We all have personal responsibilities, and when we fail in our responsibilities—by using poor judgment or making wrong choices or harboring bad attitudes, for example—we must face up to the consequences. To step in and remove the natural and corrective consequences of people's irresponsible behavior may, in fact, rob them of valuable lessons, which may be critical for their continued growth and maturity.

I can't possibly express how valuable this revelation from God's Word has been to me. When I realized that loving others as Christ loved didn't mean I was responsible *for* other people, I was set free to be responsible *to* others—and particularly to those who were hurting. I then began looking for opportunities to allow his comfort, encouragement, and support to flow through me to others because I knew that then I was loving others as Christ loves me.

LIVING OUT CHRIST'S LOVE

It was truly liberating for me to finally gain a glimpse of how Christ wanted to love others through me to bring healing to hurt people. But that didn't mean I was not to be involved in helping people solve their problems. In fact, one of the unique opportunities God gave me and my ministry was to provide ongoing humanitarian aid to the hungry and hurting people of the former Soviet Union, an effort that has brought physical healing to people, joy to me, and glory to our heavenly Father.

But I believe I would still be struggling today, living in bondage to my past, if I had not come to better understand just what God's Word had to say about Christ's love to those in need, what it really means, and how it applies to my life.

The process of coming to know God through his Word isn't always quick or easy. It takes time and effort. Bookstores are full of great helps to assist you and your young people in exploring God's Word in order to know him better. In fact, we have developed a resource to help you and your kids develop a clear and systematic approach to Scripture, enabling you to know what it says, what it means, and how it applies to life (see appendix A). And, while it isn't always quick and easy to understand the words of God, it is rewarding beyond measure. Paul was inspired with God's words when he said,

> I pray that Christ will be more and more at home in your hearts
> as you trust in him. May your roots go down deep into the soil of
> God's marvelous love. And may you have the power to under-

stand, as all God's people should, how wide, how long, how high, and how deep his love really is. May you experience the love of Christ, though it is so great you will never fully understand it. Then you will be filled with the fullness of life and power that comes from God. (Ephesians 3:17-19)

The more I comprehend who I am (that I'm a one-of-a-kind child of the King) and the more I experience why I am here (to know Christ and become more like him), the more I am filled with the fullness of life and all the power and blessing that come from God. I wish I had known all this before Sara first wrote to me. I wish I had known then how to answer her. If I had, I would have said something like this, which I now offer not only for Sara but also for any others who may be struggling:

Dear Sara,

I am so sorry that old wounds of your past have brought you such pain. I hurt with you, for I, too, have felt the pain of never hearing a daddy say, "I love you." Every child needs to hear those words over and over again from a parent. God designed for us to feel secure in that love, and my heart cries with you over the pain that has caused your lonely heart.

It's wonderful that you have forgiven your parents for the hurt they caused you. That has freed you from harmful resentment. But, as you say, it hasn't freed you from a broken, lonely heart. Yet God wants to free you from that as well, by healing the wounds of your past.

Healing a broken, lonely heart comes from being comforted. And God comforts those who mourn. Jesus said, "God blesses those who mourn, for they will be comforted" (Matthew 5:4). The Bible, a love letter to you, reveals a compassionate God who "is the source of every mercy and the God who comforts us" (2 Corinthians 1:3). I know you have prayed to God. But have you told him how you have missed the love of a father? Do you know how he has wanted to wrap his loving arms around you and hurt with you and tell you he loves you as a daddy does? Though you may not have experienced that from your earthly father, your heavenly Father's Word reveals him as the fulfillment of all that your hungry heart yearns for. Listen quietly in your heart, for he wants you to hear him say, "Oh, my beloved Sara, my heart breaks to see your heart break. I weep with you because you missed the love of your earthly father. But, Sara, let me be the Father you never had—let my Holy Spirit right now speak to your spirit and tell you that I love you with an everlasting love. Feel my arms wrap around you and hear a still, small voice say, 'I am the God of all comfort who weeps with you, who is heartbroken over your wounds and who right now is kissing those wounds with my love for you.'"

Can you hear him speak to your spirit, Sara? Can you feel his loving kiss? You're not alone. He is there, and he loves you more than you can ever know.

I know you said the wounds of a lonely heart are things you don't share. But you shared them with me. And you can share them with God. And it will please him if you will find a safe person, another Christian woman—one who knows how to comfort—with whom you can share your hurt. God's Word tells us that he has also chosen to comfort "us in all our troubles so that we can comfort others. When others are troubled, we will be able to give them the same comfort God has given us" (2 Corinthians 1:4).

Sara, I urge you to find a woman who has received God's comfort; share your wounded heart with her, and let her be an additional channel for you to receive God's comfort. As you hear her words of comfort, identifying with your pain, know that you are hearing your loving heavenly Father's words, too. As you feel her warm embrace or see her tears of grief, know that your Father is wrapping his arms around you and healing your broken heart with his tears.

The perfect love of your heavenly Father, additionally shared through one of his tender children, will help heal your heart and cast out your fear. Healing from past hurts is possible. Broken hearts are healed. It has happened to me, and it can happen to you.

Would you please write to me after you have shared your broken heart in this way? I want to hear again from Sara, the daughter of the King "of every mercy . . . who comforts us."

A son of the King,

Josh

• • • • •

Teachable Moments

Before we go back to Duane, Lauren, Megan, and the others, let's look at some practical ways to help your young people understand what the Bible truly is to their lives. The Bible is the revelation of God and his ways, and as we come to know God and follow his ways, we are provided for and protected.

The "What If" Road-Sign Game

While riding together with your family, suggest playing the "What If" game. In many respects you can consider this a "family devotional on wheels." Ask each person in your vehicle to find a visible indicator of a driving instruction—something that tells you how fast to drive, where to stop, when to go, what route you're on, etc. When someone identifies a visible instruction ask: "What if I don't follow that instruction?" Answers could include: "We might have an accident," "We could get arrested," or "We won't get to where we want to go."

Finally ask: "Why do we have driving instructions?" After discussing the answers, make the point: "God has given us his instructions for living, and he has written them in his Word—the Bible—for similar reasons. He doesn't want to see us have accidents or miss going where he wants us to go. He has given us his laws and instructions to provide for us and protect us. Let's talk about what instructions in Scripture provide for us or protect us." This is where you can probe your kids to name God's commandments and discuss how they were given for our best interest. A good place to start is with the Ten Commandments.

Paint Word Pictures

During a relaxing time with family or at a youth-group meeting ask your kids to paint word pictures of each other. A father may start by saying: "I can paint a word picture of your mother. She's got blue eyes, sandy hair, rosy lips, and a dimpled cheek. She's a morning person, very energetic, and hardworking. She loves classical music, plays the violin, loves cherry pie, and hates spiders." The idea is to describe the characteristics of the person as accurately as possible with the person being described agreeing or disagreeing with the word picture.

After a while ask: "Who can paint a word picture of God? The Bible doesn't tell us what God looks like, but it does tell us what he is like. What are God's characteristics?" Answers could include: "God is holy, just, right, pure, loving, all powerful, all knowing, perfect, forgiving, merciful, etc."

Make the point: "One of the main reasons we have the Bible is to show us what God is like. It is a revelation of God to us. And the better we know him, the closer our relationship can be with him."

The "Pass It On" Whisper Game

While traveling together or sitting around a room, suggest playing the "Pass It On" whisper game. Write a simple sentence on a small sheet of paper: "Make me a yellow fan" (for example). Don't show the paper to anyone, but whisper the sentence to a person clearly, but fast. Then instruct that person to pass the message on as quickly but clearly as possible by whispering it to the next person. Continue the process until the last person has been told the message. Then ask that person to speak the message aloud. Hand him or her the written message, and ask the person to read it aloud. The verbal message and written message will likely be different.

Make this point: "God told a few people what he is like and how we could live in relationship with him and one another, and they wrote it down. And because there were no printing presses, other people had to keep writing it down over the years in order for us to have God's written Word today—called the Bible. How do we know that people wrote all the words down just as God gave them? Some people could have left things out or gotten them mixed up, as we did in our whisper game."

After some discussion say, "We can be sure that God's Word has been passed down to us accurately because of the care the scribes took in preparing copies. They were so careful to copy everything just right, letter for letter. And then they counted every word to be sure it was just the same as what they had copied from. We can be absolutely confident that what we have in the Bible is God's message to us about himself." (See chapter 8, pages 166–78, for more details on the reliability of Scripture.)

Discovering the Real Person Is the Key to Romance

When interacting with young people about love, dating, marriage, and romance make this observation: "One of the keys to a successful romance is discovering the real person you like and letting that person know you like what you've found. Seek out what a person's preferences are—his or her favorite color, food, music, sports, and overall interests in life. When you do let the other person know you want to know the real person he or she is, it endears that person to you because it says, 'I care enough about you to want to get to know you.'"

Continue by saying something like, "God made us to want to be known by other people because he is who he is. God has given us the Bible—the revelation of himself—so we can discover him for who he really is. And when we do, he so endears himself to us that he makes us more and more like him."

Write a Thank-You Letter to God

Ask your kids to write a personal letter to God, thanking him for giving them a revelation of himself through Scripture. In the letter have them identify as many characteristics of God as they can and tell God how much those qualities mean to them. If they feel comfortable sharing what they wrote, ask them to read it to you and/or your group.

PART FOUR

THE RESURRECTION: GOD WANTS US TO TRUST HIM, NO MATTER WHAT

CHAPTER 11

The Revelation Celebration

Duane returned the motorcycle keys to his pocket.

"This discussion about the Bible has been great," Megan said.

"Absolutely," Lauren added. "I didn't realize that the Bible is one of the main ways God shows himself to me."

"I have a lot of friends who need to hear this," Megan said. "In fact, I think the whole youth group needs this."

"Yeah," Allen said. "Is there any way we can share this with the whole youth group? You know, like the Incarnation Celebration we did at your house?"

"Hey," Liz said. She turned to Megan, her eyes gleaming. "What if we found a way for you to use your acting ability to share this with the group?"

"Like what?" Megan asked. "You mean a play?"

Liz shrugged without losing the gleam in her eyes. "I don't know, exactly. But it could be fun to figure it out together."

Megan smiled back. "It could be *a lot* of fun. And I'll check with my parents so we can even have it at my house if you want."

"Great," Liz said. She glanced quickly at Allen and Lauren. "What do you guys think?"

"I'm not an actor like Megan," Allen said.

"That's all right," Liz said. "Maybe you and Lauren can work on the script, and we can get Chad to help out with other acting parts. And there'll be plenty of other things to do. The important thing right now is just to get started."

"Is that okay, Allen?" Duane said. "We want to be sensitive to your family situation."

"No, it's okay," Allen responded. "I need things like this to keep me going."

"Okay," Liz said. "It's settled, then."

The small group met numerous times the next two weeks, preparing for what they quickly started calling the Revelation Celebration. When the evening to perform the play finally arrived, members of the Westcastle youth group, along with many of their parents, began to filter into the Wagners' home. Megan's parents welcomed everyone at the door and directed them to the living room for hors d'oeuvres, while Duane and Liz arranged the dining room for the evening's events.

A new energy seemed to pervade the youth group during the last few weeks. The things Duane and Liz were teaching were really hitting home, and the youth group's numbers had been steadily increasing. As the couple watched the door, they even saw a few new faces.

"It's good to see the Franklins here," Liz whispered, nodding toward the family trio standing in the corner.

Duane nodded. "I was just thinking the same thing," he said. "I'm glad Allen brought his parents. I don't think I've seen them in church since Angie died."

It was Liz's turn to nod. "It's only been a month now. I'm sure it's been really hard."

"Yeah," Duane whispered, as Allen, Lauren, and Megan approached. "Allen pulled me aside earlier and said he had something important to talk to me about after our presentation."

"Is it about his parents?" Liz responded quickly.

"I think so," Duane said.

The trio reported that everything was ready; they could get started anytime. Duane called everyone together and asked them to join him in the dining room. An air of expectation filled the room as the young people and their parents sat around the large table. Duane stood by his chair at the head of the table, a sheaf of notes in his hand.

"Okay, you guys," he began. "Liz and the Wagners have prepared a great meal for us tonight." He nodded at his wife and their friends. "But before we begin, I'd like to ask Jennifer's father, Mr. Brown, to say grace, and then we have a short presentation to make before we eat."

After the prayer Duane cleared his throat and began. "A few weeks ago in our youth group," he said, glancing at his notes, "we talked about the Bible as a relational revelation of God, which was given to us so we can know God and become more and more like his Son, Jesus. We said that the Bible reveals God's ways, and the more we reflect his nature and ways, the more we'll experience a life full of meaning and happiness."

Several of the students around the large table nodded. Duane continued, raising his Bible in the air as he spoke. "But what if we can't trust the Bible to accurately reflect who God is? I mean, what if what the Scripture says has been distorted or diluted somehow over the years? Then we can't very well trust it to help us know God and his ways, can we?"

He elaborated further, mentioning the centuries that have passed since the Bible's original documents were written, the ancient process of copying manuscripts, the lack of printing technology, and other potential obstacles to textual reliability.

He lowered the Bible and set it on the table, next to a cloth-covered object in front of him. "So," he concluded, "if we can't trust the Bible as a reliable document, how can we trust the answers it gives us to life's problems?"

Duane nodded to Megan, who joined him at the front of the dining room as he removed the cloth from the object in front of him, exposing a small tray. The tray held several small cups. He then called Brent's name and enlisted his help.

"Brent and Megan are going to help illustrate the importance of the problem we're talking about," he said.

Megan bowed to the watching group, paused briefly, and then dropped to the floor, writhing and moaning as if she were in pain.

"Brent is a doctor," Duane said, raising his voice over Megan's caterwauling. He pointed to Megan on the floor. "And this is his patient, a very sick young woman."

Megan groaned even louder when her name was mentioned, and the crowd laughed at her melodrama. Duane then handed a card to Melissa, who sat closest to him, but he instructed her not to open the card just yet.

"Melissa," he explained as everyone listened, "Megan is dying of a rare disease; it's called *melodrama fatalis*. And you hold in your hand the only remedy. If Dr. Brent gives her that cure, she'll recover completely. If he gives her anything else, she'll die. You must open the note without having anyone else see it and as quickly as possible whisper the lifesaving remedy to Karen. Then, Karen, you must quickly whisper the instructions to Jennifer, who must pass the information to Mr. Brown, and so on, around the room, until it reaches Chad, who will whisper the cure to Dr. Brent.

"But here's the catch," Duane announced, his voice as serious as an investigative reporter. "You may say the name of the cure only once to each person. That person must relay those same words—to the best of his or her ability. And when Brent gets the information, he will come to this tray on the table and select the medicine that will cure—or kill—Megan.

"All right? Go!"

The group watched with keen interest as Melissa opened the card, read it carefully to herself, and then leaned over and whispered in Karen's ear. Karen's face reflected immediate uncertainty, but she shrugged and relayed the information to Jennifer, as Megan (who had been groaning and writhing on the floor the whole time) suddenly became louder and more animated.

Finally, the news reached Chad, who shook his head and rolled his eyes as he sprang from his seat and whispered a phrase in Brent's ear.

"What?" Brent asked, but Duane reminded him that he had to take the information just as it was relayed and do the best he could. Brent flashed a helpless look at him and then turned to the table. Duane rotated the tray to reveal to the entire group that the five small paper cups each contained a colored candy mint and bore a label on the outside. The five labels read "Hyprochloric Acid," "Hygrochloric Acid," "Hylochloric Acid," "Hyfrochloric Acid," and "Hydrochloric Acid."

Megan groaned as if death were imminent.

"Well, Dr. Brent," Duane pressed. "What's the cure?"

"I don't know," Brent said, his face reflecting his confusion. "It's one of these five medicines." He picked up each cup and read the label. "But if all I have to work with is what Chad told me, it could be any one of these."

Megan wailed. Several in the group laughed again at her melo-drama. Brent turned and appealed to the group. "What should I do?" he asked.

"Just do the best you can," Melissa offered.

Brent shook his head and finally grabbed a cup and read the label: "Hydrochloric Acid." He shrugged. "At least I've heard of this one."

"Okay, see if hydrochloric acid does the trick," Duane said, pro-nouncing the phrase carefully and loudly enough for Megan to hear.

Brent emptied the cup into his hand, leaned over to help Megan to her feet, and popped a mint into her mouth. She froze for a moment, then gazed at the group . . . and "died" a dramatic death, falling heavily to the floor.

Duane asked Melissa to hand the folded note to Brent. "What does the note say, Brent?"

He unfolded the note, and read, "A white hyfrochloric acid pill."

"Oh," Duane said, shaking his head mournfully. "Too bad!" He thanked Brent and Megan, and everyone applauded.

Then he asked the group what went wrong. Several responded at once, but all agreed that the message got garbled in the process of transmission. "Right," Duane said. "And because the information was distorted along the way, Brent had no way to be sure he was giving poor Megan the correct remedy. Without accurate, nondistorted instructions, Megan couldn't experience the lifesaving power of that information."

"So," Duane asked the group. "What's my point?"

"Uh," Melissa began shyly, "if we don't have an accurate Bible, we can't get the right medicine. Right?"

"Right," Duane said, smiling. "So it's important that we know the Bible is accurate enough to give us a true picture of the God who wants us to know him, the God who is the cure for the disease that afflicts us all, so to speak. But how can we be convinced we have a book that provides a picture-perfect lens through which we can see God? Here's how." He stepped aside, picked up three sheets of paper from one of the end tables in the room, and asked the kids and parents to form three groups.

Duane and the group spent the next part of their meeting exploring the three tests he said could be used to establish the reliability of any historical document. He emphasized that the evidence for the reliability of the Bible underscores the loving action of God, who carefully superintended the recording, transmission, and confirmation of his Word because he wants each of us to know him and his ways.

As that portion of the meeting proceeded, the group became increasingly interested. Several times someone in the group expressed surprise or appreciation in response to what Duane shared.

And at one point Mr. Brown, Jennifer's dad, asked a series of sincere questions that indicated his eyes were being opened to the strength and significance of the evidence for the Bible's reliability.

"It tells us a lot," Duane said, as he concluded the activity, "that God has taken such care to preserve and protect his written Word. And it's important to remember that he did it because he wants the Bible we have to reflect who he really is, so we can know him and become like him."

He looked around the table, paused, and smiled. "And I also believe that God would be pleased that we experience what Liz and the Wagners have prepared for us to eat tonight."

"That's what *I've* been waiting for!" Brent said.

"Me, too," Jennifer agreed. "I'm starving!"

Within moments, the meal was served, and everyone ate and talked enthusiastically. Occasionally the conversation would return to Brent and Megan's melodrama or to the activity Duane had led. Throughout the meal, however, Allen was uncharacteristically silent, and his parents seemed preoccupied and distant.

After the meal Duane and Liz cleared the table quickly as Megan, Allen, and Lauren slipped out of the room. Duane then invited everyone into the family room, which had been arranged in theater-style seating, with two chairs at the front facing the audience. Two spotlights lit the two chairs from opposite corners of the room. When everyone was seated, Duane stepped to the front.

"The Bible is a living, relational book," he began. "It's God's way of telling us not only how much he loves us and wants us to know him but also that he wants us to become like him. So the Bible is sort of a love letter from the heart of God.

"With that in mind," he concluded, backing away with a grand, sweeping gesture toward the empty chairs, "I give you 'The Case of the Unread Love Letters.'"

The youth group and their parents applauded and cheered as

Megan and Chad quickly slipped into the spotlighted chairs and faced the group. Chad extended his arm in front of him as if he were steering a car. Megan held a script over her left knee so they could both read their lines. On Duane's cue, the room lights were dimmed, leaving Megan and Chad in the spotlights.

"I'm glad we're going out again, Mary Lou," Chad read. "I sure do like you a lot."

"Thank you, Bobby Lee," Megan said, prompting a few chuckles from the group. "I like you, too."

"Yeah, I really do like going out with you," Chad said, "because of the great restaurants we get to go to with your dad's credit card. It's really nice of him to let you use it like that."

"Yeah, I know, Bobby Lee," she deadpanned.

"And I like the crowd we run with. I mean, you're so popular and all that I've got every guy in school envying me."

"Yeah, I know, Bobby Lee," Megan answered, her voice flat.

"And it's great," Chad continued, "that you're so pretty because who wants to date some dorky-looking girl? I mean, the guys would make fun of me, you know?"

"Yeah, I know, Bobby Lee."

"And it's great—," Chad began, but Megan interrupted.

"Yeah, I know, Bobby Lee, you really like Dad's car, too."

"Yeah, how did you know I was going to say that, Mary Lou?"

"Bobby Lee?" Megan asked.

"Yes, Mary Lou?"

"You haven't said anything about all the letters and notes I've been writing to you. Do you like getting my letters?"

"Oh, I sure do, Mary Lou! They smell so good!"

"Well," Megan continued, "can we talk about some of them? I mean, I've written you sixty-six letters, you know." Some in the group laughed. Megan went on. "And, Bobby Lee, you've never said a thing about a single one of them."

"Well, I'd like to talk about them, Mary Lou, I surely would . . .

but . . . but . . . well, you see, it's like this," he said. "I haven't really read them yet."

"You what?" Megan answered, spinning in her chair to stare at Chad. "You haven't read them?"

"Well, now, Mary Lou, you've got to understand," he said, running a finger under the collar of his shirt. "I'm really busy with schoolwork and football practice and video games and e-mailing my friends and—"

"But, Bobby Lee, I poured my heart out to you in those letters. I told you all sorts of personal things in them, things I truly wanted you to know. I told you about all my favorite things and things I don't like and . . . and my fears and all my dreams." She paused, and her voice dropped. "So where *are* my letters?"

"Oh, oh, you'll really be pleased, Mary Lou," Chad said. "I've saved every one, I really have. I keep them in a special place, don't you worry about that."

A long silence followed, until finally Chad spoke again.

"Mary Lou . . . I really do love you, though," he said softly.

"But, Bobby Lee," she answered, looking sorrowfully at him. "You . . . you don't even *know* me." She turned her head, then, and faced straight ahead before slowly dropping her gaze to her feet.

Immediately the twin spotlights switched off, and the room was plunged into darkness. The group hesitated a minute and then began applauding uncertainly, until one spotlight switched on again, illuminating only Megan, who sat alone on a stool in a pool of light. She glanced at the script in her hand, then lifted her gaze and looked just above and beyond the group seated before her.

"I am the Alpha and the Omega," she intoned, "the beginning and the end. I am the one who is, who always was, and who is still to come, the Almighty One." The group sat silently, listening raptly. Megan paused and looked at her script.

"I am the infinite God who knows no boundaries or limitations. My power and knowledge and greatness are beyond your comprehension. My love and holiness and beauty are so intense that to see me in all my glory would overwhelm you—for as a mortal you could not see me and live. And yet . . . I created you to know me intimately, for I am passionate about my relationship with you."

Megan shifted on her stool and slipped the script she had been reading from one hand to the other. She took a deep breath and then continued.

"But a relationship isn't complete unless the love cycle—each one of us loving and being loved—is completed. I want you to know that I love you, and I want you to love me.

"I know everything there is to know about you. I know your favorite color, your favorite food, what music you like, the dreams you have, and the future you long for. I know your struggles and weaknesses. I am glad with you when you make right choices. I am saddened when you make wrong choices. I know you better than you know yourself, and . . . I love you.

"But I want to ask you a question, not for my information, but for yours." She paused. Not even the slightest sound disturbed the quiet in the room. "Do you love me? I mean *really* love me? Be slow to answer; be sure before you speak. And before you do, let me tell you the secret to really loving me. To love me, you must come to know me. For to know me is to love me!

"Learn of my mercy and my faithfulness, and you will love me. Come to know my goodness and holiness, and you will love me. Learn of my justice tempered with patience, and you will love me. Know what I love and what I hate, and you will love me. Know what saddens my heart and what gives me pleasure, and you will love me.

"This is the way to have eternal life: to know me, the only true God. And the more you know me, the more you will become like me. The more you know me, the more you will praise and thank me and honor my name. For the more you know me, the more you can glorify me . . . and the more I will know *your* love.

"And the way to know me is through the written revelation of myself—the Word of God, the collection of my love letters to you. Read my words, hide them in your heart, and know me for who I am—the one true God, your Savior, and your friend."

Megan paused. Something had happened in the room. Everyone—including Megan herself—seemed aware of the change. She lowered her gaze, and her voice dropped in volume, to almost a whisper.

"Oh, God," she said, "you are great, but I know so little of your greatness. I know you are merciful and faithful and holy and just, but I really know so little of you."

She lifted her head and looked toward the ceiling; those who sat closest to her could see that her eyes were welling up with tears.

"I want to thank you," she said—and everyone in the room was keenly aware that she was no longer reciting from a script, no longer acting—"for your holy Word and for giving to me right now, this very moment, a longing to know you and a hunger to read your . . . your love letters to me."

She paused as if to allow the words she spoke to sink in. "And help me. Help me to see you and know you in every page, . . . so I can be like you. Oh, God, let me honor you with my life, please. *Please*," she repeated, her voice weighty with desire. She closed her eyes. "God, I sense you smiling at me right now. Thank you. Thank you for loving me. I love you, too. Amen."

A holy silence filled the room. Everyone seemed aware of God's presence. No one moved for a few moments. The only noise in the room was that caused by the soft crying of Allen's mother. Liz slipped over to Megan and embraced her. They spoke quietly to each other.

Mrs. Franklin's weeping became louder as she covered her mouth in an attempt to silence the emotions overwhelming her. She wrestled for control. "I'm sorry," she said, sobbing. She hesitated for a moment, then got up suddenly and hurried from the room. Her husband, Tad, rose to follow her but addressed the group before leaving.

"I'm sorry, too," he said. "This . . . this has all been very hard on Allison. She . . . whenever she sees people get emotional, it seems to trigger her own emotions." He paused. "And then with today's news . . . well . . ." Instead of finishing his sentence, he turned and followed his wife out of the room.

The group fell silent. Allen sank down in his chair, obviously embarrassed by the events. His face reddened as he realized that all the eyes in the room were fixed on him. "I'm sorry, you guys," he said.

"I hope I didn't do anything wrong," Megan said. "Did I get too emotional or something?"

Duane started to reassure her when Allen interrupted.

"No, it's not you, Megan," Allen said. "It's just been a real hard time for all of us, especially for my mom. We almost didn't come tonight. We wouldn't have, except my dad thought maybe we needed to keep our minds occupied or something."

He paused, and everyone waited. It seemed as if the air had been sucked out the room by the reactions of Allen and his parents to the evening's events. Finally, Liz spoke. "What's going on, Allen?"

He inhaled deeply. "This is what I was going to tell you later, Duane."

Duane nodded, and every eye focused on Allen.

"Well," Allen continued, "I guess I can say it now. You all know Angie died of . . . of Fanconi anemia. Well, today the doctor's report came back on some special blood tests that were done. I've got the same thing . . . and it's terminal."

Duane took a step toward Allen and started to speak. But Allen gestured for him to stop. The boy stood and looked nervously around the room. "Look," he said, "I don't think it's a good time to keep talking about it. I'm sorry to mess up the evening like this. I just . . . I guess we shouldn't have come." He stepped haltingly toward the door, as if every step required major effort. A moment later he was gone.

Silence reigned in the room for a few moments until Duane suggested that they take some time to pray, remembering the Franklin family . . . and especially Allen's condition.

After the prayer Megan approached Duane. "I still feel like I caused this," she said, obviously craving reassurance.

"No," Duane answered, placing a comforting hand on Megan's shoulder. "You didn't do anything wrong, Megan. It's not something any of us did. They're just going through a hard time right now."

Later that night, when Duane and Liz had returned home and gone to bed, Duane suddenly leaned over and turned the bedside lamp back on.

"What?" Liz asked. "What's wrong?"

"I've been lying here thinking," he explained. "About tonight."

"Don't let it bother you, honey," she said. "You didn't do anything wrong."

"No, I know that. I'm not worried that we did anything wrong. I just wish I knew how to help Allen. I wish I had something to say or do to help him face those, um, dark days that are ahead of him."

• • • • •

What is there to say to people facing tragedy? It's true that having strong convictions about Christ and his Word does lead us to trust in him as our Savior, comforter, and power source. It does help us to enjoy a closer relationship with our loving Father God. But there's more.

We must also gain a deepened conviction about Christ's resurrection and an understanding of what his resurrection means to each of us personally. Without such a conviction, it's extremely easy to lose our perspective, especially when tragedy strikes and life seems to make no sense. The meaning of the resurrection of Jesus Christ enables us to answer a third crucial question: Where am I going? And that gives our identity and purpose a clear and proper perspective.

The resurrection of Jesus Christ and its relational meaning to us completes the picture of reality. It allows us to see life with all its struggles from God's perspective. A deepened conviction in Christ's resurrection can equip us to face whatever happens in life—good or bad—with gratitude, courage, and optimism. That is what the Franklins needed. It's what our children need, particularly with all the challenges they face in their daily lives today. It's what all of us need.

CHAPTER 12

Because He Lives

"Thanks for coming over, Allen," Liz said. She motioned for him to have a seat in the family room. Allen smiled weakly and sat down.

"I know this has got to be rough on you," Duane began. "And I'm not sure what to say."

"You guys don't have to say anything," Allen stated. "You're both the best friends I've ever had, and there isn't anything *to* say. The doctors have said it's terminal, and that's all there is to it."

"But that's what I mean, I guess," Duane replied. "There's nothing much we can do . . . except pray."

"Well," Allen said hesitantly, "I don't want to be disrespectful to God or anything, . . . but that didn't help with Angie. For some reason, he didn't want to save her life, so I'm not sure he wants to save mine, either." Allen lowered his head in thought.

An uncomfortable silence passed between them until Liz spoke. "We may not understand these things," she began, "but we can't just give up hope."

Allen lifted his head and gazed out the family-room window. Tears glistened in his eyes. "It's torturing my parents," he said. "Mom just can't seem to stop crying. Last night she told me that she had her little girl taken away from her, and I was all she had left. And now this."

A tear welled up and trickled down Allen's face. "It's not that I'm afraid to die. I know I'll go to be with Angie." He paused and wiped his cheek. "It's just that I had so much planned, you know? Dad and I were going to the mountains to camp this summer; now he doesn't think it's such a good idea—says I need to conserve my strength. I was looking forward to college this fall. And Carrie and I have really been hitting it off. I mean, I think I'm really in love with her. I thought I really had a future. . . ." He swallowed hard and blinked back more tears.

"And probably this time next year, I'll be a memory." His voice was barely audible. "It just doesn't make any sense," he concluded.

IN A LIFE WHERE DEATH REIGNS

From Allen's perspective, the tragedy of a terminal illness is senseless. It seems pointless that a young person with such a bright future should be struck down with an incurable disease. This is but one among millions of unanswered questions we and our kids have when we face numerous trials, discouragements, and difficulties in life.

Far too many of us respond to these apparent injustices with anger and resentment, leading eventually to a cynical, pessimistic outlook on life. In fact, our studies have shown that young people who have distorted beliefs about God and truth are two times more likely to feel pessimistic than those who possess a biblical view of God and truth.[1]

We all desire—for ourselves and for our kids—the ability to face the tough realities of life with a spirit of gratitude, courage, and optimism. But a pragmatic view of reality won't help our kids navigate life's difficulties, and it may well sour them on life and relationships. A postmodern outlook will no doubt leave them facing the hard knocks of life alone, unaware that God wants them to view life from his perspective. So our approach as Christian parents, pastors, and youth workers isn't a matter of *teaching* our kids how to avoid trials or difficulties, because those things are unavoidable. We have to help them with a fresh perspective that will enable them to *handle* the tough realities of life because, as the saying goes, "We live in a cruel world," where heartache and death reign supreme.

Smiles at some point turn to frowns, and laughter gives way to crying. Happiness and joy are eventually replaced with pain and suffering. Whether or not a person has committed his or her life to Christ, personal anguish, loss, and death are inevitable. Even the earth feels the pain of death and dying. For millennia, this planet has groaned under the stress of natural disasters. Tornadoes can wreak havoc on life and property. A babbling brook can become a destructive force when it floods, destroying everything in its path. The friendly flicker of a campfire can transform itself into a raging forest fire, consuming plants, animals, and dwellings. Mountains erupt, spewing out volcanic ash. Earthquakes topple buildings. The sun parches fields, bringing drought. "All creation," Scripture says, "has been groaning as in the pains of childbirth right up to the present time" (Romans 8:22).

The disruption and decay of this earth and the inevitability of death are a living reality. Pain and loss are felt every minute of every day somewhere in the world. Yet as often as life serves up pain and heartache, we are rarely willing to accept it. Something inside us says, "This makes no sense," and we hope that life will be better tomorrow. But even if tomorrow is better, it won't mean much eventually because some day, all that we have and hold will fade from our grasp, and we will die.

The disruption and decay of this earth and the inevitability of death are a living reality.

But at one point in history, there was a band of believers who trusted in someone to change all that. A handful of devout Jewish people thought a man named Jesus was the Messiah—the deliverer—who would transform their troubled times of bondage under the Romans into a godly kingdom on earth. Isaiah had prophesied in the ancient Jewish writings that the Messiah would come and restore all things to a paradise, where there would be no more fighting, oppression, fear, or death. The entire earth would once again be a pristine garden, where everyone would live together in peace forever (see Isaiah 11 and 35).

Yet one day their Messiah, Jesus, King of the Jews, hung on a cross, dying, and their hopes seemed dashed.

Imagine the mental and emotional state of that small group of disciples as they stood watching the Messiah, their deliverer, breathing his last breath. Here was the miracle worker who could command nature, heal sickness, and produce food with a word or a gesture. Here was the King they had believed would reestablish their kingdom. Here on a cross. Dying. And dying with him were all the hopes they had placed in him.

"TRUST IN ME, NO MATTER WHAT!"

Come with me in your imagination to that moment in time outside Jerusalem. See John trying to coax a sobbing Mary away from the hill where her son hangs, nailed to a rugged cross. Imagine the contrasting view of the great dragon, Satan himself, as he crouches invisible to the naked eye at the foot of the hill called Golgotha. He watches gleefully as the very Son of God writhes in pain—dying a sinner's death. At last the great enemy can taste the sweetness of his dark victory. As Joseph of Arimathea and a few women lower Jesus' lifeless body from the cross, we can hear Satan whisper the words the carpenter had groaned moments earlier, investing them with his own meaning this time: "It *is* finished. *I* have won now," he hisses.

The evil one must have been waiting for this moment ever since God, his archenemy, had promised Eve that he would crush the serpent's head. And now, Lucifer had seemingly killed the Author of Life, and in doing so had trapped the living God in his prison of death.

But far more than the fate of the disciples—and even Israel—hung on the cross that day. The fate of the entire human race and their hope of a bright tomorrow and of life after death hung there with him. For with the death of the Son of God, death would reign forever—or so it seemed. The great dragon must have thought he had sealed the fate of every human. "Adam's sin brought death, so death spread to everyone" (Romans 5:12).

Now the hope of the promised Messiah to free humanity from the chains of darkness seemed dashed. The supposed Savior was dead. And any hope of deliverance was being buried with him.

We can't know how much Satan understood in advance—or guessed—about God's masterful plan of salvation. But at Calvary, Satan certainly appeared victorious. And the human race seemed doomed to endure pain and anguish in this life and then to die, eternally separated from God. If Calvary had been the end of the story, then "your faith is useless, and you are still under condemnation for your sins," and "we are the most miserable people in the world" (1 Corinthians 15:17, 19).

From the disciples' perspective, Christ's death gave them no cause to be grateful; there was no call for courage and no reason for optimism. Unless . . . unless, of course, they truly believed Christ for who he said he was and what he said he would do, regardless of the dark circumstances.

Because just a few days before Christ's crucifixion, when Jesus told his followers of his impending death, he also told them how he would rise again. "Truly, you will weep and mourn over what is going to happen to me, but the world will rejoice. You will grieve, but your grief will suddenly turn to wonderful joy when you see me again. . . . I have told you all this so that you may have peace in me.

Here on earth you will have many trials and sorrows. But take heart, because I have overcome the world" (John 16:20, 33).

How has Christ overcome the world? As Son of the sovereign God, he broke the power of death and rose from the dead! "I am God," says the sovereign Lord of the universe, "and there is no one else like me. Only I can tell you what is going to happen even before it happens. Everything I plan will come to pass, for I do whatever I wish" (Isaiah 46:9-10). God was not caught off guard on that frightful day on Calvary. He knew exactly what he was doing, and he was masterfully in control.

Jesus, of course, knew that everything was under control. That's why he told his disciples: "Don't be troubled. You trust God, now trust in me" (John 14:1). Yes, he knew he was about to die, but he also knew death would have no power over him. He was appealing to them to rest their troubles in him. "Have peace in me," he said. It was as if he were saying, "I want you to know I'm in control of things. I know it won't seem like it, but trust me, no matter what, for I'm going to eventually work things out for your good and my glory. And what will seem like a disaster with my death is really for your good because it is through my atoning death that I will blot out your sins and cancel *your* death notice."

An atonement for sin was necessary for a just God to forgive our sins. The consequence of sin—death—had to be conquered in order for us to be free of its power. And Satan, who rules the kingdom of darkness, also held the power of death (see Ephesians 6:12; Hebrews 2:14). When Christ entered this world, Satan's kingdom of darkness, he did so as the spotless Lamb of God, a perfect human. He willingly took on himself all the sin and wrong of the human race (see 2 Corinthians 5:21; 1 John 2:2). The sinless God-man suffered the consequences, not of his own sin, but of ours: separation from his Father and a torturous physical death (see Matthew 27:46).

But if the deceiver thought he had won that day at Calvary, he was himself deceived. For God took an apparent disastrous Friday and turned it into Good Friday—because death had no power over the righteous Son of the sovereign God. Jesus broke the power of death by rising from the grave on the third day, and in doing so pierced the kingdom of darkness with a penetrating light. "And now [God] has made all of this plain to us by the coming of Christ Jesus, our Savior, who broke the power of death and showed us the way to everlasting life" (2 Timothy 1:10). What seemed to be the destruction of Christ and a hopeless situation proved to be the very means of the hope of eternal life.

Christ's resurrection victory over death and despair not only broke the power of death but also provided the means to receive a whole new perspective of life.

Christ's resurrection victory over death and despair not only broke the power of death for all of us who trust in Christ as Savior but also provided the means—when we believe in the resurrected Christ as sovereign—for us to receive a whole new perspective of life.

WHERE AM I GOING?

It's not hard to see now, after the fact, that God was in control of the situation of Christ's death because he raised his Son from the grave. And we can see how he took the torturous death of his Son and transformed it into the means of salvation for the human race. We could chide the disciples for not trusting in Christ enough and for not believing that Jesus knew what he was doing. But it's not so easy to exhibit that kind of trust in the midst of trials or tragedy. It's hard to have a spirit of gratitude, courage, and optimism unless, of course, you actually have deepened convictions that your loving God is sovereign and that he will, in fact, cause everything to work together for the good.

In Romans 8, the apostle Paul gives us several helpful insights. He first says, "Even we Christians, although we have the Holy Spirit within us as a foretaste of future glory, also groan to be released from pain and suffering" (Romans 8:23). So it's clear here that optimism doesn't come from denying our present pain. He then goes on to say that "the Holy Spirit helps us in our distress. . . . And we know that God causes everything to work together for the good of those who love God and are called according to his purpose for them" (Romans 8:26-28). Paul had the answer: The Holy Spirit, who lives inside each individual Christian, is there to help us as our trust is placed in a sovereign God who knows what he is doing, for he will cause everything to work together for good.

This is not a belief that says everything that happens on this death-cursed world is somehow good. Allen's sickness is not good. Death is not good. Pain is not good. Sorrow, sadness, and suffering are not good. However, by trusting in God not only as our Savior but also as our sovereign Lord who does all things well, we can be confident that he will cause all things to work together for our good and his glory. Our confidence and conviction in a God who loves us beyond words and causes all things, even tragedies, to work together for good can produce within us a spirit of gratitude, courage, and optimism in the face of life—and death.

Our confidence and conviction in a God who loves us beyond words and causes all things, even tragedies, to work together for good can produce within us a spirit of gratitude, courage, and optimism in the face of life—and death.

Faith in a sovereign God moves us beyond a human perspective on life to an eternal perspective. The apostle Paul was a living example of this eternal mind-set. Listen to his heart of gratitude as he shares his God-inspired letter to the church of Corinth. Read the words carefully. Note how the hope of the Resurrection provided him with a sense of courage and optimism, even in the most difficult of times:

We are pressed on every side by troubles, but we are not crushed and broken. We are perplexed, but we don't give up and quit. We are hunted down, but God never abandons us. We get knocked down, but we get up again and keep going. . . . We know that the same God who raised our Lord Jesus will also raise us with Jesus and present us to himself along with you. All of these things are for your benefit. . . . That is why we never give up. Though our bodies are dying, our spirits are being renewed every day. For our present troubles are quite small and won't last very long. Yet they produce for us an immeasurably great glory that will last forever! So we don't look at the troubles we can see right now; rather, we look forward to what we have not yet seen. For the troubles we see will soon be over, but the joys to come will last forever. (2 Corinthians 4:8-9, 14-18)

What an amazing approach to life's problems! Paul didn't run from difficulties or try to deny they existed to avoid the pain. He acknowledged his suffering and viewed the trials of life from an eternal perspective, knowing that the God of all comfort was there to ease his pain (see 1 Corinthians 2:3-4). He trusted in a sovereign God, who would cause everything to work together for good. Paul's faith in a God who had everything under control enabled him to see the difficulties of this life as producing "an immeasurably great glory that will last forever!"

And how could Paul say that the glory and joy will last forever? Because the ultimate good is our eternal inheritance, a guarantee of living in God's presence forever. "Now we live with a wonderful expectation," Peter said, "because Jesus Christ rose again from the dead. For God has reserved a priceless inheritance for his children" (1 Peter 1:3-4). Though we may endure pain, grief, and suffering here on earth, because Christ's death was followed by his resurrection, we can know that such things are temporary—and that much greater things await us. "For Christ must reign until he humbles all his enemies beneath his feet. And the last enemy to be destroyed is death" (1 Corinthians 15:25-26).

Because of the Resurrection, we are destined to live forever in new bodies on a new earth, an existence that will be so enjoyable that anything "we suffer now is nothing compared to the glory [God] will give us later." For we "wait anxiously for that day when God will give us our full rights as his children, including the new bodies he has promised us" (Romans 8:18, 23).

Our "priceless inheritance" is a state of being in which we will be given "full rights" and where "there will be no more death or sorrow or crying or pain. For the old world and its evils are gone forever," and "no longer will anything be cursed. For the throne of God and the Lamb will be there" (Revelation 21:4; 22:3). It is a kingdom "pure and undefiled, beyond the reach of change and decay" (1 Peter 1:4).

You and I and our young people then have the answer to where we are going in life, and in death. For we—every one of us—are *destined to have our struggles, suffering, and death transformed into blessings, joy, and eternal life.*

Christ is saying to us, "Trust me. I'm alive and in control of every situation. I will take your struggles and change them into blessings. I will take your suffering and turn it into joy. I will even take your physical death and transform it into eternal life. And how can I do that? I'm the sovereign, almighty Lord of the universe, who can do all things and who causes everything to work together for the good of those who love God and are called according to his purpose for them. So trust in me, no matter what."

Christ is saying to us, "Trust in me, no matter what."

At times, we can even see the good that comes out of adversity. You can probably point to times when God's sovereign control turned your own suffering into joy or brought honor out of hardship in your own life. He has certainly demonstrated that in my life.

HONOR OUT OF HARDSHIP

After I finished seminary, I joined Campus Crusade for Christ, hoping to become a traveling youth speaker.

At that time, it seemed that I knew no fear. I was bold and aggressive in my zeal to minister to people. But years passed, and a string of disappointing assignments brought me no closer to a ministry as a youth speaker than when I had first enlisted in Crusade. In addition, I had offended some people in leadership positions. Thus, at a time when I believed I would finally get the kind of assignment I had hoped for, one that gave me the opportunity to speak to young people, I was instead assigned to Argentina.

I was more than disappointed this time. I was nearly devastated. This latest development represented more than a delay of my hopes and plans; it felt like a setback, perhaps even a reproof. (I learned later that my feelings were at least partly accurate; the few men I had offended had agreed to send me into "exile," where I could no longer cause them problems.)

But God is sovereign, and he was already working to bring honor out of hardship. I arrived in Argentina in 1967, at a time when South American universities were hotbeds of communist activity. Brash and zealous, as always, I jumped in with both feet and went head-to-head in open debate with the revolutionaries on those campuses. I traveled beyond Argentina, to campuses in Bolivia and Chile. As a result, I was given the opportunity to taste some of the hardships Paul described in 2 Corinthians 4:8-9. During that two-year period, while attempting to establish a campus ministry in South America, my life was repeatedly threatened. I was robbed, falsely framed, and imprisoned. At times I wondered if I would ever make it home alive.

But if I'd ever doubted it, I learned then that God's "power works best in [my] weakness" (2 Corinthians 12:9). News of what God was accomplishing in South America got back to Dr. Bill

Bright. The leadership I had offended had moved on, and the new leadership asked if I would return to the United States to launch a speaking tour to university students. My hopes and dreams were about to come true.

When I returned to the United States, American universities were just beginning to undergo the kind of unrest and upheaval that I had seen and studied for two years on South American campuses. My South American experience had equipped me to understand what the revolutionaries were offering as a cultural solution to American youth and prepared me to effectively counter that with a spiritual solution. Had I relied on a human perspective, I could have seen my South American experience as nothing more than an unfair "exile." But my trust in God's sovereign control enabled me to submit to leadership, however wrong-minded they might have been, and watch as God used two years for what they truly were: a "boot camp" to bring God honor for the next twenty years of ministry. Like Joseph, I could say, "As far as I am concerned, God turned into good what [others] meant for evil" (Genesis 50:20).

WHEN WE CAN'T SEE THE GOOD

Many times it is possible to see how hardship builds us up or how a difficulty brings honor to God. But, of course, that's not always the case. All of us experience times when we are simply unable to see how tragedies and hardships are working together for any good whatsoever.

In the aftermath of the September 2001 terrorist attack on America, Dr. Billy Graham spoke at the National Cathedral in Washington, D.C., in what was called a National Day of Prayer and Remembrance. He said, "I have been asked hundreds of times in my life why God allows tragedy and suffering. I have to confess that I really do not know the answer totally, even to my own satisfaction. I have to accept, by faith, that God is sovereign, and He's a God of love and mercy and compassion in the midst of suffering."[2]

He's right, of course. None of us can completely know why God allows tragedies. The answer lies, however, in our continuing to believe with conviction that a loving sovereign Lord can cause even senseless tragedies to work together for the good of those who love God. And for those things we can never understand this side of heaven, we must remember, as the apostle Paul says, that "now we see things imperfectly as in a poor mirror, but then we will see everything with perfect clarity. All that I know now is partial and incomplete, but then I will know everything completely, just as God knows me now" (1 Corinthians 13:12).

Our young people need to come to believe that a sovereign God never loses control of things, not even at history's darkest hour, on Calvary. In fact, by his sovereign power, God raised Christ from the grave, and because of that, he will one day transform *our* earthly and decaying bodies into indestructible bodies like that of Christ's, so we can rule and reign with him in an undefiled world. With a belief in the Resurrection, we can face life's difficulties with the conviction that no matter what, "if God is for us, who can ever be against us?" (Romans 8:31). We can be assured that God has not lost control and he will not abandon us (see Romans 8:32). We can be confident that he is not punishing us or condemning us (see Romans 8:34). And we can know that he still very much loves us. "I am convinced," Paul states, "that nothing can ever separate us from his love. Death can't, and life can't. The angels can't, and the demons can't. Our fears for today, our worries about tomorrow, and even the powers of hell can't keep God's love away" (Romans 8:38). If Paul were writing to our young people today, he might express it this way: "Nothing can ever separate us from his love. The death of a loved one can't. A terminal illness can't. An abusive parent can't. Terrorism can't. War can't. Joblessness can't. Famine can't. Our fears for today, our worries about tomorrow, and even the powers of hell can't keep God's love away."

As we believe with conviction that Christ as sovereign Lord rose from the dead, our perspective on life and death can change, and we can be more than conquerors. Instead of becoming angry, resentful, or losing heart, we can live our lives in the awareness of our destiny, knowing that one day all will be put right. And we can also know that until that day, God is working everything together to transform our struggles, sufferings, and death into blessings, joys, and eventually eternal life with him.

But in order to gain that sense of destiny (and its accompanying spirit of gratitude, courage, and optimism), our kids need to be convinced of the reality of Jesus Christ's resurrection.

THE HISTORICAL NECESSITY OF THE RESURRECTION

You and I—and our kids—may believe that we are destined to have our struggles, sufferings, and death transformed into blessings, joy, and eternal life. But our destiny can become a reality only if the resurrection of Christ literally took place. In fact, Paul said that "if Christ was not raised, then all our preaching is useless, and your trust in God is useless" (1 Corinthians 15:14). Why? Because if Christ didn't actually rise from the dead, it would be a strong indication that the sacrifice for sin was unacceptable to God and that Christ had not broken the power of death. For if Jesus didn't break the power of death over his own body, how could he cancel our death sentence?

"But the fact is that Christ *has* been raised from the dead," as Paul said (1 Corinthians 15:20, emphasis mine). It is a matter of historical record that Jesus literally died and that his lifeless body was placed in a tomb, but it is equally true that three days later that lifeless body was transformed into a living spiritual body. When Jesus first appeared to his disciples in this new body, they were frightened, thinking they were seeing a spirit. But Jesus said, "See My hands and My feet, that it is I Myself; touch Me and see, for a spirit does not have flesh and bones as you see that I have" (Luke 24:39, NASB).

But Paul also pointed out that "there is an order to this resurrection: Christ was raised first; then when Christ comes back, all his people will be raised" (1 Corinthians 15:23). Scripture also teaches that planet Earth will be recreated into a new planet (see Revelation 21:1). The new planet Earth and the holy city of New Jerusalem, typically referred to as heaven described in Revelation 21, are places we will bodily inhabit. We are to live in this restored new world with literal bodies. That is why our natural bodies must be resurrected into transformed spiritual bodies like the body of the resurrected Christ.

"Our earthly bodies, which die and decay," Paul said, "will be different when they are resurrected, for they will never die. Our bodies now disappoint us, but when they are raised, they will be full of glory. They are weak now, but when they are raised, they will be full of power. They are natural human bodies now, but when they are raised, they will be spiritual bodies" (1 Corinthians 15:42-44).

However, all these great and precious promises are nothing but a fantasy, a dream, unless Christ truly rose from the dead. Christ's resurrection is a historic necessity if our destiny means anything at all. That is why believing with conviction that Christ literally rose from the dead means knowing that it is actually, factually true. That is what our kids must be convinced of—that is something of which all of us must be convinced. That is the task of the next chapter.

CHAPTER 13

The Case of the Empty Tomb

Imagine with me a scene that might have occurred a few weeks after Jesus' death and resurrection.

Elizabeth of Beersheba approached her distant relative Susanna, who sat in her yard home, preparing flat loaves of bread for the large outdoor oven. Both women had been followers of Jesus of Nazareth.

"Have you heard?" Elizabeth asked breathlessly.

"Heard?" Susanna asked, as she tossed a wad of dough onto the flat stone in front of her. "Heard what?"

"The news. The wonderful news that's spreading up and down the countryside, from Dan to Beersheba. About Y'shua, the miracle worker."

Susanna's face darkened. "Elizabeth, please," she said. "I've hardly thought of anything else these last few weeks. I'm trying to forget. Some days I don't know how I can go on. I was so sure. So sure that he was the Messiah, our deliverer. So sure that he was the answer, that he could heal my heart, broken these twelve years since my husband, Eliah, died. So sure that . . . that there was more to this life than . . . than baking and washing and making do and getting by. But I was there, Elizabeth, with the other women. I saw him die. I saw him buried." Her eyes immediately filled with tears. "And with him, all my hopes."

"But, Cousin—"

"No," Susanna said. "Let me speak. I know you have tried to think of him as a 'spiritual' Messiah, dear Elizabeth, who can still live in his teachings, as other rabbis have. But a dead Messiah is no Messiah. He said he would give us abundant life, Elizabeth. But he could not even stay alive himself. And now he is . . . gone, and we must . . . we must find a way to go on. But I don't know how."

"But that's what I'm trying to tell you, Cousin," Elizabeth protested. "There are reports that the tomb is empty."

"Empty? What do you mean, empty?"

"Empty! When Mary, Salome, and the Magdalene went to complete the burial preparations on Sunday morning, Y'shua's tomb was empty!"

"Who would do such a thing?" Susanna demanded.

"What?"

"Who would take the teacher's body? And why? And where would they put it? It just makes no sense."

"Stop interrupting, and let me tell you," Elizabeth complained. "The day you left Jerusalem, the Sabbath after Y'shua was crucified, the leading priests and Pharisees went to see Pilate and asked him to post a guard at the tomb so that no one could steal the body. The tomb was sealed that day, and guards were posted outside."

"Well, then, how can the tomb be empty?"

"That's just it," Elizabeth reported. "It has to be a miracle. The women said that an earthquake occurred and an angel appeared. The soldiers fell to the ground, but the angel showed the women the empty tomb and told them Y'shua had risen from the dead!"

"Elizabeth! You must stop this nonsense. I know you loved the teacher as much as I did, but there has to be some other explanation."

"Like what?" Elizabeth countered. "Some people are saying

that some of Y'shua's disciples came and stole the body while the soldiers were sleeping, but—"

"Ha!" Susanna said. "That's not likely! You didn't see how they scattered like rabbits after the soldiers arrested the teacher? You can't expect me to believe any of *them* suddenly became brave enough to do such a thing."

"I'm just telling you what—"

"And how could they have rolled away the stone without waking at least one of the guards? Those things take two or three strong men to move. Even if they had managed that, if the guards were sleeping, how can they—or anyone else—know who took the body? And everybody knows that the penalty for sleeping on watch is death. Have any guards been executed in Jerusalem?"

"No, I don't think so—"

"I don't think so, either," Susanna said.

"But," Elizabeth countered, "if the tomb is empty, as the women say, and the body wasn't stolen . . . what then?"

Susanna blinked at her relative. At some time during the last few minutes, she had begun to realize that if Jesus' tomb wasn't empty, the religious and political elite could end the rumors by simply producing the teacher's body and displaying it in the streets of Jerusalem. And if it *was* empty, then Elizabeth's claim of a miracle seemed far more plausible than any of the alternatives.

"What then?" Elizabeth repeated.

Susanna's response was a whisper, as if speaking the words too loudly might prevent them from being true. "That," she said, her eyes glistening with hope, "would change everything."

THE STOLEN-BODY THEORY

The evidence of an empty tomb following the crucifixion and burial of Jesus Christ does not by itself prove that Jesus rose from the dead. Yet it does require explanation. One explanation that was offered within hours of the empty tomb's discovery was the theory that the disciples of Jesus stole the body. Matthew reports:

> Some of the men who had been guarding the tomb went to the leading priests and told them what had happened. A meeting of all the religious leaders was called, and they decided to bribe the soldiers. They told the soldiers, "You must say, 'Jesus' disciples came during the night while we were sleeping, and they stole his body.' If the governor hears about it, we'll stand up for you and everything will be all right." So the guards accepted the bribe and said what they were told to say. Their story spread widely among the Jews, and they still tell it today. (Matthew 28:11-15)

The possibility that Jesus' tomb was empty because the disciples stole his body may seem plausible at first glance. However, the most cursory consideration will quickly show that the stolen-body theory creates more problems than it solves. For example:

- If the guards were sleeping, how could they know whether the disciples—or anyone—stole the body? Sleeping sentinels can't reliably report what happened while they slept.
- Roman soldiers were executed for sleeping on guard duty (which explains Matthew's report of the religious leaders telling the guards, "If the governor hears about it, we'll stand up for you and everything will be all right"). How plausible is it that all the guards at the tomb would have decided to take a nap, knowing that it could cost them their lives?
- Even if the Roman guards had slept, consider what it would have taken for thieves to remove the body from the tomb. The circular stone used to seal the tomb would have weighed between one and two tons! Thieves would have had to sneak past the guards, roll the large stone up a grooved incline, en-

ter the dark tomb, and exit with the body . . . all without waking a single member of the detachment!

The notion that the disciples stole the body while the Roman guards slept certainly strains the bounds of believability.

Whodunit?

The detachment of Roman soldiers is not the only problem with the stolen-body theory. It's also difficult to imagine the followers of Jesus as the culprits in "The Case of the Stolen Body." Consider this:

- It would have taken considerable bravery—even daring—to go up against a detachment of Roman soldiers, whether they were asleep or awake. Yet the historical record shows that the disciples, in the days following the death of Jesus, were a depressed and cowardly group, running away at the first sign of trouble, denying any association with Jesus, and cowering behind locked doors—hardly the picture of a group that would risk arrest to steal their dead teacher's body (see Mark 14:50; Luke 22:54-62; John 20:19)!
- One of the first witnesses on the scene of the empty tomb reported that Jesus' gravecloth was neatly folded and arranged on the burial slab (see John 20:5-8). Can you imagine grave robbers taking the time to meticulously unwrap the body and neatly arrange the cloth on the stone slab? On the contrary, if the body had been stolen, the burial wrappings would certainly have been removed with the body.
- According to the historical accounts, the disciples were incredulous when they heard the news of the empty tomb. From all indications, they were not expecting an empty tomb, much less plotting one.
- Why would a group of men who had run and hidden when their teacher was alive suddenly decide to courageously steal

their teacher's body and begin propagating a story that would certainly bring on them the very treatment (arrest, beatings, even death) they had fled just three days earlier?

But if the disciples did not steal the body of Jesus from his tomb, where did it go? The historical record asserts that mere weeks after the death of Jesus, his followers were publicly preaching the news of his resurrection. During the week of Pentecost, in fact, thousands were "baptized and added to the church" as a result of this preaching (Acts 2:41).

But if Jesus' body hadn't been resurrected and the religious and political leaders of the day had stolen his body, they could have quickly and effectively quashed the rising sect of Christians by wheeling Christ's corpse through the streets of Jerusalem. This would have been incontrovertible evidence that would have destroyed Christianity practically before it started. But that never happened, which further bolsters the case for the empty tomb.

The enemies of Jesus had every reason to produce his body. There's no reason to believe that the followers of Jesus could or would have stolen his body. It seems clear that subscribing to the stolen-body theory means climbing a mountain of implausibilities. In short, while "the difficulties of belief may be great," as noted author George Hanson points out in *The Resurrection and the Life*, "the absurdities of unbelief are greater."[1]

THE SWOON THEORY

Elizabeth and Susanna had packed lightly for the arduous journey to Jerusalem, but it was still slow going with the aging donkey they shared. The older Susanna rode most of the time, but walking was often a relief from the uneven plod of the donkey. The women traveled in the mornings and evenings, resting during the heat of the day.

"I try not to get my hopes up," Susanna shared during one such rest period. She tore off a piece of flat bread and handed it to Elizabeth. "But if Y'shua is alive . . ." She let the thought linger for a moment, then asked, "Do you know what that would mean, Cousin?"

Elizabeth chewed and nodded her head thoughtfully.

"It would mean," Susanna continued, "that everything the teacher said is true. It would mean that all the promises he gave us, they are true. If he is alive, . . . if he can raise himself from the dead . . ."

"Would you ask him to raise your husband?" Elizabeth asked shyly.

Susanna thought for a moment. She smiled. "Why not?" she asked. "He could do it. He could raise anyone." Susanna had been with Jesus when he called forth his friend Lazarus, who had died only days before. She suddenly remembered his words to Martha: *I am the resurrection and the life. Those who believe in me, even though they die like everyone else, will live again. They are given eternal life for believing in me and will never perish.* "He could raise *you*, Elizabeth, or me—if we died."

The two women ate in silence for a few moments, each lost in her own thoughts. Then Elizabeth spoke. "I told Lemuel," she said of her neighbor. "I told him what I had heard about Y'shua."

Susanna nodded. She could tell that Elizabeth had more to say, so she waited.

"You were there, Susanna," Elizabeth said. "You saw . . . you saw the teacher die."

Susanna searched her relative's face. "Yes," she said quietly.

"Lemuel said if Y'shua is alive," Elizabeth said, speaking slowly, "that he couldn't have died." She saw Susanna flinch as if she had just been struck. She kept speaking, quickly now, to get all her words out before Susanna could interrupt. "He said that sometimes criminals are taken down from the crosses before they're dead, and he thinks that might have happened to the teacher. He said that if Y'shua's tomb is empty, there has to be a reasonable explanation, that maybe the cool air of the tomb or the pungent spices revived him—"

"Lemuel was not there," Susanna said firmly. "I was there, Cousin." Her voice broke. "If there were the slightest chance that we could have taken our teacher from the cross before life left his body, don't you think we would have done that? Don't you think a centurion—like the one in charge of the crucifixion detail that day—knows death when he sees it? Do you think he would have allowed Y'shua to be taken from the cross if he hadn't seen water and blood flow from his side when they pierced him with a spear? Do you think he would have turned over Y'shua's body to Joseph of Arimathea if he hadn't seen the shroud of death settle on the teacher? Do you think the women would have left him in the tomb for a moment if there were a single breath left in his body?" The last words came rushing out amid tears and sobs, and Susanna covered her face with her hands.

Elizabeth reached out and hugged her relative. "I'm sorry," she cooed. "I'm so sorry. I didn't want to upset you."

Susanna buried her face in Elizabeth's shoulder then and cried. After many moments, she gathered herself enough to speak again. "It's not your fault, Cousin," she said. "I cry more often these days. Not only for the teacher but also for us . . . for fear."

"Fear?" Elizabeth echoed. "Why?"

Susanna shrugged helplessly, and her eyes took on a vacant expression. "I am afraid that . . . if the stories of the empty tomb turn out not to be true, then Jesus was truly a false messiah and we have no deliverer!"

Mostly Dead?

Some people have tried to explain the empty tomb by suggesting that Jesus never really died. The swoon theory, as it's come to be called, supposes that Jesus was indeed nailed to the cross and suffered tremendous pain and loss of blood. But when he was removed from the cross, he wasn't quite dead; he was merely in shock.

Some proponents of this view even cite the New Testament record for evidence, showing that even "Pilate couldn't believe that Jesus was already dead" (Mark 15:44). They surmise that the disciples—aided by Joseph of Arimathea—took down the still-living Jesus from the cross and laid him in the tomb (Hugh J. Schonfield, author of the book *The Passover Plot*, even suggested that Jesus *planned* all this!).

Then—so the theory goes—Jesus, aided by the cool air of the tomb, by the reviving effects of the burial spices he was wrapped in, and by a day-and-a-half of rest, rose from his own burial slab, cast off his shroud, and left the tomb. When he met his disciples, they mistakenly thought he had risen from the dead (when, in fact, it was nothing more than a surprising resuscitation).

But the swoon theory has several fatal flaws.

THE "DEATH CERTIFICATE"

Jesus had undergone a vicious beating. It was typical for Romans to use an instrument known as a flagrum, which often ripped the victim to shreds (many prisoners died before they could be executed, as a result of this scourging). Jesus was then nailed by his hands and feet to a cross.

Then, because the next day was the beginning of the Jewish Passover and Jewish law did not allow them to leave a victim hanging on the cross overnight, the religious leaders asked Pilate to hasten death by ordering that the prisoners' legs be broken (see Deuteronomy 21:22-23; John 19:31). This action usually resulted in death by asphyxiation, as the victim, unable to push up on his feet to relieve the constriction caused by the weight of his body on his lungs and breathing passages, slowly suffocated.

When the crucifixion detail came to break the legs of Jesus, however, they discovered that he was already dead. Nonetheless, to be sure, "one of the soldiers . . . pierced his side with a spear, and blood and water flowed out" (John 19:34). Soon thereafter, when Joseph of Arimathea requested custody of the body, the Roman governor expressed surprise that Jesus was already dead and demanded confirmation. *Only after receiving a firsthand report* did Pilate release the body into the hands of Joseph, thus fully verifying the fact that Jesus was dead before he was buried.

THE GRAVECLOTHS

Jesus' followers prepared his body according to Jewish burial customs. Nicodemus provided "about seventy-five pounds of embalming ointment made from myrrh and aloes. Together [Nicodemus and Joseph] wrapped Jesus' body in a long linen cloth with the spices" (John 19:39-40).

The custom was to wrap the body tightly from the armpits to the ankles, layering the spices—often of a sticky, grimy consistency—between the wrappings. The spices served a dual purpose, preserving the body and acting as an adhesive for the gravecloths. The head was also wrapped in a turban-style cloth.

Yet the historical records report that when the empty tomb was discovered on Sunday morning, the first witnesses on the scene saw "the linen wrappings lying there, while the cloth that had covered Jesus' head was folded up and lying to the side" (John 20:6-7).

Accepting the swoon theory would require us to believe that Jesus, having suffered the unspeakable torture of crucifixion, awoke in a dark tomb, maneuvered himself out of the tightly wound cloths and spices, folded the cloth, laid it on the burial slab, and exited the tomb . . . naked.

THE STONE

Not only was Jesus tightly encased in burial cloths and spices, he was also buried in a rock tomb whose entrance was blocked by a stone weighing perhaps as much as one to two tons.

Let's assume Jesus had been taken from the cross in a "swoon," and the cold, damp tomb revived him sometime later. Let's also assume that he managed to extricate himself from the unyielding encasement of his burial clothes. We must next assume that once free of those constraints, he managed—from the inside of a tomb designed to be opened only from the outside—to roll a two-ton circular stone up the slotted incline (a difficult job for several men, I would imagine), while somehow propping the stone to prevent it from rolling down again and closing the tomb. All this had to be done by a man who hours before had been flogged, pierced with a crown of thorns, hanged on a cross by nails through his hands and feet, and stabbed in the ribs with a Roman spear. And it had to be done so quietly as to escape the notice of the soldiers who were guarding the tomb, allowing him to slip away unnoticed.

THE APPEARANCES

On the same day on which Jesus supposedly resuscitated in a cold, damp, dark tomb, unwrapped himself from the gravecloths, rolled a two-ton stone uphill, and snuck by Roman sentinels guarding the tomb, he also walked more than seven miles from Jerusalem to Emmaus.

Luke 24 records Jesus' appearance to two of his followers who were on the road to Emmaus, a seven-mile trek from Jerusalem. They didn't recognize Jesus until they reached their destination and invited him to eat with them. When he broke the bread in his customary way, "their eyes were opened, and they recognized him" (Luke 24:31). Walking seven miles to Emmaus is hardly the kind of activity you would expect from a man who had been removed from an executioner's cross and laid in a tomb for more than thirty-six hours.

Yet the appearance of Jesus on the road to Emmaus is only the first in a string of appearances (within days of his brutal experience on the cross) that convinced Jesus' followers that he had defeated death and risen from the dead. As skeptic David Frederich

Strauss—himself no believer in the Resurrection—said, "It is impossible that a being who had stolen half-dead out of the sepulcher, who crept about weak and ill, wanting medical treatment . . . could have given to the disciples the impression that he was a Conqueror over death and the grave, the Prince of Life, an impression which lay at the bottom of their future ministry."[2]

THE ASCENSION

If Jesus revived from a deathlike swoon, there is no reason to believe that he later ascended into heaven, as Mark and Luke record. But if Christ didn't ascend, where did he go? Is it reasonable to believe that Jesus withdrew from his followers, to live out the rest of his life in seclusion and die in obscurity?

Such a theory would necessitate the belief that while the young church was preaching the news of Christ's resurrection, Jesus himself lived in some solitary retreat, unknown to even his closest followers, while his absence perpetuated the legend of Christianity. This scenario would make Jesus Christ—whose teachings extolled the highest standards of morality—the greatest deceiver of all time and his resurrection the greatest hoax in history.

That would require believing that Jesus knowingly pursued an insane course of action: contriving his own resurrection to gain a renown he would never witness or enjoy.

THE HALLUCINATION THEORY

"I saw him with my own eyes." Elizabeth and Susanna had finally completed their journey and were reclining in the Bethany home of Mary, Martha, and Lazarus, as Mary of Magdala told them of her eyewitness encounter with the risen Lord.

"Are you *sure*?" Susanna asked. "It's not that I don't believe you," she explained. She, like the others, knew of the Magdalene's life before she met Jesus, but Susanna had always followed the teacher's lead in treating her with the utmost respect. "But is it possible you imagined it?"

Mary was not offended. She smiled, and Susanna inferred that she had been asked the question before.

"It is fantastic, isn't it?" she said. "But you know me, Susanna. I am not given to visions and hallucinations."

"I want to be sure," Susanna whispered.

Mary nodded. "I might be tempted to wonder myself, if he had not appeared that same day to Peter and to two others. And that evening to the Eleven—except for Thomas—and then again when Thomas was with them. And after that, who knows how many more saw him?"[3]

"Tell me," Susanna begged. "I want to hear all about it."

Mary smiled and agreed. She told her visitors about the discovery of the empty tomb, the words of the angel, and her encounter with the risen Jesus, whom she had at first mistaken for a gardener. When she finished, Susanna and Elizabeth both stared at her, tears on their faces.

"It's . . . it's true, then?" Susanna asked shyly.

Mary smiled again, indulgently. She nodded. "It's true."

And then Susanna sobbed, weeping openly and unashamedly. Elizabeth held her as she cried, and it was a long time before anyone spoke.

"It's so wonderful," Susanna confessed finally. "It . . . it . . ."

"It changes everything," Mary said, finishing her friend's sentence.

Seeing Things?

There are only so many ways to explain the empty tomb. If the body wasn't stolen and hidden away and if Jesus didn't swoon and then resuscitate, what else could possibly have happened? Another explanation that has been offered is the hallucination theory.

This theory suggests that those who "saw" Jesus Christ after his death and burial were actually hallucinating. They may have *thought* they saw Jesus alive, but such appearances were the results of hallucination or the power of suggestion.

Hallucinations do occur. People are often mistaken, even deluded, about the things they see or experience. However, there are certain patterns to the experience of delusions and hallucinations. They are highly individualized and extremely subjective. It is exceedingly rare for two persons to experience hallucinations simultaneously.

But the accounts of Jesus' resurrection appearances do not bear the marks of a hallucination. They occurred at disparate times. The witnesses were not expecting an appearance and were often puzzled or skeptical at first (see Luke 24:16; John 20:14, 24-25). Most appearances were to groups of people (see Mark 16:14-18; John 21:1-24; 1 Corinthians 15:6). He appeared at least ten different times following his resurrection:

1. to Mary of Magdala (Mark 16:9; John 20:11-18);
2. to the women returning from the tomb (Matthew 28:9-10);
3. to Peter (Luke 24:34; 1 Corinthians 15:5);
4. to two followers on the road to Emmaus (Luke 24:13-33);
5. to the disciples and a number of others (Luke 24:36-43);
6. to the disciples, including Thomas (John 20:26-29);
7. to seven disciples by the Sea of Galilee (John 21:1-23);
8. to more than five hundred followers (1 Corinthians 15:6);
9. to James, his brother (1 Corinthians 15:7);
10. to the eleven disciples at his ascension (Acts 1:4-9).

Another factor that argues against the hallucination theory is the record of Jesus' invitations to verify his flesh-and-blood presence with them:

Look at my hands. Look at my feet. You can see that it's really me. Touch me and make sure that I am not a ghost, because ghosts don't have bodies, as you see that I do! . . . Then he asked them, "Do you have anything here to eat?" They gave him a piece of broiled fish, and he ate it as they watched. (Luke 24:39-43)

The people who saw Jesus were not the kind of people most likely to suffer delusions. They were a skeptical bunch, who were often slow to believe. When the women came that Sunday morning with the first news of the empty tomb to the apostles, "the story sounded like nonsense, so they didn't believe it" (Luke 24:11). Peter and John's first reaction was to race to the site themselves, to see with their own eyes what the women had reported. And Thomas could not have been the victim of wishful thinking. "I won't believe it," he vowed, "unless I see the nail wounds in his hands, put my fingers into them, and place my hand into the wound in his side" (John 20:25).

The hallucination theory—like the swoon theory and the stolen-body theory—doesn't stack up against the historical record. Like the other attempts at explanation, it seems to require more faith than it does to believe the testimony of the eyewitnesses: that "during the forty days after his crucifixion, [Jesus] appeared to the apostles from time to time and proved to them in many ways that he was actually alive" (Acts 1:3).

THE TRUE FAITH

The resurrection of Jesus Christ from the dead—and his appearances to more than five hundred of his followers—changed forever the lives of those men and women . . . and millions since.

When those first disciples watched their Master and Lord die on a cross, all their hopes seemed to come crashing to the ground.

Their hopes revived when their Lord returned from the dead. But even then, it seems, they misunderstood the full import of Jesus' resurrection.

"Lord, are you going to free Israel now and restore our kingdom?" they asked him (Acts 1:6). Even after Jesus had risen victoriously from the grave, they still looked for a temporal kingdom and political deliverance from their oppressors. It wasn't until the Day of Pentecost and the indwelling presence of God's Spirit that the disciples understood what God had planned for them.

They, like most of us, couldn't really answer the most fundamental questions of life: Who am I? Why am I here? and Where am I going? But through the miraculous revelation of God it is now revealed. The apostle Paul made it succinctly plain in the first chapter of his letter to the Ephesians:

> Long ago, even before he made the world, God loved us and chose us in Christ to be holy and without fault in his eyes [our purpose]. His unchanging plan has always been to adopt us into his own family. . . . We belong to his dearly loved Son [our identity]. . . . And this is his plan: At the right time he will bring everything together under the authority of Christ—everything in heaven and on earth. Furthermore, because of Christ, we have received an inheritance from God, for he chose us from the beginning, and all things happen just as he decided long ago [our destiny]. (Ephesians 1:4-11, bracketed phrases added)

What is God saying to each of us through his incarnation, reliable Word, and bodily resurrection of his Son? And what does that all mean for you and me and our young people who believe in Christ and his Word with conviction?

1. God Wants a Relationship with Us

As aliens, separated from God, we were all adrift, without a sense of connection, not knowing who we really were. Yet Christ entered our world as the Incarnate One and revealed to us our true identity, an identity that had been lost due to sin and death. He adopted us back into his family, so that each of us can have a personal relationship with him and truly say, *"I know who I am: God's chosen child who loves him and others as only I can."*

2. God Wants Us to Know Him and Be like Him

God's Holy Spirit inhabited our very lives and as a personal "truth guide" began leading us through the relational revelation of God's reliable Word. And for what purpose? So we could know God better as his divine power transforms us more and more into the family image of his Son. We no longer live a self-serving life with actions that disgrace ourselves and our families. Rather, we live lives that are pleasing to God. No longer aimless, without a clear purpose, we gain that sense of completeness so each of us can say, *"I know why I'm here: to know God and become more like him."*

3. God Wants Us to Trust Him, No Matter What

Because he lives, we can face tomorrow—not with uncertainty, anger, or pessimism, but with a sense of destiny, confident that our risen Savior and sovereign God causes all things to work together for our good and his glory. And without a doubt each of us can say, *"I know where I'm going: destined to have my struggles, sufferings, and death transformed into blessings, joys, and eternal life."*

This kind of faith with deepened convictions in Christ and his Word results in a personal identity, sense of purpose, and eternal perspective that can help us face whatever comes our way, knowing that we are children of a King, being readied to inherit a kingdom not of this world. The writer of Hebrews recounted people of such faith and said that they "overthrew kingdoms, ruled with justice, and received what God had promised them. They shut the mouths of lions, quenched the flames of fire, and escaped death by the edge of the sword. Their weakness was turned to strength. They became strong in battle and put whole armies to flight. Women received their loved ones back again from death" (Hebrews 11:33-35).

That kind of victory is preferred, perhaps, but it is no less victorious than when we encounter oppression, mistreatment, or even death. For the writer of Hebrews goes on to say:

> Others trusted God and were tortured, preferring to die rather than turn from God and be free. They placed their hope in the resurrection to a better life. Some were mocked, and their backs were cut open with whips. Others were chained in dungeons. Some died by stoning, and some were sawed in half; others were killed with the sword. Some went about in skins of sheep and goats, hungry and oppressed and mistreated. They were too good for this world. They wandered over deserts and mountains, hiding in caves and holes in the ground.
>
> All of these people we have mentioned received God's approval because of their faith, yet none of them received all that God had promised. For God had far better things in mind for us that would also benefit them, for they can't receive the prize at the end of the race until we finish the race. (Hebrews 11:35-40)

God has a crown for you and me and our young people when we finish the race. But the race is not over. "So be truly glad!" Peter said. "There is wonderful joy ahead, even though it is necessary for you to endure many trials for a while" (1 Peter 1:6). We are here for a while longer, and God has an additional reason for keeping us in the race, a reason many people have misunderstood. But when we understand that reason, we will have discovered our sense of mission, as well as our true identity, purpose, and destiny.

CHAPTER 14

Our Mission in Life

"Thanks, guys, for meeting with me again like this," Allen said as he took off his jacket.

Duane motioned toward the family room. "It's our honor, Allen."

"These times together," interjected Liz, "are helping us as much as they're helping you—maybe even more."

The trio got comfortably seated, and Duane began.

"How have you been holding up?" he asked.

"Pretty well, actually," Allen replied. "The doctor has Dad on medication for his nerves, and Mom's getting help from a counselor at church. That's helped. I guess we're all hanging in there."

"Well," Liz said, "we've sure been praying for you guys."

"Thanks," Allen said. "I'm sure that helps even more."

"Have you had a chance to go over those Scripture passages I gave you?" Duane asked, shifting in his chair.

"Yeah, I did," Allen said, "and a couple of them really jumped out at me. I'm not sure if I understand it or not, but if they mean what I think they do—then whoa!"

"What passages are you talking about?" Liz asked.

"Well, first, this one in 2 Corinthians 4," Allen said, turning the pages of his Bible. "I'm not sure I understand verse 10. It says—"

"Why don't you read the whole paragraph," Duane said. "That way we all get a better context for verse 10."

"Okay," Allen said. "Let's see, I'll try starting at verse 8. 'We are pressed on every side by troubles, but we are not crushed and broken. We are perplexed, but we don't give up and quit. We are hunted down, but God never abandons us. We get knocked down, but we get up again and keep going.' And here's the verse I'm wondering about: 'Through suffering, these bodies of ours constantly share in the death of Jesus so that the life of Jesus may also be seen in our bodies.' What does that mean?"

"Read the next two verses," Duane said.

Allen continued reading. "'Yes, we live under constant danger of death because we serve Jesus, so that the life of Jesus will be obvious in our dying bodies. So we live in the face of death, but it has resulted in eternal life for you.'" Allen paused and looked up. "Okay, maybe I *do* get it. The way Paul responded to all his suffering and the bad things that happened to him somehow showed people what Jesus was like, right? And when they saw Christ in his life, they wanted to trust in him, right?"

"Exactly," Duane said. "Paul was a living example of Christ. People saw how he suffered, but through it all, they saw him suffer with this Christlike spirit coming through him, and that drew them to Christ."

"Look at verses 14 and 15," Liz interjected. "'We know that the same God who raised our Lord Jesus will also raise us with Jesus and present us to himself along with you. All of these things are for your benefit. And as God's grace brings more and more people to Christ, there will be great thanksgiving, and God will receive more and more glory.' Do you see that?" Her eyes danced with excitement. "Paul's belief in the resurrection enabled him to look beyond his suffering and see how God was using that suffering to win people to Christ, and that gave God glory."

"Do you think," Allen began, "that God could use my sickness, then, to get glory or something? Like, maybe my disease could end up bringing more people to Christ?"

"I think that's exactly what God could do," Duane responded. "No, on second thought, I think that's exactly what God *wants* to do!"

MISSION CENTRAL

"We are looking forward to the new heavens and new earth he has promised," the apostle Peter said, "a world where everyone is right with God. And so, dear friends, while you are waiting for these things to happen, make every effort to live a pure and blameless life. And be at peace with God. And remember, the Lord is waiting so that people have time to be saved" (2 Peter 3:13-15). We may be waiting to live on a brand-new earth, but that new earth isn't here yet. And the Lord may be waiting to usher in that final day so that those around us still have time to believe in him. But God wants our pure and blameless lives involved in that special mission.

"God has given us the task [or mission] of reconciling people to him" (2 Corinthians 5:18). During the years of Jesus' life on earth, "God was in Christ, reconciling the world to himself" (2 Corinthians 5:19). Now, Christ is in us, and Paul says that God "has committed to us the message of reconciliation. We are therefore Christ's ambassadors, as though God were making his appeal through us" (2 Corinthians 5:19-20, NIV). He wants to involve us in his ministry of drawing people to him by the attitudes we have, the things we say, and the way we act—especially in times of adversity and trouble.

God did not cause Allen's terminal illness. There is nothing good about it. But God is also not blindsided by our suffering or Allen's. Our sovereign God causes all of our circumstances to work together for good. As we make Christ more and more at home in our lives, the gracious, long-suffering Spirit of God can be seen in our suffering. And in those circumstances, people clearly see Christ.

Paul says, "We try to live in such a way that no one will be hindered from finding the Lord by the way we act" (2 Corinthians 6:3). God not only helps us fulfill our purpose by making us more and more like Christ but also draws people to himself through *us!* Because "if we love each other, God lives in us, and his love has been brought to full expression through us" (1 John 4:12).

We often seem to fulfill that mission most effectively when we are enduring times of crisis, suffering, or persecution. Nearly all of us can exhibit love, joy, peace, patience, and so on when the wind is at our back and we're sailing high. But how many people display gratitude, courage, and optimism in the midst of a storm? That is when people sit up and take notice: when tragedy strikes, when you're hurting, when you're mistreated.

Think of the trials, struggles, or suffering you may be going through right now. It's not a sin to feel discouraged or frustrated with the tests of life. But can you sense how God wants to be there for you with his love, support, and comfort? What gives him pleasure is to fill you so completely with an abundance of his joy and blessing during your difficulties that you actually become grateful for the trials you're experiencing. And when people see how courageous and optimistic you are during your troubled times, they will be drawn to Christ.

When people see how courageous and optimistic you are during your troubled times, they will be drawn to Christ.

Imagine telling your kids or class or youth group to be especially encouraged when trouble strikes or problems come their way. Imagine explaining to them that it is during those times that they have been assigned a mission, if they are willing to accept it—a mission to exhibit a Christlike spirit and share the love of Christ with those around them.

Sharing Christ with others doesn't have to be thought of as a chore or obligation. It is an opportunity to reveal Christ through our lives to others. It does require, however, a basic understanding of what to say and how to share a simple presentation of the gospel. But once that is learned, it's a matter of developing a lifestyle of being a walking example of Christ. To help you and your church fulfill your mission, we have prepared additional resources to serve as an outreach extension of moving your youth and adults alike beyond belief to conviction. These will aid you in naturally developing a great commission mentality among your youth and church (see appendix A).

Duane and Liz are helping Allen to grasp the idea that God can use Allen's suffering for good purposes. He has endured one crushing blow after another—first his sister's death, and now his own diagnosis. But such trying times give him an opportunity to glorify God through his life and fulfill his own mission. It is during such times of trial that all of us can most forcefully demonstrate to a watching world that we belong to another kingdom.

A GREAT HARVEST

It had been more than a month since Allen had learned of his terminal illness. Duane, having just completed the youth-group series on the resurrection of Christ, looked around the room. He felt good about the group's reaction to all that had been shared concerning our convictions about the reality and meaning of the Resurrection and how that provided us with a sense of destiny. He thought most of the young people had also grasped his explanation of how our new perspective on life equips us to handle tragedy and tough times, and how God uses that in our mission as God's ambassadors.

But it was the next moment that Duane had been awaiting all night.

"Allen has asked my permission to share something with everyone," Duane explained, "and I've agreed. So please give him your attention as he tells you what's on his heart and mind."

Allen began, "All this stuff we've been doing since Christmas—the Incarnation Celebration, then the Revelation Celebration, now the Resurrection—has been great, but I have to confess something to you.

"I started to struggle with it all when I found out that I have Fanconi anemia, too. I didn't really get mad at God or anything, but none of it made sense. I mean, the fact is I'm not going to live long."

Every gaze in the room was riveted to Allen's face as he spoke. Everyone listened intently.

"I started thinking about all that, and really began to feel sorry for myself. I got pretty low emotionally. But something started to change a few weeks ago. I felt like God started to reveal himself to me in his Word as the God who causes everything to work together for good. I told God that I couldn't see any good coming out of the stuff that was happening in my life, but since *he could*, I told him I wanted him to use whatever life I had left for his glory. And that's when it happened—my whole attitude began to change."

Allen glanced at the friend who had come with him to youth group that evening. He nodded in his direction as he spoke.

"Kevin was pretty much the first person to notice the change that started in me. We've been pretty close friends for a while, now, and he knew how hard I'd been taking things. And when he saw me change, he asked me what was up. So we started talking. I just told him everything, and it wasn't long before he said he wanted to know the same Jesus I did." Allen paused and smiled at Kevin, then turned to the group. "So I told him how, and he became a Christian!"

The group erupted into wild clapping and cheering. Some of them surrounded Kevin, and others mobbed Allen. An impromptu celebration ensued. Finally, Duane quieted the group and asked them to take their seats again.

"Before we end our meeting," Duane said, "I've got something to run by you. Pastor Milford asked me a few days ago if I thought the youth could put together some sort of program for Easter."

Several heads nodded, and a couple people audibly expressed their enthusiasm. Duane held up his hands.

"Well, kill me if you want to, but I told him I didn't think there was enough time. There are only six weeks to Easter, and we've got several other things going on."

"We could do it!" Megan insisted. Several others agreed.

"Just slow down, okay? I'm saying that it would be really hard. But if several key people would agree to work really hard at it—like you, Megan—I think it would be exciting to take everything we've been learning and put it into a play or something to present to the whole church. Maybe we can invite our friends and maybe even duplicate what Allen and Kevin have each experienced." He paused, and the room was strangely quiet. "What do you think?"

"I think it's a great idea!" Megan said. "And I'm willing to work as hard as I have to!"

Several others agreed, and Liz passed around a pen and paper for people to write down how they were willing to help.

"I'm not promising," Duane said. "But if I think we can do it, I'll tell the pastor, okay?"

THE RESURRECTION CELEBRATION PLAY

Megan exited the stage and gripped Lauren by the shoulders.

"Isn't this great?" she said. It was the Saturday night of Easter weekend, and the kids in the youth group had just completed the first of four acts in their program—to a packed house. Act 1, titled "The Garden," had depicted the disobedience of Adam and Eve, and how they had rebelled against God's sovereignty by "deciding" what was right for them or wrong for them. The act concluded by portraying God's heartbreak at seeing his children separated from his presence and how that separation would cause pain, suffering, anguish—and death—for the whole human race. A CD played mournful music in a minor key over the loudspeakers as the actors exited the stage.

After a few minutes the curtains parted again to reveal a nativity scene silhouetted in blue light behind a gauzy screen. To one side of the scene, separate from the others, crouched a hooded, dark figure. Suddenly a deep voice reverberated through the auditorium loudspeakers, startling some in the audience, who nevertheless kept their eyes fastened on the scene behind the screen.

"From the moment the Incarnate Son of God appeared on earth, his enemy Satan plotted against the virgin-born God-man, reasoning that God's plan to reverse the curse of sin and death could be thwarted—if Jesus of Nazareth could be destroyed."

The light behind the nativity scene faded slowly, and a light at center stage illuminated another tableau: a single robed figure, whom most in the audience immediately recognized as Jesus. Suddenly the hooded figure from the first tableau entered the scene and began to interact with the Jesus figure, reenacting the temptation in the wilderness.

"Satan's attacks intensified throughout Jesus' earthly life," the narrator said. The two figures engaged in a dialogue, using the scriptural account of Satan's tempting Jesus. The narrator continued: "But Satan's attacks failed. Jesus faced every trick and temptation the devil could devise, yet Christ did not sin. But still the battle continued—until the very last day of Jesus' life."

The scene changed again, and a third tableau was backlit on the right-hand side of the stage. A young man and three young women, dressed in first-century-style robes, struggled together to lower a body from a cross. "Satan crouched at the foot of the hill called Golgotha," the narrator's voice intoned, as the hooded figure appeared again and spoke of his victory of killing the Son of God.

The lighting on stage changed slowly from blue to a deep, dark red. The four figures lifted the limp form of Jesus in their arms and slowly left the stage in a dolorous procession, led like a drum major by the dancing, hooded figure of Evil himself.

"With that single victory," the narrator's voice continued, "the great dragon sealed the fate of every human soul. The people had hoped for the promised Messiah to free them from the chains of darkness. But that hope was being buried with Christ, the Son of the living God. Their hope was gone; their fate was sealed. Their slavery to death would now surely be eternal!"

The curtains closed. The audience sat, silent, stunned.

The stage curtains pulled back once again, and act 3, "The Great Conflict," commenced. The scene was a courtroom. A judge sat behind a towering desk, the prosecution table to his right, and the defense table on his left. Brent, wearing the now-familiar hood identifying him as Satan, stood at the prosecution table, while Jason sat alone at the defense table.

The Satan figure stood. "Your . . . *Honor,*" he sneered in the direction of the judge. "I know I don't have to tell you all the sins the accused has committed. His sins of adultery alone should be enough to convict him. Exhibit A details the times and dates the accused lusted after women—65,243 of them. Topping it all off, of course, are the occasions, marked in red, when, beginning in July 19—"

"All right, all right," Jason interrupted. "That's enough."

"How do you plead?" the judge asked.

"I guess I'm guilty, Your Honor, but . . . I do have a defense."

"Proceed," the judge said with a nod.

"It really wasn't my fault," Jason said. "My secretary was a lonely woman, and what I did was out of a heart of compassion. You see, she was abused by her husband, and someone had to comfort her. I was there, and . . ."

"Immaterial!" Satan snapped. "It doesn't matter why, or how,

Your Honor. This man's a sinner." He lifted a ream of paper into the air and shook it. "And the law says, 'The soul who sins will die.'"[1]

"I . . . I may be a sinner, but . . . ," the accused stammered.

"I rest my case, Your Honor," Satan said. "He has no defense. You have no alternative but to administer justice . . . and hand down a sentence of death."

"It is written," the judge said, certainty and sadness mingling in his voice. "The wages of sin is death."[2] He banged the gavel on his desk, and Jason was dragged from the stage, slumped and sobbing bitterly, by two uniformed guards. Satan followed, hissing at him all the way.

Suddenly Jennifer appeared at the defense table, her head lowered as if in shame.

The judge lifted a sheet from in front of him. "Case number 2308947," he read, shaking his head sadly. "Your name is Jennifer. How do you plead?"

"Innocent, Your Honor," she answered.

"Innocent?" the accuser sneered. He lifted another thick sheaf of papers and waved it in the air. "You're wasting the court's time!"

"I really do have a solid defense, Your Honor," she said.

"Proceed," the judge said.

"I know you are a fair and just judge," she said. "So I offer here all the good I have done throughout my life as a defense." Three students entered, carrying large notebooks filled with paper. "I have compiled my noble deeds of kindness. I have recorded how I helped my fellow students, gave of my time and some money to ease the suffering of others, and even made my bed . . . twice." She smiled sheepishly, then continued. "So, you see, my good deeds outweigh the bad things I've done."

"Immaterial!" Satan shouted. He faced Jennifer. "It doesn't matter how much good you've done, you're still *mine*!"

"No, I'm not," Jennifer objected.

"Are you the daughter of Jerry and Cindy Brown?" Satan asked.

"Yes," she answered. "What's that got to do with anything?"

"Everything!" Satan snapped. He spoke to the judge without taking his eyes off the young woman. "Your Honor, I appeal to the words of the court: 'Sin entered the world through one man, and death through sin, and in this way death came to all men, because all sinned.'"³ He pointed to Jennifer. "Good deeds can't erase your sin, and nothing you can do will commute your death sentence! I rest my case," he said, and sat down, exuding confidence.

The judge addressed the accused. "Do you have anything else to say in your defense?"

Jennifer, obviously shaken, shook her head.

The judge paused for a moment, then spoke. "It is written," he said. "'Cursed is everyone who does not observe and obey *all* these commands that are written in God's Book of the Law.'"⁴ Moving slowly, he banged the gavel on his desk, and Jennifer was dragged from the stage, just as Jason had been.

Even before Jennifer was gone, Megan appeared at the defense table. The judge sighed and looked at a new sheet of paper.

"How do you plead?" the judge asked.

"Innocent," Megan declared.

"Judge," Satan said, "this is getting tiresome. This one is no different from—"

The judge held up a hand, silencing the accuser. He addressed the defendant: "What is your defense?"

"I have no claim on grace," Megan began, her words no mere recitation but sincere and filled with meaning. "I have no right to plead innocence. I stand before my maker's face, condemned in thought and deed."

"Yes, exactly!" Satan said.

"But," Megan continued, "since the guiltless Lamb of God died on my behalf, I claim him as my substitute. He is my defense."

Suddenly Allen, bearded and dressed in a white robe to represent Jesus, entered the stage.

"You!" Satan screeched. "You . . . you died, like all the rest. You were buried. I saw it! A dead savior is powerless to break the chains of sin. You cannot break out of my prison of death!"

Jesus faced him with confidence. "You speak truth, but only part of it, as usual. Though I took on me the guilt of every human's sin, death could not hold me, for I did not sin.[5] I rose from the grave, conquering sin and death—" he pointed to Megan—"for her."

"Impossible!" Satan shouted and whirled around to face the judge. "You can't allow this!"

"You have there a record of her sins?" the judge asked.

"Yes, they are all here!" Satan said emphatically.

"Read them," the judge ordered.

The accuser lifted the notebook and began turning the pages, slowly at first, then faster and faster. "I . . . I don't understand. They were *here*! They were all here! Someone has erased them. It was you!" Satan pointed a finger at Jesus. "You tricked me!"

Jesus turned to the judge. "This is no trick, Father. You sent me, your Son, to earth—the prince of the kingdom of light and life entered the kingdom of darkness and death. I lived and died as a human being, shedding my blood on behalf of Megan Wagner. Her sins were buried with me. And because she has accepted me as her offering for sin and trusts in me for deliverance, I am now here— risen from the dead—to plead her case!"

The judge focused his gaze on Megan. "It is written, 'For Christ died for sins once for all, the righteous for the unrighteous, to bring you to God. He was put to death in the body but made alive by the Spirit.'[6] Christ has lived on earth in human form, died for this soul and has risen from the grave. The sentence of death . . . is canceled." He slammed the gavel on the desk.

Jesus extended a hand in Megan's direction. "Come, you who are blessed by my Father," he said. "[Inherit] the kingdom prepared for you since the creation of the world."[7]

As Megan took the hand of Jesus, the curtains closed and majestic music filled the auditorium. The narrator's voice reverberated throughout the place. "The Spirit and the bride say, 'Come.' Let each one who hears them say, 'Come.' For everything God gives to his Son, Christ, is ours, too."[8]

Duane stepped onto the stage and issued an invitation in what many church members later said was the clearest, most straightforward presentation of the gospel they had ever heard. Even before he finished, people began to stream forward, among them many young people who had seen and observed the changes in Allen's, Megan's, and Lauren's lives.

Thirty minutes after the final benediction, the youth group, their parents, and the new believers were still mingling and rejoicing over what God had accomplished that night, confident that in less than twelve hours they would have an Easter sunrise service the likes of which had never been seen in the history of Westcastle Community Church.

• • • • •

Teachable Moments

The Westcastle youth group came a long way in our story, and it's my hope that all of us have, too, as we've discovered together how the resurrection of Christ is both objectively true and relationally meaningful to our lives. Following are some practical examples of how you can convey the truth of Christ's resurrection with the young people in your life. The resurrected Christ wants us to trust in him no matter what and live our lives believing he is in control of our circumstances.

Why Do They Call It Good Friday?

Use Easter as an ideal opportunity to put Christ's resurrection in the context of God's sovereignty. Ask your kids why people refer to the Friday before Easter as "Good Friday." Say something like: "Shouldn't it be called 'Bad Friday'? Certainly crucifying Jesus wasn't good, and Jesus' suffering such a cruel death wasn't good. So why call it Good Friday?"

After discussion explain: "It is a Good Friday because God is in the business of turning bad things into good. In Romans 8:28 it says, 'God causes everything [even the death of his only Son] to work together for the good of those who love God.' Through Christ's death and resurrection, he purchased our salvation and we can have a relationship with him forever—and that's good!"

Put Death in an Eternal Perspective

Take the opportunity with older children to discuss death, perhaps when a loved one dies. Say something like, "Death is sad because we have lost a loved one. It's natural for us to grieve. And we have God and others to grieve with us and comfort us. Yet someday grieving will be over, and there will be no more death because Christ rose from the grave and will one day destroy death entirely. When our risen Lord returns to earth, he will make everything new and transform these bodies of ours into new ones so we can live with him forever. Then there will be no more death or sorrow or crying or pain."[9]

When Life Makes No Sense

At some point your children or young people may face serious troubles, not of their doing. Or maybe they will be confronted with a tragedy in which life seems to make no sense. First and foremost they need to know you are there for them to love them and comfort them. Yet they also need to realize God is there and that he still loves them and hasn't lost control. After a time of one-on-one comforting (identifying with their grief or trouble) and when the time is right, say something like: "When difficult things happen and when life doesn't seem to make sense, I'm reminded of Christ's resurrection and what it means. Because we serve a risen Christ, he is saying 'Trust me, I'm alive and in control of your life. I will cause everything to work together for good, even when you can't see how any good can come out of your troubles.'"

Consider reading the following verses to them:

We are pressed on every side by troubles, but we are not crushed and broken. We are perplexed, but we don't give up and quit. We are hunted down, but God never abandons us. We get knocked down, but we get up again and keep going. . . . We know that the same God who raised our Lord Jesus will also raise us with Jesus and present us to himself along with you. All of these things are for your benefit. . . . That is why we never give up. Though our bodies are dying, our spirits are being renewed every day. For our present troubles are quite small and won't last very long. Yet they produce for us an immeasurably great glory that will last forever! So we don't look at the troubles we can see right now; rather, we look forward to what we have not yet seen. For the troubles we see will soon be over, but the joys to come will last forever. (2 Corinthians 4:8-9, 14-18)

●　●　●　●　●

THE REST OF THE STORY

As we discovered in this chapter, we all have a mission in life to be a living testimony of how Christ can transform a life and form a vital relationship with a person. That's the rest of my father's story.

I told you earlier how his life was changed, radically, right before my eyes, as if someone had reached down and switched on a light inside him. He was infused with a sense of identity, purpose, and destiny that was so intoxicating, he touched alcohol only once after that. He got the drink as far as his lips, and that was it. After forty years of drinking, he didn't need it anymore.

But with his new life came a thrilling awareness of his mission. He lived only fourteen months after he came to faith in Christ, eventually dying from complications that arose from his alcoholism. But even in that short time, he fulfilled his mission better than many who live decades after coming to Christ.

In spite of his deteriorating physical condition—or, perhaps because of it—he played a role in helping more than a hundred people in the area around my tiny hometown commit their lives to Christ . . . because they saw the town drunk, my dad, being transformed into Christ's image.

Not even the gates of hell can prevail against one of God's children who develops that kind of conviction and experiences his or her identity, purpose, and destiny in life. And with that said, what's next? What can you do to strengthen your own faith and get started moving young people beyond belief to conviction? We have provided you with a lot of content. We hope it has been simple and straightforward.

What steps can you take now to have an impact on your own kids, your own family? How can you motivate your entire church to launch a church- and family-wide Beyond Belief to Convictions initiative? In the next chapter, we will offer practical and specific steps you can take in your family, church, church school, denomination, or Christian college to begin the exciting process of igniting a generation to live as "children of God without fault in a crooked and depraved generation, in which [they] shine like stars in the universe" (Philippians 2:15, NIV).

PART FIVE

TAKING THE NEXT STEP

CHAPTER 15

You Can Make a Difference

The alarm has been sounded.

We may lose an entire generation. Throughout the pages of this book, we've tried to show not only that our young people have distorted beliefs about God, truth, and reality but also that those distortions will certainly—and soon—steer their lives down the paths of misery and heartache. That's the bad news.

The good news is that you have a rare opportunity to reclaim this generation. You can help young people move beyond belief to conviction, empowering them to stand strong in the face of today's culture. You can pass on your legacy of faith.

The challenge is clear.

I hope that these pages have helped you to better understand that the only way we can correct a generation's distorted beliefs is by sharing the real truth—that our beliefs about God are based on what is objectively true and that a relationship with him is the key to unlocking the meaning of life. I trust that you have also had a fresh reminder of how passionate God is about his relationship with you, personally. And I pray that you have grasped a fresh way to share the Person of Truth with those around you. Are you ready to begin?

The time is now.

WE LOSE WHAT WE DON'T USE

In the past four decades I have spoken at thousands of events. I have devoted my life to motivating and challenging people to address cultural issues with biblically relevant solutions. But I learned many years ago what often happens when people are inspired by a speaker or challenged to take action after reading a book: More often than not, the inspiration fades within hours, and the challenge can easily go unheeded. It happens to me all the time. I can come away from a moving service inspired by what was said, but forty-eight hours later I may barely recall the main points of the talk. Or I can read a challenging book, and days later realize I absorbed very little of its excellent message. Why? How is it that we can read a potentially life-changing message, gain apparent insight, yet ten, twenty, thirty days later, it so quickly and easily eludes us?

The principle is this: *We lose what we don't use!* Unless we can somehow translate inspiration into practical living and transform a challenge into changed behavior, the most moving message will never become part of our lives. It will fade unless we immediately put it into practice. That is why we want to go beyond just *encouraging* you to present Christ as real and relevant to your young people to actually *empowering* you to do it!

It is my sincere prayer that you have been inspired by what you have read in this book. But we fully understand if you are still looking for that "handle" to help you lead your young people to deepened convictions. And we would miss the mark if we didn't offer you empowering resources that will enable you to accomplish that mission. Without easy-to-use resources, the majority of us may struggle to communicate a real and relevant Christ to a postmodern culture. That is why we have created over a dozen resources for the church, the home, and the school.

EMPOWERING RESOURCES FOR YOUR CHURCH

The first step we encourage you to take is to share the Beyond Belief vision with your church leadership. This is critical because leading a person to deepened convictions about Christ and his Word is to a great extent the result of a group dynamic. When the leader of a children's church, youth group, or small group has the right resources, he or she will be empowered to help each student grapple with correct beliefs about Christ and his Word, translating those beliefs into changed behavior. That's why we have developed empowering church resources in every age group: *to equip young people in this generation to become so thoroughly convinced in the reality and relevance of Jesus Christ and his Word that they act on their Christian convictions regardless of the consequences.* (See appendix A.)

You and your church have the opportunity to launch a congregation-wide emphasis for every family and age group that will ground each person in the Christian faith as perhaps never before. These resources are far more than a "Christianity 101" course in what we believe and why we believe it; they also include an evangelistic component. Your youth and adult groups will be challenged to invite their nonchurched friends to a nonthreatening series that will answer their deepest questions about the meaning of life: "Who am I?" "Why am I here?" and "Where am I going?" As a group, you will be able to demonstrate to a relationally needy generation of young people that the God of creation is passionate about a relationship with them and has gone to extraordinary lengths to make that relational connection.

EMPOWERING RESOURCES FOR YOUR FAMILY

The primary responsibility of training up a child to believe in Christ and his Word (and to teach why we believe what we believe) belongs to parents. And if there was ever a time when parents desperately needed empowering tools to help them in the task of leading their children to deepened convictions, it is today. That is why we have developed an array of resources for the home and family.

The Beyond Belief family of products also features resources that will prepare parents to go home and lead their preschool, elementary age, or teenage children through a step-by-step process that will give them a clear understanding of the foundation of the Christian faith and how to stand strong in the face of today's culture. Taking advantage of these empowering resources will help parents guide a child or teenager to a life-changing encounter with Christ, a personal discovery of who God is, and an understanding of how trusting in him will unlock the very meaning of life. (See appendix A.)

EMPOWERING RESOURCES FOR YOUR CHRISTIAN SCHOOL AND HOMESCHOOL

Although the education and upbringing of our children is a task that belongs primarily to parents, much of the educational process takes place in a structured classroom setting. Many parents have elected to place their children in Christian schools or engage in homeschooling. The ideal way to help our kids not only to reject the postmodern worldview but also embrace deepened Christian convictions is to align church, home, and school into a unified whole that arms our children with the truth and protects them from distortions.

That is why we also have developed empowering resources for

Christian schools as well as homeschooling families and coopera-tives that will reinforce the practical teaching our kids get from church and family. If you are homeschooling your children, take advantage of the material developed for your setting. If you send your children to a Christian school, go to your school's teachers and headmasters and share the Beyond Belief resources that are available to them. (See appendix A, under the heading Christian School and Homeschool). Let your Christian school teachers and headmasters know you are committed to cooperating with them in countering the postmodern cultural influence on your children. Explain your desire for a three-pronged approach that will strengthen your children and ground them in the faith . . . at home, church, and school.

THE BATTLE IS THE LORD'S

Over the next decade, by God's grace, I—along with an extensive team of committed believers—will be launching a Beyond Belief campaign. I will make myself available to the body of Christ to help you reach your goal of leading your children into a vibrant re-lationship with Christ, a relationship that is real and relevant to life. As a team we will not only be creating numerous resources but also traveling around the world to assist churches, schools, and communities in this crucial mission of grounding our kids in the faith. We will all need to be repeatedly inspired and equipped to rise to the challenge before us. We will need ongoing empowering resources to reach our goal. But more than anything, we will need the empowerment of God himself.

This campaign for the hearts and minds of our young people will be a tough battle. But we can't win it simply through an educa-tional—or even reeducational—process. It is more than a mental war; it is a spiritual battle. As the apostle Paul said, "We are not fighting against people made of flesh and blood, but against the evil rulers and authorities of the unseen world" (Ephesians 6:12). That is why we need to "use every piece of God's armor . . . truth . . . righteousness . . . peace . . . faith . . . salvation . . . the word of God . . . [prayer]" (Ephesians 6:13-18).

We are engaged in a great conflict, but we have a great God on our side. We need to entrust our children to God and use every piece of the armor he has provided for us. It will not necessarily be easy, and we are not guaranteed that every person we reach out to will be won. But the battle is the Lord's, and he will not be defeated.

As you and I remain faithful, we will be amazed at what God can accomplish through us. As insignificant as our individual efforts may sometimes seem, you and I can make a difference in the world around us. As the apostle Paul wrote: "Now glory be to God! By his mighty power at work within us, he is able to accomplish infinitely more than we would ever dare to ask or hope. May he be given glory in the church and in Christ Jesus forever and ever through endless ages. Amen" (Ephesians 3:20-21).

Campaign Resources

APPENDIXES A–D

Launching a Church- and Family-wide Beyond Belief Campaign

You Help Call the Shots!

If you're a parent, pastor, youth worker, or Christian educator, we want you to be our "Associate Director of Empowering Resources." While this book does actually initiate the *Beyond Belief Campaign*, the many resources needed to launch it in your church, home, or school have not yet been fully developed. In fact, the first family of resources will not be released until September 2003. That is where we need your vital input.

"Help Me Help You before May 2003!"

My team and I need your help in order for us to provide the most relevant resources possible. You can be involved as much or as little as you'd like. You can collaborate with us on the design of the key resources or simply vote on proposed resources, titles, and cover designs. My team has developed a strategic master plan for launching this campaign. But the point is this: You and your youth are why we do what we do. And the more input we receive from you, the better able we will be to develop relevant and easy-to-use resources for your family or group. So, in order for us to get the best resources into your hands by September 2003, we need to hear from you now . . . and until May 2003.

Our Goal Is to Help You Reach Yours

As we receive your input and feedback, we hope to hear your heartbeat and understand what you need so that we can serve you with greater relevance and excellence. So, let's get connected with each other.

Simply go to **www.beyondbelief.com** and sign on. There is no charge or fee. There you will be able to:

- Receive the free *Beyond Belief* booklet, articles, and other helps

- Download free *Beyond Belief* sermons and youth talks

- Participate in on-line evaluations of proposed resources—even vote on resource titles and cover designs

- Discover effective ways to motivate your group to launch a family-wide and church-wide *Beyond Belief* emphasis, beginning in September 2003

- Take advantage of youth-worker and Christian-educator training

- Help mold and shape the proposed design of the *Beyond Belief Tour* with Josh . . . and learn how you can bring the tour to your area

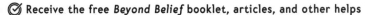

 # Go to www.beyondbelief.com

Working alone, we can each accomplish some things . . . but if we work together, we can accomplish things that are beyond belief! Because when "his mighty power [is] at work within us, he is able to accomplish infinitely more than we would ever dare to ask or hope" (Ephesians 3:20). SO LET'S GET CONNECTED AND STAY CONNECTED!

www.beyondbelief.com

Your Kids' Deepened Convictions Depend on a Relational Connection

Your child, student, or youth group needs a relational context in which to develop deepened convictions and live out those convictions in relationship with others. The following are existing resources that can help you connect—and keep on connecting—with your kids.

For Adults & Adult Groups

In this five-part video series (with companion book), Josh provides biblical insights for relationally connecting with your youth on a deep level—in ways that will last.

For Youth & Youth Groups

This eight-week youth group experience helps kids make a vital connection with God and each other. Each lesson, supplemented by an optional video, is built upon scriptural teachings that will bond your group together and help them draw others to Christ.

For Youth Workers

This handbook brings together over forty youth specialists to share their insights on what makes a successful youth ministry.

For more information on these resources and how to obtain them, go to www.josh.org and click on "Resources."

More about the *Find Your Fit* and *LifeKeys* Courses

The *Find Your Fit: Dare to Act on God's Design for You* book and workbook provide a comprehensive career exploration tool for your teenagers. Whether used in a classroom, youth group, or in individual counseling, *Find Your Fit* will help young people realize their God-given uniqueness by discovering their specific talents, spiritual gifts, personality type, values, and passions.

The *LifeKeys* book and workbook are designed for adults of all ages. This comprehensive course will help you discover who you are, why you're here, and what you do best. Using the latest in self-testing indicators, you will be able not only to know yourself better but also to lead your children or young people to know who God designed them to be.

Available wherever Christian books are sold.
Published by Bethany House Publishers, Minneapolis, Minnesota
www.bethanyhouse.com

MORE ABOUT INTIMATE LIFE MINISTRIES AND THE GREAT COMMANDMENT NETWORK

Several times in this book we have mentioned the work of David Ferguson. David's ministry has had such a profound effect on us in the past several years that we want you to have every opportunity to be exposed to his work and ministry. David and his wife, Teresa, direct a ministry called Intimate Life Ministries in Austin, Texas.

WHO AND WHAT IS INTIMATE LIFE MINISTRIES?

Intimate Life Ministries (ILM) is a training and resource ministry whose purpose is to *assist in the development of Great Commandment ministries worldwide.* Great Commandment ministries—ministries that help us love God and our neighbors—are ongoing ministries that deepen our intimacy with God and with others in marriage, family, and the church.

Intimate Life Ministries Serves

- *The Great Commandment Network of churches and ministries,* seeking to fortify homes and communities with God's love;
- *A network of pastors and other ministry leaders* walking intimately with God and their families and seeking to live vulnerably before their people;
- A team of *accredited trainers* committed to helping churches establish ongoing Great Commandment ministries;
- A team of *professional associates* from ministry and other professional Christian backgrounds, assisting with research, training, and resource development;
- A team of Christian *broadcasters, publishers, media, and other affiliates,* cooperating to see marriages and families reclaimed as divine relationships.

HOW CAN INTIMATE LIFE MINISTRIES SERVE YOU?

The Great Commandment Network is an effective, ongoing support network for churches, ministries, and Christian leaders. There are at least four ways ILM can serve you:

1. Ministering to Ministry Leaders

ILM offers unique two-day "Galatians 6:6" retreats to ministers and their spouses for personal renewal and for reestablishing and affirming ministry and family priorities. The retreat accommodations and meals are provided as a gift to ministry leaders by cosponsoring partners. Thirty to forty Galatians 6:6 retreats are held throughout the U.S. and overseas each year.

2. Partnering with Denominations and Other Ministries

Numerous denominations and ministries have partnered with ILM by "commissioning" them to equip their ministry leaders through the Galatians 6:6 retreats along with strategic training and experiential resources for ongoing ministry. These unique partnerships enable partner organizations to use the expertise of ILM trainers and resources to perpetuate a movement of Great Commandment ministry at the local level. ILM also provides a crisis support setting where partners may send ministers, couples, or families who are struggling in their relationships.

3. Identifying, Training, and Providing Resources for Leaders

ILM is committed to helping the church develop relational leaders through

- *Sermon series* on several Great Commandment topics to help pastors communicate a vision for Great Commandment health as well as identify and cultivate a core lay leadership group.
- *Experiential, user-friendly resource packages* for deepening Great Commandment love. All courses are video-assisted and complete with detailed workbooks and leaders' guides.
- *Weekend Workshops* for enriching relationships and implementing

Great Commandment ministry in the local church through marriage, parenting, or single adult workshops. Conducted by Intimate Life Trainers, these workshops are a great way to jump-start Great Commandment ministry in a local church.

- *Great Commandment Living Conferences* help the church be relevant in a postmodern world by shaping both a "fresh message" and "fresh methods" according to a Great Commandment standard—loving God and loving people.
- *Regional Training Conferences* to address critical leadership issues for church and ministry.

4. Providing Crisis Care and Support

The ILM Enrichment Center provides support for relationships in crisis through Intensive Retreats for couples, families, and singles.

For more information on how you, your church, or your denomination can become part of the Great Commandment Network and take advantage of the services and resources offered by Intimate Life Ministries, write or call:

Intimate Life Ministries
P.O. Box 201808
Austin, TX 78720-1808
1-800-881-8008

Or visit the Web sites at www.ILMinistries.org or
www.GreatCommandment.net.

BOOKS BY DAVID FERGUSON
OR DAVID AND TERESA FERGUSON

THE NEVER ALONE CHURCH (Tyndale, 2002) explains the Great Commandment Principle, which can forever change the way you relate to God, the way you love those closest to you, and the way you "do" ministry.

NEVER ALONE **(Tyndale, 2001)** takes the Great Commandment Principle into the marriage relationship. Marriage experts David and Teresa Ferguson bare their hearts and show how God transformed their empty marriage into one in which they not only meet each other's needs but also become vital partners with God in loving the way he loves.

NEVER ALONE DEVOTIONS FOR COUPLES **(Tyndale, 2001)** is a 365-day devotional that helps couples give and receive love in a whole new way. The devotions focus on 52 themes such as appreciation, affection, consideration, forgiveness, harmony, intimacy, respect, and trust.

Available wherever Christian books are sold.

Published by Tyndale House Publishers, Wheaton, Illinois, www.tyndale.com

MORE ON EVIDENCE FOR CHRISTIANITY

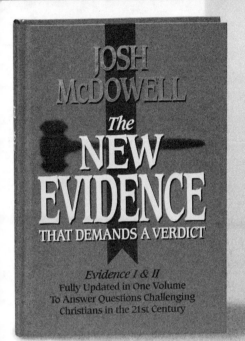

Throughout this book we have referred to and quoted material from *The New Evidence That Demands a Verdict*, the revised and updated version of the classic *Evidence That Demands a Verdict*, which has served as a comprehensive Christian defense resource for more than thirty years. The revised text provides detailed evidential documentation for the reliability of Scripture, the deity of Christ, his resurrection, the case for and against Christianity, and much more.

Specifically in this book we have referred to and drawn from the following chapters of *The New Evidence That Demands a Verdict*:

Part One: The Case for the Bible
3. Is the New Testament Historically Reliable?
4. Is the Old Testament Historically Reliable?

Part Two: The Case for Jesus
5. Jesus, A Man of History
6. If Jesus Wasn't God, He Deserves an Oscar
7. Significance of Deity: The Trilemma—Lord, Liar, or Lunatic?
8. Support of Deity: Old Testament Prophecies Fulfilled in Jesus Christ
9. Support of Deity: The Resurrection—Hoax or History?

Part Four: Truth or Consequences
32. The Nature of Truth
33. The Knowability of Truth
34. Answering Postmodernism

Available wherever Christian books are sold.

Published by Thomas Nelson Publishers, Nashville, Tennessee
www.thomasnelsonpublishers.com

NOTES

CHAPTER 1—A CRISIS OF BELIEFS

1. Glen Schultz, *Kingdom Education* (Nashville: LifeWay Press, 1998), 39.
2. Ibid., 40.
3. "The Churched Youth Study" (Dallas: Josh McDowell Ministry, 1994), 69.
4. Ibid., 65.
5. Barna Research Group, "Life Goals of American Teens," study commissioned by Josh McDowell Ministry (Ventura, Calif.: The Barna Research Group, Ltd., 2001), 6.
6. Ibid., 8.
7. Ibid.
8. Barna Research Group, "Third Millennium Teens" (Ventura, Calif.: The Barna Research Group, Ltd., 1999), 47.
9. Rob Rienow, as quoted in John Leland, "Searching for a Holy Spirit," *Newsweek* (May 8, 2000): 61.
10. Barna, "Third Millennium Teens," 48.
11. Ibid.
12. Ibid., 51.
13. Josh D. McDowell and Bob Hostetler, *Right from Wrong* (Nashville: Word, 1994), 263.
14. Leland, "Searching for a Holy Spirit," 62.
15. Barna, "Third Millennium Teens," 44.
16. Ibid.
17. Ibid., 43.
18. Jim Leffel, "Our New Challenge: Postmodernism," in *The Death of Truth,* ed. Dennis McCallum (Minneapolis: Bethany House, 1996), 35.
19. Barna Research Group, "How America's Faith Has Changed Since 9-11," Barna Research Online (November 26, 2001); <www.barna.org/cgi-bin/Home.asp>.
20. Andy Crouch, as quoted in Andres Tapia, "Reaching the First Post-

Christian Generation," *Christianity Today* 38 (September 12, 1994): 18–23.

21. Barna, "Third Millennium Teens," 44.
22. Ibid.

CHAPTER 2—BELIEFS TO CONVICTIONS

1. *Merriam-Webster's Collegiate Dictionary*, 10th ed., s.v. "believe."
2. Ibid., s.v. "conviction."
3. Wendy Murray Zoba, *Day of Reckoning: Columbine and the Search for the American Soul* (Grand Rapids: Baker, 2000), 78–92.
4. Ibid., 85.
5. Ibid., 180.
6. Lenny Savino, "Suspect's Letter Gives Hijackers Instructions," *Akron (Ohio) Beacon Journal*, 29 September 2001, A1, A5.
7. Text of Osama bin Laden's videotaped remarks aired on U.S. television stations on October 7, 2001, reported in *Akron (Ohio) Beacon Journal*, 8 October 2001, A7.
8. *Merriam-Webster's Collegiate Dictionary*, s.v. "true."
9. Clark Pinnock, *Set Forth Your Case* (Nutley, N.J.: Craig Press), 1967, 6–7.
10. J. P. Moreland, *Love Your God with All Your Mind* (Colorado Springs, Colo.: NavPress, 1997), 25.
11. Barna Research Group, "Third Millennium Teens" (Ventura, Calif.: The Barna Research Group, Ltd., 1999), 37.
12. David Crary, "Attacks Strengthen Family Ties," *Akron (Ohio) Beacon Journal*, 22 October 2001, A7.

CHAPTER 3—THE TRUTH ABOUT TRUTH

1. Fernando Savater, *El Mito Nacionalista* (Madrid: Alianzu Editorial, 1996), 16–19.
2. Thomas A. Helmbock, "Insights on Tolerance," *Cross & Crescent* (Lambda Chi Alpha International Fraternity, summer 1996): 2.
3. Barna Research Group, "Third Millennium Teens" (Ventura, Calif.: The Barna Research Group, Ltd., 1999), 39.
4. Ibid., 16.
5. See John 18:33-38, emphasis mine.
6. *Merriam-Webster's Collegiate Dictionary*, 10th ed., s.v. "truth."

CHAPTER 4—HOW TRUE ARE CHRIST'S CLAIMS?

1. For a detailed treatment of this prophecy, see Josh McDowell, *The New Evidence That Demands a Verdict* (Nashville: Nelson, 1999), 195–201.

2. Peter Winebrenner Stoner and Robert C. Newman, *Science Speaks* (Chicago: Moody Press, 1976), 106–12.

3. Ibid.

4. Origen, *Contra Celsum*, trans. Henry Chadwick (Cambridge, England: Cambridge University Press, 1980), 32.

5. John 9:3.

6. John 9:7.

CHAPTER 5—THE RELATIONAL MEANING OF THE INCARNATION

1. Barbara Kantrowitz and Pat Wingut, "How Well Do You Know Your Kids?" *Newsweek* (May 10, 1999): 38–39.

2. William Damon, quoted in Sharon Begley, "A World of Their Own," *Newsweek* (May 8, 2000): 54.

3. Barna Research Group, "Third Millennium Teens" (Ventura, Calif.: The Barna Research Group, Ltd., 1999), 51.

4. Horace, *Horace's Satires and Epistles*, trans. Jacob Fuchs (New York: W. W. Norton, 1977), 89.

5. Charles Caldwell Ryrie, ed., *Ryrie Study Bible* (Chicago: Moody Press, 1976), 25.

CHAPTER 6—RELATIONALLY CONNECTING THE DISCONNECTED

1. My friend David Ferguson has written extensively about this idea in his book *The Never Alone Church* (Wheaton, Ill.: Tyndale House, 2002).

CHAPTER 8—THE BIBLE: RELATIONAL AND RELIABLE

1. Josh McDowell, *The New Evidence That Demands a Verdict* (Nashville: Nelson, 1999), 74.

2. Ibid., 78.

3. Ibid., 79.

4. Adapted from McDowell, *New Evidence*, chart, 38.

5. Ibid.

6. Ibid., 38–39.

7. Ibid., 8.

8. Ibid., 8–9. For more information about the Bible translations and distribution, visit the Web site for the United Bible Society, <www.biblesociety.org>.

9. Ibid., 42–44; 53–54.

10. Ibid., 61–68; 91–116.

CHAPTER 9—THE MEANING OF GOD'S WORD TO OUR LIVES

1. Barna Research Group, "Third Millennium Teens" (Ventura, Calif.: The Barna Research Group, Ltd., 1999), 44.

2. Ibid., 43.

CHAPTER 10—INTERPRETING THE WORDS OF GOD

1. See 2 Timothy 2:15, NASB.

CHAPTER 12—BECAUSE HE LIVES

1. "The Churched Youth Study" (Dallas: Josh McDowell Ministry, 1994), 69.

2. Billy Graham, "Billy Graham's Message," (homily given at the National Day of Prayer and Remembrance held at the National Cathedral, Washington, D.C., September 14, 2001); © 2001 Billy Graham Evangelistic Association, <www.billygraham.org.>

CHAPTER 13—THE CASE OF THE EMPTY TOMB

1. George Hanson, *The Resurrection and the Life* (London: William Clowes & Son, 1911), 24.

2. David Friedrich Strauss, *The Life of Jesus for People*, 2d ed., vol. 1 (London: William & Norgate, 1879), 412.

3. See Luke 24:34; 24:13-35; 24:36-49; John 20:24-29; Matthew 28:16-20; 1 Corinthians 15:6-8.

CHAPTER 14—OUR MISSION IN LIFE

1. Ezekiel 18:4, NASB.

2. Romans 6:23, NIV.

3. Romans 5:12, NIV.

4. Galatians 3:10, emphasis added.

5. See Acts 2:24; Hebrews 4:15.

6. 1 Peter 3:18, NIV.

7. Matthew 25:34, NIV.

8. Revelation 22:17; Romans 8:17.

9. See 1 Corinthians 15:25-26, 52; Revelation 21:3-4.

About the Authors

JOSH MCDOWELL never intended to be a defender of the Christian faith. In fact, his goal was just the opposite. As a skeptic at Kellogg College in Michigan, he was challenged by a group of Christian students to intellectually examine the claims of Christianity. He accepted the challenge and set out to prove that Christ's claims to be God and the historical reliability of Scripture could be neither trusted nor accurately verified. The evidence he discovered changed the course of his life. He discovered that the Bible was the most historically reliable document of all antiquity and that Christ's claim that he was God could be objectively verified. When Josh was brought face-to-face with the objective and relevant truth of Christ and his Word, he trusted in Christ as the Son of God and his personal Savior.

Josh transferred to Wheaton College and completed a bachelor's degree in language. He went on to receive a master's degree in theology from Talbot Theological Seminary in California. In 1964 he joined the staff of Campus Crusade for Christ (CCC) and eventually became an international traveling representative for CCC, focusing primarily on issues facing today's young people.

Josh has spoken to more than seven million young people in eighty-four countries, including more than 700 university and college campuses. He has authored or coauthored more than sixty books and workbooks with more than thirty million in print worldwide. Josh's most popular works are *The New Evidence That Demands a Verdict*, *More Than a Carpenter*, *Why True Love Waits*, the *Right from Wrong* book, and the *Right from Wrong* workbook series.

Josh has been married to Dottie for more than thirty years and has four children. Josh and Dottie live in Dallas, Texas.

● ● ● ● ●

BOB HOSTETLER is a writer, editor, pastor, and speaker. His thirteen books include the award-winning *Don't Check Your Brains at the Door* and *The New Tolerance* (coauthored with Josh McDowell). He has won two

Gold Medallion Awards, two Ohio Associated Press awards, and an Amy Foundation Award.

Bob is a frequent speaker at churches, conferences, and retreats. He has been a disc jockey, pastor, magazine editor, freelance book editor, and (with his wife, Robin) a foster parent to ten boys (though not all at once). He and his wife are among the leaders of Cobblestone Community Church in Oxford, Ohio.

Bob and Robin have two children, Aubrey and Aaron, who are currently attending Miami University in Oxford, Ohio.

● ● ● ● ●

DAVE BELLIS is a ministry consultant focusing on ministry planning and product development. He has pioneered an interactive video and workbook educational design used by more than 100,000 churches and small groups worldwide. For over twenty-five years as a campaign coordinator, writer, and producer, Dave Bellis has directed Josh McDowell's many campaigns, developing more than 100 products. He and his wife, Becky, have two grown children and live in "the house that Meech built" in Copley, Ohio.